# THE GREAT
# FRAGMENTATION

# THE GREAT FRAGMENTATION

## and why the future of business is small

STEVE SAMMARTINO

WILEY

First published in 2014 by John Wiley & Sons Australia, Ltd
42 McDougall St, Milton Qld 4064

Office also in Melbourne

Typeset in 10.5/13 pt Myriad Pro

© Steve Sammartino 2014

The moral rights of the author have been asserted

National Library of Australia Cataloguing-in-Publication data:

| | |
|---|---|
| Author: | Sammartino, Steve, author. |
| Title: | The Great Fragmentation : why the future of all business is small / Steve Sammartino. |
| ISBN: | 9780730312680 (pbk) |
| | 9780730312703 (ebook) |
| Notes: | Includes index. |
| Subjects: | Business enterprises. |
| | Information technology. |
| | Information society. |
| Dewey Number: | 658.4062 |

Cover design by Wiley

Cover image © iStock.com/ pavlen

Printed in Singapore by C.O.S. Printers Pte Ltd

10 9 8 7 6 5 4 3 2 1

**Disclaimer**
The material in this publication is of the nature of general comment only, and neither purports nor intends to be advice. Readers should not act on the basis of any matter in this publication without considering (and if appropriate, taking) professional advice with due regard to their own particular circumstances. The author and publisher expressly disclaim all and any liability to any person, whether a purchaser of this publication or not, in respect of anything and of the consequences of anything done or omitted to be done by any such person in reliance, whether whole or partial, upon the whole or any part of the contents of this publication.

# CONTENTS

*Preface*                                                                                          *vii*
*About the author*                                                                                  *xi*

1   The industrial deal: the shift from industry to technology                      1

2   A global revolution: industrial leapfrog                                              9

3   The social reality: beyond the surface of social media                          19

4   Life in boxes: the industrial formula for living                                       29

5   Rehumanisation: words define our future                                              47

6   Demographics is history: moving on from predictive marketing           63

7   The truth about pricing: technology and omnipresent deflation           79

8   A zero-barrier world: how access to knowledge is breaking                  91
    down barriers

9   The infinite store: rebooting retail                                                         103

10  Bigger than the internet: 3D printing                                                    115

11  Screen play: post–mass media                                                             129

12  Too big to fail?: the great financial disruption                                      153

13  The 3-phase shift: a closer look at the web                                          167

14  The big game: an introduction to gamification                                     179

15  System hacking: a great idea with a bad reputation                            197

16   The job, the factory and the home: how location              205
     follows technology

17   A stranger from Romania: building a real Lego car            217

18   Market-share folly and industrial fragmentation:             231
     industrial metrics

19   The externality reality: is this the end of privacy?         241

20   Business = technology: the 4Ps revised                       249

Recommended books and documentaries                              259
Index                                                            263

# PREFACE

Over the past 10 years I've been a keen observer of the business landscape. I had an inkling something was going on when I left corporate life for the first time in 2005. It was a time when the web 2.0 era was gathering a head of steam. A real sense of empowerment was sweeping the entrepreneurial community. Many of the tools of business were all of a sudden becoming accessible and easier to use. You didn't need anyone's help to find out how to do something because information was entering the 'on-demand' realm. While most of us still had VCRs in our houses with the time blinking on 12 am, some savvy tech geeks decided to refocus their efforts externally. They decided to not just build something for themselves, but to build something for all of us — something end users could play with, improve upon and even use to build something else. The insight of creating for further creation and humanising and socialising business was inspired.

This was a bit unexpected because after the dotcom crash a lot of us (me included) had doubts about the technology utopia the internet promised to provide. But, while it was delayed, it has arrived. What's arrived has turned out to be far more widespread and structural than most people predicted. It turns out that information that's freed up and accessible by all has an equal and opposite impact on the physical world. Information becomes objects. Information changes the shape of the physical world. Information changes the social and physical world and inevitably the economic structure.

In many ways, it's the opposite of what business had been about up until this point. Business was a zero sum game of producers and consumers: an 'us' and 'them'; a server-and-receiver structure. But most of all, it was a definitive power structure where the people who already had wealth and access had much of the economic power. And I know what you're about to say: 'But what about the 1 per cent, the ever-increasing wealth of the wealthiest few?' The truth is that we're just at the start of a bigger revolution where everything important in life and business is becoming cheaper and more available to everyone. It's a time when our standards of living will increase exponentially via the dissemination of powerful technology; a time when the power flips back to the populous as tools of all sorts are democratised. It will be an entire revision of the factors of production, the way business is done and the power structures around our economy.

As this book is written at the intersection of technology and business, there will be concepts that may not be from the business world you live in. The good news is that the definition of much of the new terminology is provided in the book and the rest is a mere web search away from a quick definition. Let your curiosity take you away from the book and on a non-linear journey — something that matches life. It's also worth remembering that what matters is not so much how any of this technology works, but how it reconfigures commerce. It's the patterns that matter. As business people, we only need to concern ourselves with what technology can do, not how it does it.

The main economic pattern is the increasing fragmentation of industries. Everything in business is breaking down into much smaller pieces. More access is resulting in more players and in more options being available for everything we do and make; in other words, a more decentralised economy. The delineation between makers and buyers is evaporating. We're moving into a phase of highly distributed crowd-powered business systems. The parts that make up our economy are shifting and while the final structure is not knowable, the trajectory is. We're entering a phase in business where things are moving so quickly that we need to avoid the pretence of claiming to know the outcome. Instead, what's needed is an open-source strategy that matches the technology and the newly empowered populous: a world where there are very few trade secrets.

Business is facing its own climate change, but it seems to me that much of the thought and analysis to this point has been about keeping the water out of the front door, or building a better boat to keep a business afloat. As business leaders and entrepreneurs we have to go wider. In times of significant change, what's really needed is a thorough analysis of the landscape and a topographical assessment of the new world. Even the big players — the new 'big' — became big by creating highly distributed networks of small pieces that are more loosely tied together with many more fragmented products and services. The new digital dominators all live deep inside the long tail.

\* \* \*

There's no shortage of books available with tactical tips on how to use the latest tech tool. If that's what you're looking for, this isn't the book for you. If you're lucky enough to be reading this preface in a bookstore prior to purchasing the book and you want a tactical 'how-to' summary, please buy another book. This one will only disappoint you. What you can find in this book is deep understanding of the technological landscape that's about to infiltrate our world, both from a business and social perspective. Let's be honest: the two can't be separated anyway. And why should they be? All business books that are strategic in nature have to cover the breadth of life. They have to cover anthropology, technology, commerce and culture.

By the time you've finished reading this book, you'll have a philosophical base about the direction in which the world is moving. This will serve you more than a bunch of disposable digital tactics would, especially given the pace of change. The disrupters are already being disrupted by the next-generation startups. Tactics are short term. Philosophy is enduring. I hope you'll develop your own philosophy on the future as we examine the marketing mix and how it's shifting and fragmenting around us.

Steve Sammartino

# ABOUT THE AUTHOR

Steve Sammartino had his first startup before the age of 10, running an organic egg farm in the early 1980's before the words *organic* or *startup* had been invented. The first phase of his 'adult' career was in marketing, working his way into senior executive roles in global consumer goods companies and advertising agencies. He escaped his cubicle for the first time in 2005 and went on to found rentoid.com — a peer-to-peer renting portal that became a leader in the collaborative consumption movement. After a successful exit he embarked on a number of crazy side projects including putting a Lego space shuttle into actual orbit, building a jet-powered bicycle, and crowdfunding the build of a full-size Lego car that runs on air and uses an engine made of Lego — all to prove what's possible in a connected world with low cost technology.

He does some serious stuff too.

Steve also travels the world helping companies transition from industrial-era thinking into the digital age, writes on business and technology issues and blogs to over 30 000 readers a month.

His latest startup project is Tomcar Australia — a seven-person car company which makes and sells all-terrain vehicles. It is Australia's first car startup in over 30 years and a company that practises what Steve preaches.

Connect with Steve, check out his latest projects or read his blog via www.stevesammartino.com.

Or maybe just say hi to @sammartino on Twitter.

# CHAPTER 1

## The industrial deal:
## the shift from industry to technology

The industrial revolution was a pretty good deal. Here's what we got: stable jobs with better pay, paid annual leave and union-improved working conditions; improved housing with automated heating and cooling; homes filled with labour-saving devices and disposable widgets; free entertainment projected directly into our living rooms; personal motorised transportation and a national transport infrastructure; a garage filled with toys; air-conditioned supermarkets selling packaged goods with long shelf lives; big box retailing; government sponsored education, medical innovation and public hospitals; jet aircraft that could fly us through the clouds; and a life expectancy beyond the age of 35.

It's no surprise that people living in industrialising countries clamoured to gain the benefits of a longer and wealthier life. The only rational choice was to sign up for it. The benefit of an improved life expectancy on its own was quite compelling. But when we added the layers of conspicuous consumption and free entertainment on tap it was a real human high ground.

So we handed in our craftsman and artisanal skills to help build the one-size-fits-all economy and the consumables that fill it up. It was the only way all of us would be able to own everything. It meant we had to trade in the very personal touch of a craftsman and become part of the machine itself. By becoming part of the machine we were able to have more. We were handed everything earlier generations could only dream about, a standard of living beyond that of gentries and kings when we take into account the upgraded living standards we all acquired. But there was a price to pay: we had a job to do. Our job was to help churn out the items that built the industrial world and to buy the items we churned out. We had to become consumers.

## Terms and conditions

The industrial revolution didn't come with a set of terms and conditions; however, there were some unspoken rules that weren't covered in the text book. The textbook was so focused on how to make widgets and money, it forgot about why any of that mattered.

We abided by these terms for the best part of 200 years. The two most important terms were:

We'll enable a more materialistic lifestyle

*but*

You'll need to follow the rules set by the owners of the capital.

This was a simple way of saying that our individual creativity can't compete with the industrialists' aggregated efficiency. It's something that goes against the basic human spirit — our need for collaboration, creativity and nuance, which is imbedded deeply into our past and, thankfully, our future.

Consumers and creators were two different classes in the industrial world. The industrialists owned the factors of production. The ability to create independently was taken away from workers and re-engineered so it belonged only to the capital class. Without saying it, the deal was: 'You let us design, make, distribute and advertise and in exchange we'll give you a higher standard of living.' They left out the bit about keeping all the profits for themselves.

This economic model worked well until we reached the point where we owned everything we needed. But now the deal has entered its final phases and the gig is up. The industrial revolution is putting itself out of business. I wonder if they had a planned-obsolescence in mind.

## Unlearning

The methods used by corporations became so effective at generating more for less that they're making their own era an obsolete business method. Companies that want to thrive during the technology era need to seriously revise their economic playbook. The efficiencies these corporations generated have made high-end technology disposable, or at the very least, low cost. It's difficult to make a profit when products have to improve each year *and* cost less than they did last year.

**This means that in the new economy we're all required to do some unlearning to stay profitable and relevant.**

It means the only way of achieving revenue upside is to sell more units, but there are only so many mobile phones and televisions a person can own. This means that in the new economy we're all required to do some unlearning to stay profitable and relevant.

## A new business infrastructure

The entire economic, political and social infrastructure is going through a 200-year shift from the industrial era to the technology era. All of the elements that make up our economic infrastructure are experiencing a technological disruption. These changes are not the comfortable, incremental ones we're accustomed to, but step changes that — for the unprepared — hurt careers and kill businesses. Products and services, distribution systems, pricing methods, advertising and promotion are all following a transition away from clustering and aggregated power structures. They're moving from a one-size-fits-all model to small, distributed, specific, customised platforms that deliver to a one-size-fits-one model. Previously stable economic systems are now fragmenting rapidly.

## The 4Ps

In order to understand the changes in our economic system, we need to investigate the changes in parts. The simplest way is by looking at the parts that make up what's known as the 'marketing mix'. This is called 'the 4Ps': Product, Price, Place and Promotion. While modern marketing mavericks will try to displace these simplest of production-related business factors, there's nothing in business that can exist outside of these four parameters. We're limited to using the 4Ps when it comes to configuring what we hope to sell. User experience, community, interface, responsiveness — take your pick — they all sit inside and are part of the marketing mix and they go back to the foundation of economics, the Ws: What, Where, Who, How much and for Whom. The 4Ps are the only levers we can use for building anything in business for a profit: they're the factors of production in their simplest form. All four parts are changing rapidly and forever. A simple explanation of each of the 4Ps will help create a context for the journey in this book.

- *Product.* This is what we sell, whether it's a widget, a service, an event or an idea. It's what we use to generate revenue from.

- *Price.* This is the price we sell a product for, even if that price is attention or privacy. Price also includes the impact of demand and supply, finance, currency considerations and payment systems — anything that must be considered when money changes hands or there's a transaction.

- *Place.* This tells us where we can get the product and how it's delivered to us, both physically and virtually. It includes all considerations for distribution systems in exchanging goods and services between people and organisations.

- *Promotion.* This is anything to do with communication about what's available and why people may want it; for example, the tools of information exchange and media among people, brands, organisations and governments.

The 4Ps form the interdependent system, or 'mix', from which we do business. In fact, it's the same marketing mix that people employ when they earn their living, but most people don't have the presence of mind to see it in such simple terms. While certain brands and companies often focus heavily on a particular part of the mix to create a point of difference, it's getting them to work in concert that leads to a profit advantage. And when all of them are changing rapidly we need to pay attention and reset our mode of operation. What it comes down to today is that a business is either disrupting these factors of production or it's being disrupted by a new competitor trying to put the incumbent out of business. When the factors of production change, the world we live in changes too. Where we work changes, so where we live also changes. It impacts the support systems around the economy as well: the financial system, the education system and even government policy.

The greatest innovation we've seen since the commercial internet was born in the early 1990s has been the rebuilding of infrastructure. That's why everything is up for grabs. Until now, many industrial legacy organisations have remained unaffected by the change. It was a temporary situation for them. But all of the 4Ps are — and will continue to be — disrupted.

The first example of disruption affected the fourth P, promotion. This was to be expected, given the world wide web (the web) is all about interacting in a new way; it's a form of media in itself. It was the easiest of the 4Ps to disrupt, thanks to our new internet technology.

**legacy media:** the traditional media outlets that were common before the internet, including television, radio, newspapers and magazines

The biggest and first P to be hit hard by the technology revolution was legacy media. But open communication does more than just disrupt the media: it's the bellwether for rapid innovation. Knowledge exchange affects everything and redesigns the systems and infrastructure around us. The corporate infrastructure that used to provide a layer of protection now forms a legacy of financial burden in the form of assets that can rapidly become redundant and costly to carry. Probably for the first time since the commencement of the industrial revolution in the late 1700s, it's better to be small than big in business. So the question any company should be asking is:

**Probably for the first time since the commencement of the industrial revolution ... it's better to be small than big in business.**

*Would I build this same infrastructure today given the choice of a clean slate?*

6

The simple reality of the technology revolution that we're living through is that it requires 'clean-slate' business strategies. Piecemeal legacy adaptation is the fast track to irrelevance and financial disaster.

Clean-slate business strategies are not only needed because everything around us is changing. They're needed because, unlike other revolutions, this one will be a global revolution. The change is so rapid and global this time that developing nations will skip right past their industrial era and straight into technology-driven economies.

## What is fragmenting

The power base of industrial companies is breaking up. It's flipping from the 'few' to the 'many'.

## What it means for business

The industrial business playbook is being rewritten. Industrial legacy infrastructure is no longer a business advantage.

# CHAPTER 2

## A global revolution:
## industrial leapfrog

The global revolution is underway and it's far more significant than the industrial revolution.

## Beyond the fortunate few

The benefits of this revolution will not be confined to a number of wealthy, Westernised countries with existing infrastructures and stable governments (which, to provide a level of quantum, excluded more than 80 per cent of the population). The entire globe will participate in the technology revolution, not just the billion or so fortunate people who live in western Europe, Nordic regions, North America, Australia and certain parts of Asia. And this will happen because the cost of entry and adaptation is so low.

This revolution is about accessibility, and it's driven by the low cost — disposability, even — of technology, costs low enough for people within developing nations to access mobile technologies, often before the true industrialisation of the nation even occurs. The most cited example of this phenomenon is that there are more mobile phone subscriptions (approximately 4.6 billion) around the world than there are toothbrushes[1] in use (approximately 4.2 billion). While this point is debatable, what matters is that this revolution has the potential to create a leap-frog effect and that the path to economic development will no longer be linear. Countries could circumvent certain industrial technologies altogether. For example, industrialised, government-funded schooling could leap directly to cloud-based, open-source learning. This is something large conglomerates in the packaged goods, power generation and other industrial stalwart categories should take note of. A corporate strategy that relies on growth from selling to developing nations as they industrialise is fraught with short-sighted danger. The speed of development of certain technologies means that industrial methods of production may never eventuate in tomorrow's non–BRIC countries' developing economies.

> **The entire globe will participate in the technology revolution.**

**BRIC:** Brazil, Russia, India and China

3D printing (discussed in detail in chapter 10) has the potential to circumvent manufacturing altogether. Exponential advances in solar, wind and other power-generating technologies may mean that houses will become

---

[1] http://60secondmarketer.com/blog/2011/10/18/more-mobile-phones-than-toothbrushes and also www.chartsbin.com/view/1881

self-sufficient with regard to their energy needs. As we saw for media and communications, the ability to create products that enable us to own the tools is where the economy is headed.

It's what technology wants. It fragments down to the micro level and becomes personal. The job of the corporate hero of tomorrow is to provide a platform for customer independence.

## The multi-generational shift

The reason why it's hard for companies to cope with this shift to micro businesses, is that it's a multi-generational shift. Given that the dawn of the industrial revolution was in the late 1700s, and if we use 30 as an average age for a new parent (it used to be much lower), we're living through a nine-times generational shift in lifestyle and economic understanding. This is a significant amount of indoctrination handed down from parents and employers of how things should be done and what works in this world. It's pretty hard to unlearn all of this, especially when most of it has been proven empirically.

We can thank Fredrick W. Taylor and his scientific management techniques[2] for the overly rational and logical approach to business. Taylor believed that workers could be regarded as cogs in the overriding industrial machine and that the tasks undertaken by workers could be analysed down to a minute level of movement and time and then designed, iterated and improved for the ultimate in efficiency. For physical tasks this can be a valid approach. What's unfortunate is that the 'humans-as-machine-cogs'-based management ethic leaked its way into knowledge work over the past 100 years, while creativity and human judgement took a back seat to the idea of spreadsheet-based or quantitative decision making — an ironically irrational approach to managing many creative decisions. An example from my working life is the involvement of a procurement department in the choice of advertising agency. And I'm not talking about the negotiation or contract element at the end of the process, but full involvement from the start.

## Changing habits

This rationality, while being potentially useful for gaining efficiencies in systems, has inappropriately become the preferred approach in all business

---

[2]Frederick Winslow Taylor, *The Principles of Scientific Management*: http://books.google.com.au/books?id=HoJMAAAAYAAJ&pg=PA3&redir_esc=y

arenas and even in career paths and corporate strategy. It probably had a greater negative impact on our schooling and education process than we give it credit for.

Employers want to see linear, rational progressions in all their inputs, even their staff. They want your schooling to be linear; they want you to work in the same industry; they want to see progressive upward steps that validate your company performance. Forget that it's most likely your internal political performance that defines your success, rather than what you actually deliver for the company.

They prefer all replacement staff to have the same industry experience, the same education, the same previous job title, the same customer experience, and experience in the same channels of distribution, which is essentially a risk-reduction strategy for the hiring manager if things turn out badly rather than a growth strategy for the organisation. It's not surprising, given that the primary role in large organisations is to protect against the financial downside rather than chase a revenue upside. This course of action works as long as the business and technology environments remain stable. The problem is that our business environment is changing quickly and the habits of large organisations are not.

 **The problem is that our business environment is changing quickly and the habits of large organisations are not.**

## Lifetime employment

It used to be that you'd get a job and stay with your employer your whole working life. Smart employers, and certainly startups, are now beginning to look for people with wide experience, otherwise known as 'horizontal personnel'.

A thin experience base of vertical climbing is not robust enough in a world that's facing shake-ups in every economic arena. It's not going to augur well when things get shaky. The more specialised any person or company is, the higher the risk they can be replaced in a technology revolution. We've been encouraged to diversify our investment portfolio since the beginning of investment and portfolio theory. And yet, people are not encouraged to do the same thing with what's most often their primary form of income for life — their salary.

This puts employees into a career paradox: the obvious strategy for achieving high office in a company is ultra-specialisation and vertical climbing. Yet, the probability of being successful this way is low. At the same time it reduces the value of the employee who doesn't make it to a corner office and has to follow another career path because they have what I call a thin market proposition. In the end it often becomes an all-or-nothing bet. Companies creating employment didn't care about this while all the risk was with the downsized or stagnant employee. However, these days the risk of not having employees with wide experience is starting to impact the future performance of companies. It's not a very future-proof human-resource plan.

Over the past 20 or so years, since the internet has been opened up for use as a commercial platform, the strategy of staying in the one industry and trying to climb the corporate ladder hasn't served the humble employee well. It has displaced many employees and many employers who couldn't see the error in their ways. While many employers espouse that their employees make the company, it's sometimes hard to believe they really mean what they say.

## From employees to projecteers

Over the past 10 years I've transformed myself to de-risk my career and income. I've made a transition from a consumer-goods marketing executive to something I haven't quite been able to define as yet. The most apt description is probably 'entrepreneur', although it doesn't always translate to my advantage on an immigration card when travelling overseas.

**projecteer:** a person who works independently for others on projects

Essentially, I've gone from a thin, singular career base of 'marketing person' to a range of income-generating activities including business blogger, web startup founder, startup investor, university lecturer, technology journalist and radio commentator, viral video maker, public speaker, car company board member, industrial era company consultant, government technology adviser and business author—none of which involved vertical climbing, but horizontal hopping. What I try to do is find the Venn-diagram overlap in each opportunity. Each overlap invents the right to step into another realm, which then overlaps with the previous one, and so on. It's something businesses have been doing for a long time: related diversification. Unfortunately the people working within these businesses rarely adopt the corporate strategies they implement for their own careers and income purposes. When it comes to careers in the technology age I always tell people that Venn is Zen. (It must be true because it rhymes!)

The important point to note is that I didn't have the right, or permission, to do or learn any of this. I just went ahead and did it. I did it because I could. There was no gatekeeper and I could do most of it for free using the gift of democratised knowledge and connection tools. Now it makes me antifragile. 'Antifragility' is a term coined by author Nassim Taleb to describe something that improves when it breaks or is disrupted by shocks so it can reconfigure and grow stronger. I have multiple sources of revenue and the relative diversification of a personal index fund of tech revolution-proof skills. It's what both employees and employers need to do: focus less on functional departments and more on connecting seemingly disparate skills and overlaps.

## Industrial education

All of this comes back to the education system. It's not surprising, given our current government-funded education systems are a child of the industrial age. The industrial template was used to design a schooling system that could produce great workers for the industrial era and promote orderly political behaviour. This model has indoctrinated people's thinking. From the government, to parents, to kids, to companies, to their eventual employees. Learn the syllabus, reproduce it in tests, do well at school, get into university, get a qualification employers want, get a job in a good, stable (preferably big) company, climb the hierarchy, get paid more and, finally, retire in a reasonably independent financial state. It's the path most people I know are on. Yet most people on this path agree that it rarely leads to riches. It's a linear and rational B-follows-A method for educating our children and grooming them for their working life plan. It doesn't work now, and it's only going to get worse as new systems and technologies increasingly disrupt the workplace. I'll go into detail about this in chapter 16.

> The skills that get someone to the top within a company are, unfortunately, not the same as those needed when they get there.

The skills that get someone to the top within a company are, unfortunately, not the same as those needed when they get there. This may just be a contributing factor to the highly paid, please-take-this-money-and-go-away exits of corporate CEOs.

The two imperatives for success as an employee in a large organisation are financial risk mitigation and internal political performance; in other words, don't blow the budget, and make the quarterly number for Wall Street. Regardless of the long-term impact of their decisions, the high-performing corporate executive must find a way to get the number. No brazen careerist would push out a game-winning launch if it risked their position at the firm or if the probability of its success wasn't high, regardless of the benefits the company could receive from a significant innovation. They'd rather research the goodness out of any innovation, 'wait and see' how the technology emerges and incrementally refine what they already have in the market. It's what their employer rewards, so it's the right choice for staff in most organisations.

## Startup culture

The reason we see so many startups doing well isn't because the entrepreneurs are necessarily smarter than their corporate-dwelling counterparts. It's because the reward structure for entrepreneurs is different. As a startup founder, you win if you create value and invent revenue. The corporate executive plays an entirely different game, one of reducing cost and protecting against losing market share. The prize in the corporate executive game is a relative wages contest against fellow staff members, which endures regardless of the company's performance.

Yes, there's an obvious difference between a large existential revenue base and trying to build something from scratch. Some may even say comparing the two types of organisation is irrelevant because they're at different life stages and trying to achieve different outcomes. But this is no longer the case. How people operate within these different structures matters more than ever because when eras come to an end, the rules change and we all have to start again, regardless of how big or established we are.

The culture of big is 'don't make an error on the big project'. Mistakes are bad and costly, or they're perceived to be bad and costly because that's the way it was for a very long time. This thinking is largely driven by the history of where companies emerged from, rather than the reality of the market they compete in today. It was super expensive to get a factory design wrong. It was (and is) expensive to get your product ranged in a national retail chain. It was downright scary to run a national advertising campaign that didn't resonate with the audience. It was a disaster if the new warehouse had design flaws. If a company failed to launch something, it hurt financially. In an industrial world, all the things that major brands and companies did had a lot riding on them financially. And that's why we mostly see incremental innovation — which is an oxymoron, if you ask me.

In a technological world, the cost of mistakes is lower. If you happen to be running a nondustrial company, mistakes are actually good. The cost of getting it wrong in digital firms becomes low-cost iteration, a form of market research that's actually tested in the market, rather than in some contrived, demographically profiled research group. And the mistakes we make are sometimes invisible. Perhaps no-one used whatever was launched; it most likely didn't have national advertising support; and it most certainly can be replaced by reconfiguring the computer code that went into building it.

**nondustrial company:** a company whose DNA is not of the industrial era, but the new technology era

# The truth about competitors

Sure, not every business will be digital. Sure, factories, mills, warehouses and other complexes and expensive business infrastructure will still exist. And yes, it's clear that not every business will be involved in technology. Hard costs that come from delivering industrial-level, hard, physical goods are valid, needed and will remain a part of the business landscape. But the reality is that every legacy industry is competing against its digital brethren. They're competing even if they're not chasing the same customers or revenue pool.

During a transition from one age to another, companies don't just compete for market share. During a shift in ages we start to compete heavily in a way that's indirect and difficult to perceive. We don't just compete for customers or shelf space either. We compete for a wider set of fundamental business resources.

We compete for awareness and interest in what we're doing. The more boring the item we're selling, the more we need to spend on media.

We compete to get high-quality personnel who understand the emerging landscape and people who can provide intellectual horsepower in a changing landscape. If our industry or brands are undesirable to work for it becomes difficult and expensive to attract the people who can create the changes needed to escape the boring downward spiral to irrelevance.

We compete for financial capital. In a market where funds are being raised in non-traditional ways (crowdfunding, for example, which I cover in chapter 12), we compete against industries whose financial upside is greater. It starts to increase our cost of capital as we're limited to traditional and more expensive methods of financing growth.

We compete for the ability to collaborate with others. The new platform orientation in business means brands need to collaborate more often. Brands without in-market cache will find it increasingly difficult to find collaborators. Mash-ups and corporate marriages of value tend only to occur when both players get positive rub-off from each other.

We compete for the future and making it through the transition to the emerging landscape as if we're competing for the primary resource of sustenance just to stay alive.

The global nature of this revolution has conspired to give us a global voice. And what's most interesting about the voice is that it hasn't just been magnified, it has also been unified.

## What is fragmenting

This revolution is a truly global one. It's affecting every person, not just the fortunate few in developed economies.

## What it means for business

Business can't simply try to implement industrial-era strategies in emerging markets. The technology revolution means that many industrial-era ideas and markets will be leap-frogged by developing economies.

**CHAPTER 3**

The social reality:
beyond the surface of social media

Social media is only a small part of the change we're living through; it's a surface indicator or a symptom of the times. The fact that all of it has been enabled by an omnipresent and ultra-cheap space race in technology tells us much more about why it matters. The wormhole goes deep, and social media is just the entry point to the hole that we've recently entered. We'd do well to think of social media as the introductory 101 course for something much more significant.

A focus on social-media strategy is flawed by definition. It's too focused on the tool and not enough on the reason. The obsession that people, brands and companies have with followers, fans and friend accumulation won't be the panacea to any marketing problem. The clues are even in the words we use to describe it. It's a simple social conversation that's digitally enhanced. Having a social-media strategy is akin to asking people whether they have a conversation strategy when they talk to people. While it may be overtly planned at some kind of networking event, it's far from the way most people behave on a day-to-day basis. What we're actually looking for is human interaction that makes us feel good, solves our problems and speaks with a human voice, rather than that of a corporate PR department or a telecentre. What we want to have are the interactions we never could pre-web. What we don't want to hear is the voice that's owned by those with the largest media budget. That's a bit like high school when the class loud mouth got all the attention. Just as in our analogue life, we'd rather hear from those with something that's worth listening to and conversing about.

In recent years the 'social-media expert' has arisen: the early adopter who makes a living from teaching others how to use the tools of the day. People and agencies have made big and quick money doing this. Showing companies and people how to get the most out of Facebook, or any new powerful tool, has always been a profitable endeavour. Let me make it easy for anyone who's still curious about social strategies. The five, simple, human rules worth following are:

1　Speak with a human voice.

2　Listen more than you talk.

3　Be a resource to others and help them.

4　Be nice to people.

5　Don't say anything you wouldn't want on a daily news report.

The end. It's a bit like life really.

Focusing on one node is a very tactical approach to a revolution. If social media is the focus of a business, it means we're missing the bigger shift. It's a bit like becoming an expert in the use of lathes at the start of the industrial revolution, or even worse, a particular model of lathe. Being expert at using a tool puts business people into the technician space, rather than the strategic space. It's far more valuable to build a philosophy that can be layered on top of any new tool that happens to appear. Once we have a philosophical framework, the tactics become easy.

Tools are made redundant all the time. They're replaced by new models and technology without notice. This time it's likely to happen more quickly than it would have in the industrial era because we're dealing with the non physical. This means we have considerable control over today's social-media tools. We can move from one app to another in a matter of seconds with practically no switching costs.

There's also the other complexity that comes with trying to grow fruit in someone else's garden. We're at their mercy if they change the game rules. Simple changes to algorithms by the owners of digital media can render a significant corporate investment useless overnight. Our best approach in this instance is a portfolio approach that de-risks the connections we're forging. This must also include the development of direct connections with an audience.

## It's permanent

We can't ignore social media and hope that it will go away. It's equally foolish to intimate that it's not useful in life or in business. The direct connection provided by digital social tools has incredible globe-changing benefits. Instead, the best way to think of social media is as another layer in natural human language. Social media — or digitally enhanced conversation — is really just part of the evolution in human conversation.

First we had body language: hunters and gatherers would act out scenes to describe a situation or occurrence using facial expressions, arms and legs, much as we do today. Then came grunts and sounds, which evolved into words, phrases and an audible language structure. After this came visual references such as cave drawings and pictographs and these eventually formed into written language types, enabling the development of permanent and transportable language through scripture, and eventually books. Each new form of code was built upon a previous layer.

It's not unimaginable to consider early Mesopotamian people lamenting the arrival of the written word. I can imagine them discussing the latest trends around the campfire of an evening and saying how this writing thing is giving away all their secrets and will certainly result in the end of privacy and the decline of their civilisation. Or maybe this new form of written language would disrupt a thriving Mesopotamian business which, in some way, was based on the audible word, not this new written version. It sounds a lot like the tabloid fodder regarding social media we hear today, doesn't it?

With each iteration of human communication tools there's resistance, just as there's resistance to any emerging and scary technology. But when the usefulness is greater than the fear, its eventual uptake is inevitable.

Regardless of what caused the evolution of language (there are currently a number of competing theories of how language arrived), it's clear that those who mastered its use built themselves an evolutionary survival bias. The ability to master language has been the 'killer app' when it comes to hunting, farming, defending and all forms of civilisation development. Even today the mastery of a language — whether it's one of a populous, the language of an industry or a particular computer code — usually comes with social and economic benefits. There's a reason why autocratic nation states have historically restricted education, discussion and free speech: they stifle human activity and restrict change. What's interesting from a social perspective is that when each new evolution of language arrived, it lived alongside the previous forms of communication. None replaced entirely the previous methods; they only added to the interconnected structure of how we communicate. Digital conversations are simply the next phase in the evolution of people. As for the languages that arrived before it, digitally enhanced conversation will live among them in a deeper mesh of human connection possibilities.

## Digital conversations = collective sentience

Digital conversations enabled by social media take us deeper than any other form of publishing. The immediacy and geographic implications of being able to communicate with anyone or any collective tip us into the arena of collective sentience. It's not so much reporting the story of what happened, or how to do something. It's real-time communication about what's happening. Twitter does this exceptionally well due to its brevity and ability to tag itself to other live conversations in distributed media by reaching the minds of people who are not within earshot but need to know something right now. Or, we may want to tap into a collective's mind right now because we know that they know something we need to know at this very moment. People within our digital collective hold the answer we need. In this sense, semantic search is already here. I find myself asking Twitter the nuanced, complex and invariably human questions search algorithms are not quite adept at answering just yet. In some ways, these algorithms may never need to do this as we've now developed the technology to tap into the collective connected brain in real time.

From a business and social perspective, this is our best way of understanding what social media means. It's a path to the collective brain and real-time human activities. This is what makes social media permanent and notable, not the digital distribution of the written words, images and video. We've had that for some time with email and other digital forums, but it didn't inspire the same global transformation and attention that social-media proliferation has.

> I find myself asking Twitter the nuanced, complex and invariably human questions search algorithms are not quite adept at answering just yet.

## Social media as an industrial-system protest

The seminal moments in social media that made global populations sit up and pay attention weren't the heady valuations of the technology companies serving up new social tools. (Remember when Microsoft bought a microshare of Facebook, valuing it at US$15 billion?) They weren't even the moments of celebrity endorsement resulting from celebrities using the new tools and gathering swarms of followers. It was the instant global awareness brought to events that impacted real people's lives, such as the Miracle on the Hudson, which was first reported via a tweet by people escaping an airbus sinking in New York's Hudson River. It was the immediate global reporting of the terrible tsunami in Japan and the initial reports of explosions during the Boston marathon.

But most of all, social-media uptake is an industrial-system protest that says we want more than the one-way monologue served up by traditional media during the 'TV-industrial complex'.[1] This couldn't be better exemplified using social media tools than in what we saw during the Arab Spring. The

---

[1]Phrase coined by Seth Godin to explain the top down system of media-driven coercion and consumption paradigm that shaped the post–World War II consumer era: www.fastcompany.com/events/realtime/miami/blog/godin.html

Iran election protests in June 2009 and the revolution in Egypt in February of 2011 were the strongest demonstrations of the power flip we're entering. Now we all have a published voice that can reverberate as far as a population is willing to carry it, rather than as far as a marketing budget will extend. Prior to technological and digital conversation tools, all our voices were largely private unless we were lucky enough to be picked by a powerful media conglomerate or publisher who would lend us their audience. It didn't matter whether our voice was written, spoken or audio visual, if we didn't have coverage, we didn't have a voice. Now everyone is, or can be, a media company. We all have a technology-enabled megaphone for voicing an opinion, whether it's courageously rising up against a tyrannical government or performing a micro protest to an industrial company delivering a poor customer experience. People have as much potential power as any organisation. It's only now that most people — and companies for that matter — are starting to recognise the depth of the media power flip. Gathering attention in democratised media does take a compounded and consistent effort, but if someone publishes a view worth listening to the people-driven networks will do the rest. In the new media of today the most trusted voice is an independent one, something a corporation can never be.

## Network diffusion

In simple terms, Metcalfe's law[2] states that the power of a network is proportional to the number of connected people using the system. So, the power of a network increases as a function of the number of people using it. This law was first used to describe the network effects of fax machines or the number of telephone lines, both of which are useless with only one device. But the value of the network increases with each device because the total number of connections is increased. For example, two telephones can only make one connection, five can make 10 connections and 12 can make 66 connections. It offers a vast and noticeable difference from the one-message-to-all broadcast model of legacy media. Of course, this works the same way for internet connections and the social services and platforms that live on top of the internet. And everyone with electricity will be on this network in a short time. This is a certainty given that many technological companies no longer make money from the goods they offer; it's the use of these goods that creates their largest revenue stream, being

---

[2]http://www.cs.umd.edu/~golbeck/downloads/Web20-SW-JWS-webVersion.pdf

the advertising they serve up and data they sell. What this means is that companies that make the digital tools will do everything they can to get them in the hands of people. It's not pure altruism that drives projects such as Google's Project Loon and Internet.org.

> **Project Loon:** a proposed network of high-altitude balloons travelling on the edge of space to widen internet coverage

> **Internet.org:** a consortium of Facebook, Samsung, Ericsson, MediaTek, Nokia, Opera and Qualcomm aimed at bringing affordable internet access to the two-thirds of the world yet to connect with high-quality, low-cost mobile technology

That said, the human benefits driven by these commercial imperatives can't be understated. The web will reliably appear in every global corner where electricity is available. This will result in a rapid distribution and connection of people the world over.

Digitally-enabled conversations and social media matter because conversation is the starting point for the diffusion of ideas and innovation. It's the primary human method for releasing our creativity. The primary idea coming from the already connected societies is that we don't just want to consume; we want to create. We have something to offer the world and it's time we participated in the production process. We want to co-design the world we live in.

**We want to co-design the world we live in.**

## Soul-crushing corporations

Corporations were originally set up to protect people and to promote innovation via the removal of personal financial risk resulting from the behaviour of others we do business with. As we entered the industrial era, corporations grew to the point where they dominated the social landscape and shaped opinions. It's not uncommon to read someone's online social-media bio supported by the phrase, 'Opinions are my own'—who else's would they be? Translation: 'Please don't sack me for allowing myself the luxury of some independent thought'. People have become so afraid of the corporations they work for—dehumanising the people they were invented to serve—that they hesitate to voice their opinions. Corporations became their own organism and forged a path, as a virus does. Cells came and went, but the thing itself grew and had its own agenda.

But people are back. And this time we're armed with all of the technology and tools the corporation has. We can do anything they can do, but we can probably do it better, faster and cheaper. And the reason we can do anything they can do, is because we can access anything they can access in the commercial world. The only way organisations will survive through the great fragmentation is by building platforms that enable people to build on top of them and within them. Look at all the new media darlings, such as the free global television channel otherwise known as YouTube or the global production hub access directory known as Alibaba. They have spent the past 10 years providing us with platforms to produce on. Using these platforms we can get on with the more human needs of connection and creativity.

Now that we can all access the factors of production, access is greater than ownership. Now that we're over our consumption obsession, we can aim for deeper meaning in our days than spending them filling up our spare rooms and garages with stuff.

Now that we're re-connecting, we're starting to realise we can create our own paths, not ones designed by the industrial system. It means that how we do business and live life won't be defined by chance and proximity, but by desire and interest.

## What is fragmenting

The means of communication are expanding into multiple layers and formats. Social media is effectively the natural evolution in human communications.

## What it means for business

Social media is not the next means of blasting messages. It's a human form of conversation that primarily serves human interactions.

# CHAPTER 4

# Life in boxes:
## the industrial formula for living

The post–World War II era in Westernised, developed and relatively democratic countries was a cosy existence, as cosy as any time in the history of humanity. Standards of living increased constantly, year upon year. Despite a few shocks and interruptions along the way, we had steady employment growth, increasing incomes and all the trappings that go with classic suburban living. It seemed as though this type of existence could be the answer people had been looking for. A decent-sized house with space around it. Close access to our place of employment. Government-funded schools nearby. Shopping malls filled with shiny gadgets we didn't know we needed. A quarter-acre block with a driveway. A lush, green, grassed backyard in which to play with growing families. Actually, it sounds pretty damn good. I still think it's an incredibly deluxe way of living, especially compared to the nondustrial alternative. It was predictable and packaged. I like to call it 'life in boxes' and it looks something like figure 4.1.

**Figure 4.1: life in boxes**

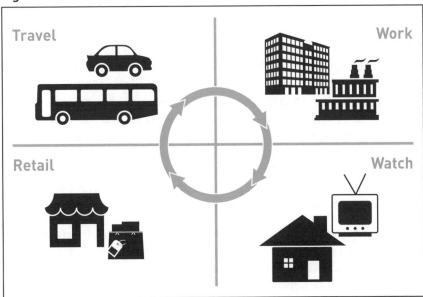

Here's how an average week would go for suburban dwellers between 1950 and 1995: wake up; get ready for work; hop into your transport box — a bus, a train, but more likely a car — and sit in that box for up to an hour. In that box, we'd listen to songs on the radio chosen by someone else in the hope that we might buy the album (which, incidentally, usually only contained three good songs out of 12, but was a terrific way for music stores to garner $30 revenue).

In between the songs we'd be told by way of advertisements about other amazing products we could buy once we'd finished our work for the week. We've got to spend our money on something, right?

Then we'd arrive at our second box for the day. This was either a factory or an office. Of course, everyone hoped to graduate to an office from the factory floor, but either was fine as we were better paid than our parents and our parents' parents. Better conditions too. We'd do what we were told in this box and make sure we helped our employer ship out its little brown boxes of goods for sale at the end of the day. The objective of working was to get to be in the corner box — a pretence of privacy for corporate dwellers with the primary objective of company cost efficiency — but sometimes we had to settle for the cubicle-style box. Many would try to be the last to leave the corporate box, or ensure they left after their boss, to further promote their corner-box aspirations. It was also vital that we had an empty 'in' box or pigeonhole box pre–desktop computer. Leaving the factory or office box late had the additional benefit of fewer boxes on the road in the race back to the suburbs.

We'd get back to our family box at the end of the day for a bit of rest and relaxation. Dinner would be cooked using many labour-saving, pre-packaged food boxes. Since the commencement of the 1980s we've had a little microwave box to save time, important, given we stayed so late at the corporate box while chasing the corner box. We'd eat and then sit down for a night of curated entertainment on the television box. Sure it's flat now, but it's a box that owned most families for hours a night for decades. In my country (Australia) we had four choices of what to watch. The box would entertain us. More subtly, it shaped us and our opinions and told us what we should buy from the big box retailer.

On weekends we'd visit the retail box hoping to see the objects of desire that we saw on the entertainment box that week. We'd hope to see something we didn't expect that would provide us with new consumption opportunities of delight. We'd buy from the big box retailer what we could — or couldn't — afford. We'd buy it because we'd worked so hard in our employee box that it made all the effort worthwhile. It was a reward that got us through the week. It gave us something to look forward to between the drudgery of following orders. We needed and deserved these things.

Our whole economy was designed around these boxes as our world rapidly transitioned from the simple industrial economy into the great era of conspicuous consumption. We didn't just live in and around the boxes, we helped build and fill them. There's a very good chance we worked for one of the companies that created the boxes: transport, housing, consumer goods, retailers, media, durable goods. It makes me wonder if we had a perverse yet subconscious need to facilitate our life in boxes by telling ourselves to buy more of something, forgetting the need the boxes served and instead allowing the boxes themselves to become the need. By knowing at a level that the more stuff we bought, the more we facilitated our so-called improved living standards. We raced the Joneses to have more boxes, but we and the Joneses both knew that the benefits of the race to have more would be shared regardless of the diminishing returns of box living.

It was obvious to me that we'd reached the end of the line when self-storage boxes started to appear across the Western world. In the US alone, self-storage generates annual revenues of more than $24 billion, and it's been the fastest growing segment of commercial real estate for the past 38 years.[1] At first I thought this may be due to the rising cost of real estate in our primary place of residence and the increase in apartment living. Yet 68 per cent of self-storage-box occupiers live in free-standing houses and 65 per cent even have a garage. This is an industry that only exists because we've decided to consume to such an extent that we need to outsource our excess. Another classic reminder of our back-to-front boxed lives is the irrationality of the garage. It's not uncommon to have a garage filled with once-loved, unneeded superfluous stuff worth next to nothing while the new and relatively expensive car stands on the street instead of in the garage. Yes, much of what came in the boxes was and is good, but the things we own are starting to own us.

> Yes, much of what came in the boxes was and is good, but the things we own are starting to own us.

All of this doesn't even take into account the downtime created by the boxes, such as traffic, waiting in lines and having to be in a box somewhere. While we can talk all day about the impact the boxes have on our lifestyle, our finances and our economy, it's the impact they have on our minds that matters most. During the post–World War II era of box living, our minds became boxed in by thinking that was defined by consumption and production. We allowed the purveyors of box living to own our thinking, to limit our desires and output to what fits in the box and to turn us into box zombies. Our society developed a volumetric mindset, where more of anything was better. And the boxes made this possible.

---

[1] Data retrieved from the Self Storage Association fact sheet: http://www.selfstorage.org/ssa/content/navigationmenu/aboutssa/factsheet

# Parasocial interaction

It's not surprising that this lifestyle led to a number of weird human behaviours. Celebrity worship is one such behaviour, for which we probably can't be blamed. People staring directly into our faces, talking to us in a very personal manner inside the box in our lounge room on a daily basis via the television is going to engender a natural human response. And that response is that we're going to feel as though they're talking directly to us: that we're having an interaction of sorts and that it's a real and valid relationship.

A term that describes this phenomenon is 'parasocial interaction'. First coined by Horton and Wohl, parasocial interaction describes a one-sided relationship in which one party knows much about a person, while the other person has no knowledge that the party even exists. It's easy to see how it happens. It's interesting to prophesise why it's happening. Is it a form of vicarious living? Is it people filling the void created by shallow daily corporate interactions? Is it that until television and radio arrived, storytelling was delivered via trusted family and tribe members? It's impossible to know, but it does indicate that the one-way conversation provided by traditional media and life in boxes is something we were not designed to cope with.

# The homo sapiens operating system

Just like computer systems, people also have an operating system (OS). It's known as our deoxyribonucleic acid, or DNA. DNA is a molecule that holds the code to our genetic instructions. It's used for the development and function of all known living organisms. The DNA of homo sapiens is about 200 000 years old. Therefore our operating system is also about 200 000 years old. We haven't had a software upgrade in some time!

And yet the world around us since the industrial revolution — a world that anatomically modern human beings have not been designed to cope with or adapt to via the evolutionary process — has changed rapidly. The evolutionary process moves quite slowly in relative terms. If we take industrial life as we know it today and divide the approximately 200 years we've been living this way into the 200 000 years we've been in our current human design, it only amounts to 1 point of 1 per cent — yes, 0.001 per cent of human existence. It's a tiny proportion of our time on the planet, and if you ever feel as though you just can't cope, it's with good reason. Is any system ever designed in life or on earth to cope with events that occur 0.001 per cent of the time? No, it's not.

## The humanity externality

So it's very 'human' to feel as though the modern world wasn't designed for us, even though it's the result of our behaviour. We're social creatures in nature. Our ability to communicate and our social structures are key reasons why we sit atop the food chain on earth. But the industrial world was in many ways antisocial, driven largely by the rational and logical requirements of a system that places efficiency above all else. A loss of humanity is the price the system pays — an externality that's spat out by the industrial machine as it forges ahead.

## The shallow social pool

The time we invested in living in boxes changed the social structure of who we spent our days with. We've all had times in our lives when we've had to work and trade with people we don't truly care for. Large tracts of our daily social cohort were filled with people we wouldn't choose to invest time in if it weren't for economic reasons. In other words, while it may not be our choice to have personal interactions with the people we work with, it's necessary for survival. However, this takes up a lot of our time, leaving only so much time available for real human interactions of our own choice.

# Dunbar's number

Social researcher Robin Dunbar contended that we can't have meaningful interactions with more than 100 to 200 people at any one time in our lives. Known as Dunbar's number, his research suggested that there's an actual cognitive limit to the number of stable social relationships we can physically maintain. This specifically refers to relationships where both parties know and can relate to each other on a personal level. Dunbar contended there was a link between the size of the neocortex and its processing capacity, which in turn limited functional group sizes. Proponents also assert that group sizes that become larger generally require more restrictive rules to maintain cohesion and enforce accepted group norms. In other words, smaller groups and those within the Dunbar limit can keep an organic structure, which is a structure of successful social relationships built around unwritten and unenforced social boundaries. Dunbar's number isn't about all the people we've ever met in our life, or even the people we've previously had periods of consistent contact with. It's about our circle of close acquaintances in life at any one point in time.

As new people come into our social cohort, others — by physiological necessity — tend to drop out of our lives. People come and people go. It's good to know that we no longer have to feel guilty about not calling up an old high-school buddy or an ex-colleague you bumped into at a conference. It affects us all, and it is largely beyond our control. The number of people any one person can maintain contact with does vary depending on their personal capacity, but the entry and exit of social relationships is a reality for all of us. It's an interesting point to note given our ability to stay in touch, especially in a digital era that isn't limited by technology or communication methods. The only limit we have on maintaining contact today is our personal ability to keep the lines of connection open. Yet, Dunbar's number persists.

It's also evident in internet social networks among people. Dunbar has recently been scientifically frolicking in the anthropological goldmine of Facebook and has revealed his early findings that digitally, as well as in the real world, our species is incapable of managing an 'inner circle' of more than approximately 150 'friends' or meaningful social relationships.

## Enemy territory?

Dunbar's number is more about frequency of interaction than choosing with whom we'd like to interact. Many of the relationships that fill up our personal capacity have been designed by the industrial machine we live within, and the people we work and deal with on a daily basis. In the modern era these people are not always a function of who we like, trust and want to hang out with. Rather, they're often the cohort that's economically necessary but socially unpalatable — bosses, teachers and trading partners as opposed to the trusted family, tribe and community members who once made up our cohort. And as the industrial machine demands more and more of our time, we find ourselves in a cohort we wouldn't choose if we stopped to design it. The reality of who we have our close relationships with is based on two physical realities: frequency and proximity. How frequently do we engage with other people? How often do we interact with them (all types of interactions, both physical and geographically displaced digital conversations)?

What is our proximity to a particular person? (In this case proximity pertains to the physical closeness and real-world interactions we have together.) Do we meet in person? Are we getting to know each other without the use of technology and by simply meeting in the same location?

The more of the above two things we have, the stronger our relationships become. If we think about who we have strong relationships with, we'll see we have both frequency and proximity with them.

The thing we need to be careful about is that these facts point to the reality of how isolated we've become from those we care most about. If you're a hard-working industrial participant, then it's true that your co-workers have both a higher frequency and a higher proximity than any of your family members. We can only hope there are some people in the group we really enjoy being with. It's probably why a lot of people take jobs — and leave bosses.

## Digital clustering

In recent years, since the social web arrived, we've started escaping our geographic realities. Facilitated by these tools, there has been a classic emergence of digital cohorts based around shared value systems and interest. We can now choose the people we want to increase our frequency with even if we're geographically constrained. Our permanent and daily digital connections enable us to circumvent our geography.

**Our permanent and daily digital connections enable us to circumvent our geography.**

We do a form of border hopping to connect with those we enjoy collaborating with, rather than collaborating with those who are merely profitable.

What evolves from here are displaced networks based on connection, creative intention and the new ability to collaborate digitally. It removes the previous demographic boundaries that shaped us, based on physical constraints rather than desired behaviour. When you were a child at school, you became best friends with the kid who sat at the desk next to you, and this seating arrangement was probably decided by alphabetical order of surnames (ironically, early web-based search engines were based on alphabetical order too, rather than the actual needs of the searcher). Or you became friends with your next-door neighbour, or other kids on your street, regardless of whether you actually shared any interests. While these options of friendship and physical connection still exist today, we're not limited by them. There's nothing stopping a 12-year-old gamer becoming best friends or a playing partner with another kid half a world away who shares a passion for the latest massive multi-player game. They can have all the frequency and interaction they would have had with their next-door neighbour playing a daily ball game in the yard just a generation ago. This is not just limited to the digital natives of the day; this reality is open to anyone, and it's likely to become the norm in that we'll choose desirable connections based on value systems and interests, rather than geographic constraints and economics. The shift in the type of work we do and the places we stay will start to represent what we first create virtually in the digital world. It will then eventually graduate to become part of our entire world, the one we shape in our own vision, first made possible by what these new digital connections afforded us.

## Virtual is real

While it's clear we're living through a revolution, most people still create a weird kind of separation between what they call the real world and the virtual world, almost as though they're two separate planets. It's easy to understand why people feel this way. It's because much of what's arrived is so radical and new. It takes time to adjust to the new reality, but it's still part of the single reality we all live in. Because much of the technology is so obvious and has changed human body language, the way we touch and interact with smartphones is a very different type of human movement, one not seen before. In this way it's kind of clumsy and inhuman. This facilitates a human response that says, 'This is not us. This is separate from us. We're not used to it, nor that type of interaction from our species. So it must be a new world — a different one. We need to give it a new name so that we can segregate it while we work out how it all fits together and in our lives'.

## IRL vs AFK

Since the web became a daily part of most people's lives, the term 'In Real Life' (IRL) has been coined to let people know whether an interaction was virtual or physical. It's a term hardcore netizens revile. They much prefer AFK, or Away From Keyboard, the inference being that the internet is real life — and it is. When we think about it, even this can only be regarded as a temporary descriptor for being connected at a point in time. Keyboards, like all technology, will eventually supersede themselves, and that process has already commenced. While high-quality voice recognition software seems to be forever promised 'next year', the keyboard has in many places been usurped. Most smartphones and tablets, while they have a visual replicator for a keyboard, are infrequently used. The user experience design high ground seems to be centred around making a keyboard an unnecessary interface. If we take it to an even deeper level, this distinction of being at some kind of 'connected terminal or device' will evaporate as well. Everything in our world — from packaged goods, to the windows in our homes — is on the verge of being connected. There will be no separation from the network unless we make a clear decision to 'go dark' in a distinct and purposeful manner.

> **netizen:** a person who is a citizen of the internet (inferring that the internet has an expected set of collaborative behaviours just like our physical communities do)

## Virtual is the physical preamble

From a social perspective, the displaced digital connections we make — those connections with people we've never met in person, or with whom we started a relationship digitally — are merely a preamble to a future physical interaction. We find that if we don't enjoy a digital interaction with someone, we won't continue the frequency of that interaction. If we do enjoy the digital interaction, then our basic human need for connection and physical contact will take over. We'll find a way to connect with them, to meet with them and to break bread in the physical world. The digital interactions we create through our interest-based networks become a type of sampling campaign for meeting and interacting in the traditional human way: a way of finding souls who share something metaphorically to make it a physical reality.

## Let's go surfing

Often when I go surfing I take a photo of what the waves look like and post it on Twitter or Instagram. I like to let people know when there are great waves for surfing. When I do this I always add the hashtag #surfing. Some of my non-surfing friends (the large majority) like to live vicariously through my habitual and filter-enhanced picture of the beach.

I've noticed that this is also a habit of other surfers who live in my area. I live in Melbourne, Australia, which is more than one hour's drive from the nearest breaking waves. For such a distance from the surf, Melbourne has a surprisingly large surfing population. I started to have some conversations on Twitter with other surfers who shared my passion. We'd first find each other by 'surfing' the hashtag of #surfing, and then we'd connect every weekend by sharing pictures of where we surfed that day. The crazy thing is, we'd all be leaving the same city, around the same time, to go surfing in many of the same places, but travelling in separate cars.

A now friend, previous stranger and fellow surfer, Simon, would talk with me online about the surf forecast even before the weekend arrived. He'd share with me where he thought the best waves would be and he became a really terrific resource, helping me enjoy my pastime more because he thought I might appreciate the information. And it probably made him feel good sharing his expertise because he could, not because he had to or had some financial reason to. Eventually we became comfortable enough with each other to organise a meeting at a particular beach to share some waves. I remember not knowing what he looked like (his profile picture was of a wave). He did tell me what car he had and his type of surfboard. In a way, meeting at a location and going in separate cars was a safety mechanism.

After a few surfs together we eventually started meeting in the city and driving from there to the beach in one car. We discovered that we share the same business interests and even work in the same industry. The new digital tools helped our like minds to find a cluster of relevance, a way to connect on what matters to us. It's often the case that the tools we adopt say more about the values and experience we hold and the life we lead. Simon and I even share the same family circumstances. We've become good mates and we do various business projects together.

## Digital replicates physical

The process I've just described replicates the exact way we connected with people before the digital possibilities. A certain topic would come up in physical conversation. We'd share some ideas. We'd talk about meeting around that topic, catching up and focusing on the issue. It's exciting to meet someone who cares about what you care about. We'd agree to catch up at the next event for the topic of interest, then we'd do that thing together, and finally form a relationship beyond the thing, and delve into the human side of connection. It's all the same behaviour, just being started via different tools. Our social patterns and norms are unchanged; just the tools are new.

Interacting is a human social need; it's a deep-seeded need to connect and feel the warmth of a valued association. A virtual existence that doesn't cross the physical chasm is a lonely one indeed. We have to remember that everything we invent needs to be invented with people in mind, regardless of the business or industry we operate in. The tools that enable us to be more human are simply becoming more important.

# There is no 'digital'

Digital tools and how they change what's possible have created the birth of a new set of jobs that often have the D word (digital) in front of them. New types of jobs are one of the good things that come with disruptive change. They replace redundant jobs such as 'woolly mammoth hunter'. But it's when these so-called new digital roles are generalist in nature that organisations have got it severely wrong. They behave as though digital is a separate thing, something we attend to and then close the door on. While it's clear that the omnipresence of the world wide web has changed our business infrastructure, it's **There is no digital; there is only life.** not clear that most people understand the truth about digital as it pertains to business strategy. Here's a simple phrase to help remind us: 'There is no digital; there is only life'.

We seamlessly move among a variety of technologies during our day, as we have done since the beginning of time with all forms of technology. We don't have a digital life and an analogue life any more than we have a 'sitting on a chair' life or a 'sitting on the floor' life. A chair is just a piece of technology, just as the latest shiny device in our pocket is. And it's about time we started recognising that a digital strategy is a flawed one by definition.

> **digital strategy:** a flawed and simplistic strategy that involves only the web-based parts of a business

All that exists is a strategy. And just like any good strategy, it ought to take into account all of the potential inputs and considerations of our business environment. A good strategy should be technology-agnostic. It doesn't care about the technology of the day. It only cares about serving the market. A good strategy, then and now, only cares about achieving objectives via consideration of all of the methods at its disposal.

# What's your electricity strategy?

As I write this, successful companies are still littered with digital XYZs: digital marketing managers, digital strategists, digital sales managers … the list is endless. Just go into any job-posting site and type in the word 'digital'. Everyone in business is in 'digital'. If we want to participate in the new economy, we have to be in 'digital', just as we have to be able to read and write.

The days of digital strategy are over. The days of digital anything in a job title are over as well. They should never have existed in the first place. Anyone who doesn't get digital, doesn't get strategy. Any person or organisation that has not invested the time to understand and embrace the changes is saying, 'We're not serious about surviving the present-day upheaval'. Having a digital strategy is a bit like having an 'electricity strategy'. It just doesn't make any sense. Referencing the infrastructure in the direction means the focus is not where it should be; that is, on the customer.

# The market doesn't care when you finished school

Anyone who works in a strategic or marketing capacity in a business, and who does not understand and naturally integrate digital into what they do, is not keeping abreast of how things are changing. Even worse, it means that the leadership team within the organisation that commissions these new roles is also out of touch. It's incumbent upon management and staff to self-educate. The fact that all this stuff arrived after we graduated from university is not an excuse anyone will buy. The cost of not being across digital is just too high. It's ironic given how easy it is to learn all the new 'stuff'. None of it is hard. None. Yes, the technophiles took a while to get their act together in making the technology easy enough for us to use, but they got there in the end. Every tool on the web worth using for business includes a personalised hand-holding process that teaches us how to use it. It's super marketing really — something VCR manufacturers could have used in 1981, and many remote-control designers could do with even today as you can see in figure 4.2.

**Figure 4.2: a remote control**

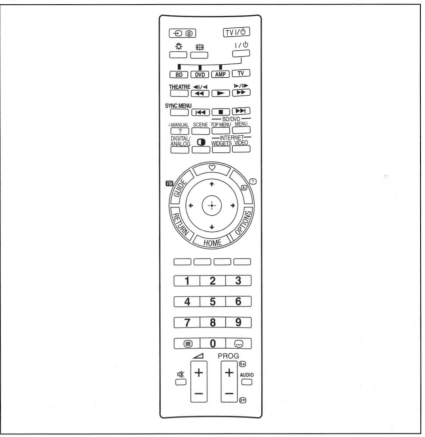

If you can turn on a computer and read, then you can learn anything you need to know for business use in digital. The new landscape — that is, the new technological, internet-based economy — even comes with simple-to-follow learning instructions in the shape of online videos and user-friendly interfaces. We need not know more than how to read and how to be a human being to learn how to use the tools to a ninja level of effectiveness. It's a terrific reminder that this revolution is one of connection, not technology. Technology is merely the facilitator.

# Getting your digital *on*

It's important to note here that I'm not talking about the deep-level digital skills required for, say, building a smartphone app. I'm talking about the knowledge needed by people who are in a similar job now to the one they had before the digital revolution arrived; that is, the generalist business and marketing executives of this world. Generalist business people don't need to convert their entire skill base to become code monkeys or development engineers. We don't need to know what makes the tools work, we just need to be able to use the tools. We only need to drive the metaphorical digital car. In business we only need to be concerned about whether the tool can get us to our desired destination, not the mechanics of what makes it possible. We can leave all that to the people providing the tools.

# It's not my job

A simple argument for any business executive is that their job is to manage people, strategy and finance, not be an expert in managing a bunch of tools. The problem is that business and tools are inextricably linked. Tools mattered just as much in production during the agrarian era as they did in the industrial era, as they do today.

Let's take the example of a job type we all understand, that of a general practitioner (GP, or doctor). What they do has been impacted as heavily by technology as any business, maybe even more so. When we want to get diagnosed, be advised of the latest treatment options or be prescribed medicine by our doctor, we expect that they are up with the latest technology available to us as their patient (or customer). If a doctor told you during a consult that they didn't bother to learn about MRI scans because it happened after they finished medical school, and they preferred to only rely on x-rays, you'd go and look for a better doctor pretty damn quick, one who cares enough to learn what they need to know.

# Welcome to med school

The cosy period of being able to work at a stable job — a job that doesn't change much for your entire working life — is over. While there will be times when we have to call in a specialist, we still need to know which one is best, and what they should be able to do and solve, as doctors do. We're all general practitioners in our own industry, so it's a requirement of the marketplace that we're familiar with the latest tools and methods we need to achieve the outcomes we need for our business, regardless of when these tools arrived in the marketplace. The new general practitioners of business need to make the decision to keep up, just as doctors must with their journals and conferences. There's no choice. It's what the new market demands; every youngster entering our industry keeps up to date by default. It's not even a task for them; they enjoy it. It's the world they were born into. So unless we decide to enjoy it too, and go for deep learning by using the tools, we'll not only be left behind, but probably replaced.

Now that we're escaping the industrial machine, it's about time marketers realised that people are not interchangeable widgets and that they would rather be spoken to and about by a human voice.

## What is fragmenting

We're being freed from our life in boxes. Where people live is no longer defined by where the infrastructure is because everything is so widely dispersed now.

## What it means for business

The power to decide is back in the hands of the populous and no longer with the industrialists.

# CHAPTER 5

## Rehumanisation:
## words define our future

I hear a man's words, and I see into his soul.

The words we use shape the values we have. They shape the values and belief systems of the societies we live in. It's also true that the people around us (correctly or otherwise) judge where we fit into their world based on our words. Think of a job interview, for example. It's nothing more than a truncated language test used to determine how capable or smart a candidate is for a particular function.

This could possibly be the worst way to assess a potential employee's suitability for any role other than a direct sales or public speaking post. Yet we use this method as the default because we define almost everything we do and believe through what we tell ourselves and each other. Language permeates our entire commercial ecosystem and is also a significant arbiter of brand success.

# Aiming for mindless consumers

The language used in corporate environments tells us much about the true value systems and culture of an organisation. When Facebook says it wants a more open and connected society, it's really talking about its desire to peek into your underwear drawer because that may just be a profitable move. Turns out it is — for now.

We hear a lot of double-barrelled language so that the organisations in question can't be accused of lying or misleading. They like, and even love, words that leave things open to interpretation. There is, however, some language that's been used in corporate environments, and especially within marketing circles, that's downright ugly and has nothing to hide behind. During the transition from a corporate-driven economy to a human-driven one, there are some words we should leave behind as redundant relics. Two words that need to be at the top of the pile are 'target' and 'consumer'.

## Targets

A target is something to aim for, shoot at, maybe even kill. It's something someone wants because it suits their needs. I much prefer the terms 'audience' and 'community'. An audience is something or someone we try to impress. It gives us a chance to prove our worth, it invests its time in us and we must respect it by trying to over-deliver to its expectations. An audience isn't passive; it provides feedback and input that's part of the show. Really great performers even know how to get an audience onto the stage to become participants, something we've seen smarter brands do in recent times. With an audience, the onus is on us. We hope they throw flowers on the stage, cheer and ask for an encore. We want the show to live beyond the showing time. We want it to have a before (people anticipating and looking forward to the engagement) and an after (people raving and sharing the story with their friends). If we do well with an audience who gave us our attention, then we have a chance at building a community. With an audience, we enter the stage knowing we may get rotten tomatoes thrown at us, if that's what we deserve. We need to think of the flow of interaction for doing business in more human terms. We garner some attention and gather an audience. The audience participates in our show. From this, a community may emerge. Within our community will be customers who pay us money for providing value to them as people. (Note that they are not called 'consumers'.)

## Consumers

Consumer. What a terrible way to refer to a person or group of people. Even pond scum can be defined using the word 'consumer'. It's such a detached way to refer to people, it's as if all that can be seen is a mouth, a set of teeth and a gut. And it's a classic example of large corporations forgetting they're doing business with real people who have emotions, dreams and aspirations by defining them as a kind of parasite of commerce. If it sounds ugly, we need look no further than the definitions of the word 'consume' as a reminder.

Here are my 'top-5' definitions, taken from various dictionaries.

### con~sume:

1   to destroy or expend by use; use up

2   to eat or drink up; devour

3   to destroy, as by composition or burning

4   to spend (money, time etc.) wastefully

5   to absorb; engross.

(Based on the Random House Dictionary, © Random House, Inc. 2014.)

## Markets follow conversation

The words we use are of vital strategic importance. It's not just a matter of simple semantics. It has an important strategic impact on the way we approach the marketplace. As soon as any brand or company defines the people it sells its wares to as 'consumers' it impacts the overriding corporate culture. The rot sets in. It creates a cadre of behaviours that lead to poor business decisions. It's a volumetric, non-human measure by nature, so it leads brands down a path where they want that faceless mass to buy and use more. It entices companies to build an infrastructure around serving masses and reducing input costs. This invariably leads to a corporate factory mindset where brands must sell more, prices must be reduced and market share must grow in volume terms. This leads to the inevitable death spiral of commoditisation and price focus.

Defining people in this way stymies innovation. It creates an illusion of what a company should be doing in the first instance. It shifts the company focus onto the products they sell instead of the solutions they create. By defining people as the 'absorbers' of what is made, they're hardly likely to find a better way to serve the needs of people. How can anyone possibly connect to and understand who they serve when those they serve are objectified into a product-usage behaviour?

# Dead-end products

In some ways, it's not surprising the words 'target' and 'consumer' appeared as key marketing parlance. Most things from the industrial age were dead-end products. Dead-end products are those that arrive to the end purchaser in their final format. A price is paid and the benefit of the product is that it can be used as it is. Sure, we may be able to re-sell it, or even use it for an extended period of time, but it's designed in a way that its primary purpose is to finish its lifecycle at that point.

But more than that, dead-end products are not intended to be reinterpreted, mashed up and released back into the market with our input. The time-saving devices of the industrialised world fit very much into this space. Time is saved because someone else did the hard work to prepare something for you. If you think about life pre-internet, it was filled with dead-end products — packaged goods, fridges, cars, washing machines, sneakers, ducted heating, instant coffee, glossy magazines, sitcom television programs — all sit-back-and-receive scenarios.

# A future of unfinished products

The world we live in now is about handing the brand back over to its rightful owners: the audience. Companies believe they own their brands, but in reality they don't. A brand depends on those who purchase it for sustenance. If we stop feeding a brand, then the brand dies. The same is true for so-called 'free' products that advertise our attention as a revenue source. The price we pay in that situation is the price of our valued time and limited attention. Our attention is very valuable commercially when we have an unlimited number of places to direct it. If a brand depends on those who use it for its survival, they must have a form of ownership claim on it; a kind of dual dependency. And what people are telling us is that they want to help create the things they use. There is a clear shift towards people preferring products that are not finished. They want products where they get involved in the making process. Everything from slow food to high-end technology is transitioning to the malleable marketplace.

# The malleable marketplace

It's worth reminding ourselves what software does. Software allows us to interpret its capabilities to create an output specific to our needs. At first software was for corporations, where the end user would create a different output. The tiny insight that the end user should be able to change functionality on demand, way back in the late 1970s, was the bellwether for an impending age of end-user control.

Today the best technology devices arrive with the need for our input. Even better, they arrive with an open door for tinkerers and garage heroes to show us what they're capable of. They're designed to be reconfigured by the end user, to be customised. Our phones are a canvas for our own creation and the imagination of others in the market. No two smartphones end up with the same configuration once they're active in the market.

## Software to soft-retail

If green-screen, corporate-born software can become more human, surely any product can. Now we can design our own shoes and clothes and pay a premium for the experience, remembering, of course, that the design decisions when it comes to fashion items are where a large part of the product value is created. In fact, it's now the anomaly for a shoe brand to not have a custom creation option. And the malleable marketplace doesn't need to be limited to products that are designed online and then shipped. Brands have to remember that people don't see the online world as anything separate. We want the same visceral experiences everywhere that we do commerce. We're agnostic in that sense. Even boring old retail can participate in the malleable marketplace.

## Component retail

Component retail is where brands ship product components and raw materials to stores to be assembled on site, all as part of the retail experience. It's a model where customers will become the theatre at store level and are happy to provide labour because they've been given the very personal gift of creating something for themselves. We'll see this sign a lot more on shop windows:

*Build it yourself instore.*

This retail model is far less about a price point and product and far more about the experience and the story it invents.

## The album with no sound

The most extreme and inspiring example of the malleable product comes from the musician, Beck. A recent album, if you can call it that, was released without any sound. Yes, there was no music with the album. Known as the *Song Reader* project and released at the end of 2012, it consists of 20 songs of sheet music. Beck presented the skeleton of the album for other musicians and fans to use to create their own version of the 'songs'. So the first version of the album users would hear is the one they created themselves. After the launch of the album, Beck embarked on a number of live *Song Reader* performances, with other musicians playing as guests. But more importantly, fans embraced the idea, posting their versions online and on YouTube, some achieving many thousands of views. With this counter-intuitive move, Beck managed to give birth to infinite iterations of his music. By handing over his so-called intellectual property, instead of fighting piracy, he gave others the blueprints for his songs: 'How should this sound? Go make some music!' It gave me some reborn faith in humanity. It made me believe again that money follows imagination. Why don't companies release blueprints for their products in a similar way? Maybe the audience can take it somewhere miraculous. Individuals may just see something that companies never did, in much the same way as social media was taken to places the media conglomerate could never quite imagine.

## But we make cars

It's difficult to imagine a car coming to market unfinished and being co-designed or even co-created by the market. But that doesn't mean it's impossible. While we may have heard of the glass cockpit, surely there's no reason why cars couldn't have glass dashboards — dashboards designed by the people who actually drive them. Imagine the front half of the dashboard — or cockpit of the car — as being a large, rendered screen. All we'd need is a screen-enabled or head-up display interface that connects to the cloud or a smartphone. Most cars already connect with smartphones via bluetooth and other forms of connectivity. It would be an app store for cars and extra revenue for stuff people actually want, rather than ripping customers off with aftermarket products. There's no reason why any major car company couldn't create an app store or tap into the existing application ecosystems and platforms to provide apps built either by the car company or opened up to the audience to re-imagine the dashboard. Malleable driving experiences could be made possible by software (smartphones) that already lives in our pockets. Apps could enable the driver to change dashboard visuals, designs and colours, as well as controlling music, tracking devices, voice-activated enhancements, and general driving efficiency and enjoyment hacks. Who knows, the crowd may come up with significant safety enhancements that use sensors to wake sleepy drivers.

**glass cockpit:** an aircraft cockpit that features electronic (digital) instrument displays, typically large LCD screens (Wikipedia)

Moreover, cars are very soon going to evolve into lounge rooms once self-driving cars become the norm. The technology for safe self-driving cars already exists. Millions of kilometres have been driven without incident. The cost of the technology that makes it possible is in rapid freefall. It's hard to predict when autonomous driving cars will be available to the public, and estimates range from a few years to up to 20 years.[1] Google, a leading developer of the technology, claims its technology will be ready to commercialise with major auto manufacturers by the year 2018. When this happens, the possibilities of

> **The technology for safe self-driving cars already exists.**

---

[1] Driverless car prediction dates by various respected auto and technology firms: www.driverless-future.com/?page_id=384

dashboard technology will no longer be restricted by safe driving practices. Given we're talking about years, rather than decades, car companies should probably prepare for the inevitable now. A world of entirely new revenue streams awaits the auto industry if they follow the playbook already evidenced in both media evolution and personal computing technology. All they need is to have the courage to let other people get involved.

## From products to platforms

Being able to thrive going forward is about removing the finality that comes with the launch mentality: not assuming that a product is finished when we deliver it to the market. Brands that survive the current reconfiguration of economics will understand that a product or service is a continuum of development, a continuum that people take from the company and invent the next stages of. Brands are evolving into platforms for audiences to perform with and upon. This is the human input that the industrial system didn't allow or even want. What's interesting is that what the brand evolves into with the creativity of outsiders is usually better than what the corporate committee would have decided on. It's certainly more varied because instead of one-size-fits-all, it's one-size-fits-one.

# Corporate skulduggery?

In some ways corporate skulduggery sounds like something we've already seen in the classic corporate playbook: large corporations taking advantage of an unsuspecting public to get free labour and fatten the bottom line. The serendipity with which it arrived is evidence it was beyond the thinking of most organisations. While it may sound like an evil corporate trick, it's actually a humanising process of letting people do what they do best. And that's to be part of the creative process, add their spin and potentially be rewarded, both emotionally and financially, as the product extends beyond when they touched it and had an input into it.

Companies didn't ask people to mess with their products. They resisted, and they still do. But when digital tools first arrived, people started mashing up everything they could get their hands on. The compulsion was deeply seeded into what people do. They wouldn't stop, and companies—doing what companies do (the smart ones at least)—decided to get onboard to make a profit. That said, the very large majority still dismiss this shift as a niche, a nuance, a cute little sideshow to the real corporate play. And they are very, very wrong.

# Outsourcing logic

'Computer' used to be a job title. The word first entered parlance to describe the job of people who had to spend all day calculating stuff, adding things up, quantifying and providing the numbers that went into our modern world. It actually comes from the word 'compute', which has French origins and was borrowed from the Latin word *computare*, meaning 'to count, sum up; reckon'. It was only from 1946 that it began being used as the word for an electric machine that could undertake these computing tasks. The machines that were developed to replace human computers (at first they were mechanical adding machines) came along for a very good reason: that people should be doing more important tasks than calculating and adding. Not only are we not very accurate at doing it, it's an inane, boring process that has little human spirit and enjoyment associated with it. For a while there though, we couldn't kick the habit of trying to turn people into machines or organic beings that served the machines. I like to call it the 'spreadsheet era'.

# The end of bison hunting

If we were to ask a seven-year-old how to find the answer to $13 \times 7$, there's a chance the answer would be, 'Put it into the calculator on your phone'. That's a correct answer. It's one of the methods that can validly be used to find the answer. Increasingly, this will become the way it's done. There's a chance kids of tomorrow won't know how to do their times tables. So the real question is, do they really need to know how to do them? It may seem like an extreme example and something that's too important in modern life to let slip. You're probably thinking they won't be life ready, and that this would be a travesty to human education. But there are so many things I never learned to do that would have been life ending pre–modern civilisation. I can't ride a horse. I can't catch a fish, let alone scale it. I wouldn't know how to grow a crop, build a shelter or kill a beast to feed my family. I'm pretty much useless when it comes to life-saving skills of the pre-modern era. Put me in the Savannah to forage and hunt for my own food and I won't last very long at all. So, is it worth being able to calculate anything in the post-industrial era? Maybe. Is that what we get paid for these days? Is it where anyone adds value? With the advent of ubiquitous computing, is it worth memorising anything? In a world where everything the world knows is available on demand any time with perfect accuracy, I'd argue that we're better off outsourcing logic so we can get back to the more human and creative tasks of doing this:

*Making connections with the seemingly disparate elements in our world.*

That's where the value lies today.

Here are some thoughts:

- We can't split test our way to a better world. If we test two bad ideas against each other, a bad idea still results as the winner.
- An algorithm can't intuitively predict something outside of its ecosystem parameters.

The point is, we're slowly outsourcing left-brain logic to the CPU (central processing unit), not because knowing stuff isn't important, but because putting things together in creative ways is more rewarding emotionally and increasingly more rewarding economically. Technology is creating the asset of human connection. The industrial age removed the necessity of lifting heavy objects; the technology age is removing our need to calculate stuff. It's time we all embraced the human side of the revolution and stopped worrying about which skills may evaporate.

# The tastemakers

The major success factor for the pre-web modern marketing era was mass: mass manufacturing, mass consumption, mass machines, mass media, mass merchants. When you bundle all of these together in an organised fashion you end up with a mass pop culture. The system itself required pop-culture hits to be self-sustaining. The system needed and supported a macro pop culture. It didn't support niche. What this means is that we had a set of tastemakers who decided what we liked: the television program managers, the magazine editors, the news curators, the retail buyers and the marketing managers. They would decide which alternatives we'd be given to choose from. They decided this by virtue of the fact that we had no way of knowing what else was available. If it wasn't in our personal geography, we wouldn't know about it. All the things we did know about were hokey and local, or the same thing our entire nation knew about because the tastemakers decided to make it, advertise it and pay the price to put it on the retailers' shelves. Only the tastemakers could afford the reach that goes with mass. We got to choose one of the options available on the shelf. We got to choose one of the few shows on free-to-air television. The system didn't support niche like it does now. The cultural phenomena that resulted from the system were powerful indeed. The Rubik's cube, breakdancing, BMX bikes, cabbage patch dolls, sitcoms, teenage mutant ninja turtles, video cassette recorders, the walkman, aerobics, legwarmers, Coke vs Pepsi, Band Aid, hair metal, Beverly Hills Cop, Nintendo, PAC-MAN and glow worms were all picked by someone else, someone who decided we needed them to enhance our human existence. And they were right. Of course we wanted them. We wanted to express our human emotions and this was what was available at the time. We had to have the latest widget of desire, see the show and participate in the fad. Fads were rad. They formed part of the lore that made our so-called community, a community that was a substitute for natural human inclinations.

# The selfish era

Mass marketing was a selfish modality of marketing designed by and for the owners of capital, and not only financial capital, but mind capital. The average suburban dweller became everyone and no one. We had all loved and believed in average products with the edges rounded off.

There are a lot of examples of selfish marketing occurring on a repetitive and formulaic level beyond that of the fads mentioned above. Some selfish industries are still getting away with it — for now. Here's my all-time favourite example of selfish marketing, entirely designed to inconvenience people and trick them into spending more money than they set out to.

## Milking customers in retail

In traditional bricks-and-mortar retail there's something called the 'retail cold spot'. It's the far-away-in-the-back-corner-of-the-store places that not many customers would typically walk to or past. The bigger the store, the more likely it is to have them. So, in their infinite wisdom, retailers decided to put the most important items (the traffic generators) in their retail cold spots. This is why, whenever you go to buy milk at a large supermarket, or even the local corner store or 7-Eleven, the milk is always in the back corner, even to this day. The truth is that it works financially. People walk past the other aisles and see things they didn't know they needed, the impulse-purchase items such as chocolate bars and corn chips. The net result is more revenue for the retailer. Who cares about the stupid customer. Very selfish stuff indeed.

Let's imagine for a moment that an online retailer behaved the same way. Seriously, what if someone who sells widgets online decided to hide what people really wanted behind all the things people didn't have any intention of buying when they entered a website. You came to buy a certain book and they made you click through 23 separate web pages just to get to the page with the book you were searching for. You simply wouldn't bother. They wouldn't have the chance to lure you in before you clicked out of the website thinking, 'This is the worst user experience in history!' And you'd find another place to spend your money.

It sounds totally ridiculous when we overlay certain physical retail strategies into the virtual world. The reality, though, is that if it doesn't happen online then it shouldn't happen offline. Plain and simple. Strategies that work over the long haul are human, not selfish. Business should be about value creation, not value extractions.

# So how do we survive?

Sure, companies need valid business models. And there's an art to making more money through execution tactics. But deep down in any retailer's heart, they know their job is to make people happy to spend their money with them without any retail chicanery where the environment tricks people into subconscious behaviour. It's not cool, and I think the new tools will continue to expose it and hurt businesses that use these tricks.

## Marketing mantra

Rant warning ...

Here comes a truth bomb. It may sound a bit ranty, but it's totally true. I lived the first 15 years of my employed life working for the world's biggest packaged goods companies, listening daily to the marketing language I'm about to detail for you. I know most people are aware of this language, but I really feel it needs to be expunged from the business tactics of tomorrow, so much so that I feel the need to rant about it.

Marketing-specific language also had its fair share of self-language. These were terms that companies would never use directly with their customers, but that form a large part of their conversations with agencies and in boardroom discussions. But the gig is up, and just in case you don't know which terms you should banish from the boardroom, here they are with my own personal definitions in some real, human language:

- *The planned obsolescence.* We're going to make this thing in a way that it breaks on purpose. We're going to leave out features we've already made so that our customers have to buy it again and/or upgrade.

- *The roadblock.* We're going to buy media on every single channel all at the same time when we launch this product. If you watch television, or any form of traditional media, we're going to block every input so that you have to listen to us shouting at you even if you don't want to.

- *The AWOP (average weight of purchase).* We're going to get people to buy more of what we sell, even if they don't need it. Every year we want people to have more of this product because it makes our system work more efficiently. We'll trick them by giving two-for-one offers and discounts that their rational minds can't refuse, even though we know they can't use or eat what we sell and it will probably end up in the trash.

- *Brand loyalty.* We'll make sure our customers only ever do business with us. They must be loyal to us (not we to our customers). We'll make loyalty a one-way street that serves the brand and we won't return the favour.

- *Household penetration.* We need to bust our way into people's homes — and as many homes as possible. We're not going to knock on the door, be nice or build a relationship of trust and service. We're going to do whatever we can to bust our way in. We don't care whether they want our products or not.

- *Cannibalisation.* We'll only ever launch a new product if the new version won't eat into our existing sales too much, even if a new one would serve our customers better. We'd rather make money than serve people. But if the new replacement product makes more profit than what it substitutes, we'll delete the old one from our range and force people into the new one.

There are more of these marketing terms. You can probably buy a book that espouses the virtues of them strategically. But I think they're ugly and they're for amateurs who don't see or want to play the long-term game.

# Creative types

We were tricked during the industrial era of television into thinking that producers and marketers had some kind of magical talent when all they had was access to the tools that we didn't. The proof is everywhere around us in the digital world. There's an internet full of bloggers who write as well as — and with as much thought as — *The New York Times* journalists. There are viral video makers on YouTube who are every bit as creative as the directors who work in the world's best advertising agencies. There are designers on Etsy who have the flair and sensibility of the famous Eames office.

## Give me that hammer

When the necessary tools entered our hands we realised that we're at least as creative as all of them. We can do whatever they can do given half the chance, and with even fewer resources. In fact, when people are given tools and opportunity, it changes things. Access is everything. There's often something very special that happens to creative output when it's a gift to an audience, rather than a sell job. A person hacking away at a blog post on an issue late on Saturday night because it matters to them and their community … this has every chance of being the article we should read on that topic because of the purity that comes with it. It's this approach that brings out the human side of endeavour. And what we all want are things that are more human.

# Collaboration, creative orientation and counter intuition

The key difference we see online and with newer businesses today is that they give first. The ethic is to collaborate first (thus providing resources) and then transact. The flow of the user experience is to give the end user something of value, build trust in the relationship and then engage in commerce once we're comfortable with each other. The industrial ethic had the opposite approach. Its approach was to say, 'Here's this item and this is the price. So let's transact. You buy something and if you buy it often enough I might reward you for your loyalty later on'. Airline frequency flyer programs operate in this way.

In contrast, the burgeoning co-working-space approach, is very much to trust and interact first and then transact much later. Most co-working spaces around the world have an attitude of, 'Come in; hang out; do some work; have a coffee on us (the espresso machine's over there) and here's the wi-fi password. If you like it after a few weeks we'll work out an agreement to rent a desk'. It's collaborative in nature: human first, commercial second.

Sometimes we have to remind ourselves of how dramatic these changes really are. So many of the things we're seeing are counter intuitive to what we'd expect from large corporations. Let's take the simple example of the two biggest global social-media competitors, Facebook and Twitter. Both of them have cross-platform sharing. The entire social web has this. This means that users can choose to publish on one platform and have it automatically posted on the other platform. It's very hard to imagine a six-pack of cola coming with three cans of Pepsi and three cans of Coca-Cola. But in the new world, there tends to be more focus on coopetition than there is on competition. Not only does it put the user's needs first, it also populates the social-media ecosystem to benefit both brands.

> **coopetition:** cooperation between competing organisations to build a stronger ecosystem

Now that we've been set free creatively, marketers are starting to realise that our statistical profiles are a very poor predictor of behaviour indeed.

## What is fragmenting

People are no longer a component of the industrial machine. They're escaping the cubicle and factory to build something more humane.

## What it means for business

'Tell and sell' is over. Now it's about connecting in a non-corporate, human manner. Corporations have to start acting more like people and less like evil organisms with their own agenda.

**CHAPTER 6**

Demographics is history:
moving on from predictive marketing

If you learned your marketing trade any time in the past 60 years, there's a very good chance a large part of what you learned was related to demographic profiling, the statistical art of putting people into behaviour buckets. These were clusters created to define what people believe and how they're likely to behave so that they could be 'targeted' with financial efficiency. It was the marketing diet I was brought up on, and I believed it to be accurate in most ways, until I realised that everything I saw in the 'real world' flew in the face of demographics. It's not surprising, when we have a close look at what makes up our demographics, to see that it's no longer an accurate measure. Once marketers start to dig deep, it's apparent that demographics is a tool that's past its marketing 'use by' date and that there are better ways to engage with an audience that actually wants to hear from us. Rather than mind-spamming a large group of people who may be interested in what we offer because some demographer has said they behave a certain way. Actually it's even a bit more sinister than that. The truth is that the large majority of demographics were self-perpetuating. Choice in the market was limited, self-expression was limited, the ability to connect was largely geographically based and culture was defined by gatekeepers and tastemakers. The way demographics 'got fed' shaped the beast itself, rather than the other way around. And now that we choose what to feed ourselves, the shape is turning out to be vastly different.

Business methods have limitations, and we could only use what was available at the time. The tools weren't great, but it was probably the best option we had to market with during the post–World War II consumption explosion — and it worked. But when something better arrives, it's time for the responsible people making decisions in business to adapt and move on. And that time is now.

## How to get profiled

Demographics have typically included the following measures for creating clusters or profiles to market to: gender, age, income, education, ethnicity, location, language spoken, mobility, home ownership and employment status. These are all classic weapons in the demographer's and marketer's arsenal. But today, many of them are less relevant than ever.

On closer observation, they're more like forms of human discrimination than decent marketing tools. Many of these measures go beyond political incorrectness and are closer to downright rude or even illegal ways of discriminating. I'm relieved we're also graduating from this nonsense. Yet most boardrooms and marketing strategies are yet to evolve.

Why does it take so long for old, ineffective tools to disappear from strategy documents? The reason is that senior management believes in them, and they're too busy managing the balance sheet to notice their tools need replacing.

It's not that some of these on their own are not predictable measures of what people do; it's when they get used at a layered psychographic level that we start to get false positives. This is a test result which wrongly indicates that a particular condition or attribute is present. When it comes to behaviour prediction in an omniconnected, choice-driven world, demographic profiling is starting to deliver a barrage of false positives. Predictive data lies; real data is what we need because it's much more reliable.

## The price of pop culture

In 1968, famous late artist Andy Warhol claimed that in the future everyone would have 15 minutes of fame. It was a nice idea based on what we knew about the world at the time. Limited access to the tools of fame (mainstream media) and the need to be selected by a tastemaker along the way meant we could only ever hope for a slither of fame. It turns out, however, that fame is now permanent for those who choose to be selected. It turns out it's not that hard to be famous within a selected sub group who care about what we care about. It's a very different picture from when Andy was in town.

The price of pop-culture success is that you had to be prepared to roll the financial dice if you wanted to play. That price was the cost of super-expensive infrastructure, or renting out expensive parts of the infrastructure — not just the factories and the systems, but the price of renting eyeballs seconds at a time (in the form of expensive television commercials) and renting space on a mass retailer's shelf. The incredible cost of these two end points in the business supply chain meant they were only available to the well-financed few.

## The best average

Mass retail by definition needed mass media to pull products from the shelf. It meant producers had to make the 'best average' (oxymoronic, I know) products they possibly could — average products for average people to support the price of the system. Pop culture could simply not support niche because niche is invisible and niche has no voice in a world defined by mass-media monologue. Big brands were created more by big budgets than by big ideas and amazing products. As marketers, the desire was for conformity of the masses. It made things easier and helped the balance sheet work.

# The weapon of choice

The financial cost of failure was high, so risk had to be mitigated. It's the way any program in an organisation gets approved: not by the potential upside, but by understanding and minimising the downside risk. The weapon of choice for reducing the risk was demographics. Companies would project who the audience 'might be' based on mashing up a set of parameters. They would then select a set of media programs to find the agreed demographic and 'shoot to kill' with a good dose of target marketing, all the time knowing that the majority of the investment would be wasted. In fact, it would often be regarded as a success if 30 per cent of the audience fell into the profile. It's a pretty weird definition of success to have a 70-per-cent failure rate. While any media buyer could argue that the media-purchasing company buys based on a cost–benefit ratio, the reality is they're also paying for the people who aren't the desired audience. Worse still, it doesn't mean that those in the desired demographic who actually are exposed to the message aren't annoyed by the interruption. The reality is, demographic media buying is a very expensive guessing game.

## Don't fence me in

The curious thing about demographics is that they were actually shaped by the media, rather than the media reacting to what the demographics liked and believed in. The media loved the idea of demographics so much that they invented pet names for different groups to define them in neat, saleable clusters: the baby boomers, Generation X, Generation Y, the sea changers. They were all designed to simplify the selling process. The media shaped the demographics itself according to what it chose to expose the demographic to. Did young families really like watching sitcom television shows between 1950 and 1995, or did young families watch and learn to like sitcoms between 1950 and 1995 because that's what was on every television channel from 7.00 to 10.30 pm? Did teenagers in the US like American top-40 music, or did teenagers like music and that's what was on the radio for the last 50 years of the twentieth century?

The probability of aggregating an audience was higher at that time because the media was part of the shaping process itself. The choice of what any demographic group would see was determined by a very thin line-up of media. They all aired the same types of program at roughly the same time. They all ran the same advertisements for the products they thought a demographic may buy, and the retailers would choose to only put those products with national advertising support on their shelves. The limited choice created the profile more than the attitude and desires of the people inside the profiles.

It was also hard to escape the 'norm'. We all worked and went to school at normal and predictable hours. It was hard work just escaping the message. For want of a better term, people got brainwashed into fitting into their pre-defined demographic behavioural pattern. But this system is breaking down, and beyond age and a few limited geographic constraints, demographics is totally finished as a useful marketing tool.

## How do you define a teenager?

How would you define a teenager today? What do teenagers like in a world of infinite choice, global connection, pricing parity and high disposable incomes? How is their behaviour different today from 1985? Defining a teenager and their behaviour is no easy task, but the reality is that teenagers would associate themselves with interest groups that fly in the face of geographic boundaries and even the actual age bracket they fall into. So the question marketers need to ask themselves is this:

*How similar are teenagers who live in the same suburb, go to the same school, with the same ethnic origin profile, with the same average income who are also these different things: goths, punks, surfers, skaters, geeks, ravers, jocks, musicians, hipsters, preps, emos, gamers [insert your preferred teenager genre here]?*

Would any of these groups listen to the same music, wear the same clothes, hang out in the same places, eat the same food, read the same books or watch the same movies ... let alone like the same brands?

Probably the only thing we can reliably contend is that they all purchase the technology that keeps them connected with their peer groups.

# Stealing music or connecting?

One of my favourite examples of this shift — that is, how kids connect across interests rather than demographics — is the story of two of the co-founders of Napster, Shawn Fanning and Sean Parker. They were online friends for three years without ever meeting each other. They 'met' via an internet chat room called IRC (Internet Relay Chat) and only met in real life when they went to pitch to investors after Napster took off and gained traction. They built Napster as a way for people to connect over music.

Fanning claims that the connection of like minds was one of the key things that made Napster work in the early days. It wasn't about stealing music. It was about accessing the music you liked and couldn't find in the physical world, and finding other people who liked that music too. It facilitated what teenagers have been doing with music since the days when they listened to 45s and shared them with their friends. Digital files simply made the process ridiculously more efficient and enabled micro-interest groups to form around the music. All of a sudden, punk rockers could find punk music and goths could find their favourite goth bands that weren't ranged in record stores. It was like border hopping digitally. It spawned the idea of sharing things online: first music, then interests, and now most of life.

# Marketing 1.0

The marketing process during the mass-media era was linear and it had a deep predictive orientation that could be followed relatively easily as long as the company behind it had the courage to make the large and risky financial investments required to play. It went something like this:

1 Define the target demographic.

2 Research the concept with said demographic.

3 Design the mass product.

4 Tweak the mass product with qualitative research.

5 Gain mass distribution.

6 Buy mass media.

7 Rinse and repeat.

8 Innovate incrementally using existing infrastructure.

But the linear process just doesn't work anymore. The environment and resulting go-to-market methodology has fragmented into non-linear, unpredictable pieces. We now operate in a world where a smartphone game designed by an independent game manufacturer can end up being a major motion picture with global licensing that can compete with the likes of Disney (think Angry Birds). Or where a crowdfunding campaign can result in enough financial backing for a new wearable computing device — such as the Pebble — to be launched before Apple or Google enter the smartwatch market space.

## Marketing revised

A simplified view of the old marketing world compared to the new marketing world could be defined by making this comparison in table 6.1.

**Table 6.1: old marketing vs new marketing**

| Then: industrial complex era of mass marketing | Now: digital era of omniconnection |
|---|---|
| Guess | Connect |
| Make | Know |
| Advertise (massively interrupt) | Co-design |
| Hope | Transact |

The feedback cycle in business today isn't a segmented part of the process or a period of time for interaction after which no more questions or input are allowed. Now it's a fluid and never-ending process that involves the brand stewards — the audience — and they're the people who feed it. Technology facilitates a fragmented process that's hard to define and requires constant experimentation and iteration. It requires a process where it doesn't really start and end like it used to. The needed approach from marketers today is to remove the launch mentality.

## The new intersection

If we're not going to use demographics as a marketing tool, then how do we make a connection with a potential audience? How does business go about doing business if we throw out the old methods of going to the market and marketing to people? (Mind you, marketing isn't evil. It's beautiful and powerful, it's just that it needs to be used in a more human way.) If marketers embrace this philosophy, we'll all end up better off after the interaction.

The way we replace demographics is with social and interest graphs.

## Social graphs

The social graph is the network that results from relationships that are digitally facilitated and maintained through virtual connections, which can now be spread more quickly using social-media tools. These connections are, theoretically, easier to make and easier to maintain than when our connection methods were all physical in nature.

## Interest graphs

The interest graph is the online representation of the stuff we really care about. It's based on the real values we have and the things we do and support, hence forming a more genuine identity. The interest graph matters because it doesn't just track the activity undertaken by people, but also what they hope to do — where they want to go, what they want to buy, who they want to follow and meet, and what they want to change.

## Social + interests = intention

It gets interesting where these two ideas intersect. The overlaying of the social graph and the interest graph tells us much about a person's intentions. When people develop relationships based on a connection of interests facilitated by social-media connections we can see the true predictive persona. It's actually how the best and most enduring relationships have always been formed; it's just that now we can form them more quickly, develop larger cohorts and there's less luck involved in finding similar souls. And if marketers are nice, collaborative and helpful, most people will welcome them into their cohort. Modern-day marketing just has to have good manners, something all good relationships do well with.

# The story of cities

The social and interest graphs are redefining cities, not just social cohorts. In a type of paradox, cities are becoming more alike and more different at the same time. Let me explain.

Globalisation and the collective mind have facilitated a shift where things are not as different as they used to be in cities. Cities, or more accurately the behaviours that occur within them, are becoming more and more alike. New York City, Shanghai and Warsaw are more similar than they have been at any time in history. And I'm not talking about the availability of McDonald's and Coca-Cola. Cities are experiencing a move to niche, yet global, trends — interest by interest,

**People are self-organising themselves into groups around passions.**

social group by social group — into a massive subset of connected communities that exists in most geographies. People are self-organising themselves into groups around passions. They can do this now because they can connect easily and find each other, but more importantly because the culture vultures (mass-market tastemakers) have finally left the building. It's a fragmentation into subcultures that are replicated on a global scale, facilitated by the network connections people have. All cities now have a local startup community, a clear subculture that was the domain of San Francisco's Silicon Valley.

There are now more niches in every city maintained by a group itself, not by mass marketers looking for the next pop-culture hit. In fact, niches can now build themselves sustainable micro-economies around their interest. The community itself becomes the designer, producer, promoter and end user. They can do this because the barriers to entry are inconsequential. Chances are we can find that niche — whether it's the local break-dancing scene or drone flying club — wherever we go. All cities are fragmenting to have it all. But at the same time each city has never been more fragmented and differentiated within its walls. Figure 6.1 depicts this fragmentation of cities.

Figure 6.1: the behaviour of cities has evolved as people are self-organising themselves into groups around passions

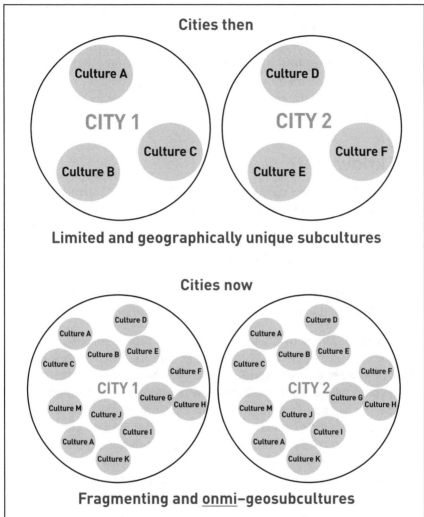

No city is immune. Whereas cities would once have had their own macro identity driven by geographic realities or history and localised influencers, whether human or media based, now their key influencers and influences are interest based. They follow the output of the interest group. And they listen to the personal micro celebrities from those groups. My economic and political philosophy is more influenced by Seth Godin and Tim O'Reilly than it is by my local members of parliament. The people we revere within our interests shape us, and it's we who choose who can be part of our shaping process.

# Do I know you?

Apart from my family, I didn't know any of the people I spend time with today 10 years ago. I didn't know 80 per cent of my social group just five years ago. We found each other digitally. By following certain interest groups that popped up in my city I met people at events and through discussing issues of importance to us online first. Simple metadata search terms helped me find an entirely new cohort: people I didn't work with, people I didn't live near and people who have a different education profile from me. One powerful tool for doing this was simple hashtag surfing.

A hashtag is a word with # before it to denote a topic thread. For example, the topic 'startups' would be represented as '#startup'. Then anyone posting things of interest on social forums could add the hashtag to their post so others could follow the topic. These new relationships blossomed quickly because we already had something in common. Unlike for pre-digital connections, we didn't have to work out whether we had something in common after serendipity brought us together. What is significant is how my life stage says that this shouldn't be true. I'm a 40-year-old married man living what should be the stable part of my life, a life filled with old friends and colleagues who play golf on Saturday mornings. And yet, I'm meeting new people and pursuing the interests that weren't available to me during the first part of my adult life.

# The interest graph in action

If I think about the things that matter to anyone these days, there's a very strong chance they're unexpected and unpredictable demographically. We're all progressively heading towards having what might be regarded as weird interests. The social network Pinterest is a place that provides the perfect example of this. Pinterest is a visual-based network. In its own words, it's 'a tool for collecting and organizing the things that inspire you' — a tool where you can 'pin' only pictures and videos to separate, topic-based boards. It's the stuff we really care about, desire and aspire towards. My Pinterest page says much about me (my reality) and nothing about my demographic profile (the 'target market' I belong to).

Here are some of my current boards:

- *Aviation:* I can't fly a plane, I don't have an engineering degree and there is no other evidence that I like planes. Yet, I've watched every documentary that exists on how to fly a plane, even though I have no intention of ever flying one.

- *Surfing:* I live a one-hour drive away from the nearest surf beach. I live in one of the coldest cities in Australia. I don't read surfing magazines, but I do check the surf every morning on my phone at daybreak. I refuse to wear surf clothing (everyone knows that real surfers don't wear surf brands unless they're paid to) and yet I go surfing multiple times a week. Billabong, Quiksilver and Rip Curl can't find me because they're fishing in the wrong pond. And I guarantee I spend more on surfing every year than the teenage girls these companies chase with their clothing ranges, a chase which also damages their brand in the eyes of real surfers.

- *BMX bikes:* I'm not 12 years old and I don't own a BMX bike. However, I'm about to invest about two thousand dollars on the bike I could never afford as a working-class kid. Demographically, I'm invisible.

- *House stuff:* This is the Pinterest board where I'm statistically and demographically predictable. It's the board that I fit the demographic profile for. It has all the items I need for my house renovation and fantasy garden in it, the stuff brands try to sell on free-to-air television gardening programs and magazines. They're the programs I don't watch because my free-time attention is elsewhere. I've fragmented away from the mainstream media even when I'm undergoing my own so-called predictable behaviour.

## Radical (old-school BMX term) micro marketing

After I made my BMX Pinterest board, I sent a tweet out saying how excited I was about my new project to build the ultimate retro BMX powered by the connections the internet makes possible. I already had a few posts of bikes for sale on eBay and links to old-school BMX forums. The tweet had a link pointing to the Pinterest board. After I got back from lunch I checked my Twitter feed to find someone had sent me a reply tweet about the BMX project. It was from a local BMX store. They informed me they had an old-school BMX section in their store for big kids like me. The way they did it was really cool. The tweet said, 'Cool project Steve. Here's a link to the best forum for Old School BMX … If you wanna reminisce, pop in some day'.

Needless to say, I went in the very next day to get some advice on the project, on where to get parts (it's a bit like car restoration) and on how to get the genuine stuff. They earned my business in 140 characters.

This was such a clever play on so many levels. There are a lot of subtle marketing lessons to be learned from this tweet. I'll spell them out clearly.

- *Make it personal.* They addressed me as Steve. You'd be surprised how few people do that when they find you online, even though your name is a mere click away.

- *Offer resources first.* They provided me with something of value to help me: the link to the forums. They didn't try selling to me on the first connection.

- *Focus on an ecosystem.* They didn't stress about where I went to solve my problem. They chose instead to embrace the fact that I was entering their market space. In some ways they recommended a competitor (the online forum that happens to sell old BMX parts).

- *Use real language and culture.* They spoke the natural language of the group. It wasn't corporate brochure-ware PR speak. It was human and real.

- *Find tools of connection.* I asked the owner how he found me. I mean, unless I was in his stream how would he know about my project? He said he does a social-media search every day with only two simple data parameters: the hashtag for #BMX and the geography of Melbourne. Very clever stuff.

- *Focus on one customer at a time.* They focused on direct connection, one new fan at a time. They didn't try to build an audience. They helped a person, which is a very different approach. It seems old-school BMXers are a little bit smarter than old-school marketers. What a great way to build a community; one that I'm now a part of.

While everyone gets enamoured with 'big data', there's probably a lot more we can do with 'little data'.

# The anti-demographic recommendation engine

A lot of e-commerce platforms and social-media engines seem to be able to do what mainstream marketers could never quite pull off. Every day, I'm exposed to products and services that I have zero interest in ever purchasing, mainly due to the laziness of the marketers who allocate the budget behind them. But occasionally I'm utterly inspired and thankful when great marketers (with permission) introduce me to things that are just perfectly suited. Twitter is terrific at this with its who-to-follow recommendations. But the best example has to be Amazon's 'Recommended for you' books. It's always spot on, sitting perfectly in the centre of my personal interest graph, based on the simplicity of what I've bought, looked at, wish listed and what others have in their list when there are overlaps. For me personally, it's very accurate indeed. What's interesting is that this recommendation engine is what I'd coin an 'anti-demographic' profiler:

- It doesn't care what sex I am.
- It doesn't care where I live.
- It doesn't care or know how much I earn.
- It doesn't care if I finished school.

None of this matters. What matters is the direct connection and the reality of my interests based on my digital footprint. It's the type of efficiency that mass can never achieve. The smart marketing money now lives in a node-by-node approach.

Not only did the industrial-era mass marketers try to fence us in, but they also tried to trick us into buying *today*, saying, 'Tomorrow is too risky. Prices might go up'. The reality is just the opposite because everything is getting cheaper.

## What is fragmenting

Behaviour no longer clusters around the demographic profile of people. We're all moving close to the edges and away from expectations.

## What it means for business

Demographics is becoming a poor audience predictor. The intersection of the social and interest graph is where it's at.

# CHAPTER 7

# The truth about pricing:
# technology and omnipresent deflation

For all of its flaws, the industrial mentality has given us the gift of efficiency, of doing everything we do better, faster and cheaper than we did it yesterday. The machine mentality of getting better by increments has led us to a point where the tools that matter are free. They cost so little that they basically cost nothing. Or, in fact, they actually cost nothing in real terms and are given to us in that the thing of real commercial value comes from the person at the end of the technology, rather than the technology itself. The technology still doesn't make the decisions that matter. We do. From a commercial perspective the decisions that matter are those that involve expenditure, which is still largely a human decision. Two hundred years of churning and competing on price got us to a point where it almost no longer matters. And we should be thankful because that's how we reached the age of 'disposable technology'.

## Technology deflation

The default example of how technology is getting ever cheaper and ever more powerful is Moore's law. For the uninitiated, Moore's law was an observation made by Gordon Moore, co-founder of Intel, who contended that over the history of computing hardware, the number of transistors on a circuit board would double approximately every two years, effectively doubling the power and halving the price of computing power. But it's not Moore's law in itself that's so defining. It's that the output capabilities of many digital electronic devices follow closely the pattern of Moore's law. The principle applies to processing speed, memory capacity, pixels in digital cameras, GPS devices, network capacity, solar panels … and an extensive list of other technology device inputs. And even if we look at the pre-digital era it also remains true for vacuum tube circuit computers. They all follow the law of accelerating returns of technology.

The rate of improvement we see in all of these technologies has been exponential and a key force in the dramatic democratisation of the modern economy. Many previously unattainable technological goods and services — computing and communications devices only affordable to the largest organisations — are now at disposable price points, often even free. This doesn't just change the kinds of gadgets we own; it changes the entire economic structure. All of a sudden, advantages large firms used to have, barriers to technology, and large financial hurdles begin to diminish. We end up in an economic environment where people can own whatever a company can own. The new game becomes less about the tools and more about the creative adaptation of those tools—that is, the human side of the technology.

## Real-world technology deflation

One gigabyte (GB) of external hard-drive memory cost about fifteen dollars to purchase in the year 2000, and only a few cents today, but in real terms it's free. It's free because myriad cloud-based computing services will provide anyone with up to 10 GB upon signing up, with no payment plan.

But it's not just the prices of the technology that are dropping. It's also the prices of the functional pieces of technology inside the devices. The prices of entire gadgets are rapidly falling. These price declines are also assisted by production-line improvements; that is, globalisation—the opening up of low-cost labour markets in the production of technology products. It's staggering to observe the law of accelerating returns when we look at it in real terms; in other words, the real things we use every day, not just the techie bits that live inside them. Let's consider the following examples as reminders of how far we've come.

- *Television.* A 42-inch flat-screen LCD television now costs 10 per cent of what it did 10 years ago. Not only is this a mere fraction of the former price, but the television is better in every way. It's now high definition, web enabled, thinner, lighter and more energy efficient.

- *Laptop.* This is the one we're all most familiar with. I recently bought a new MacBook Pro. It was half the price of the previous model, and all the key specs have twice the capacity of the old one. But it's also lighter, stronger, and it has better screen resolution, more features and better software.

- *Digital camera.* In 1990 a 0.077 megapixel camera cost almost $2000.[1] Today, high-resolution digital cameras come free with every smartphone. In fact, the camera as a separate device is becoming a rarity. Like film, it's becoming redundant, which is not surprising given that smartphones now come equipped with cameras of up to 41 megapixels.

- *GPS.* The first hand-held GPS receiver, which was launched in 1989 (the Magellan NAV 1000), was the size of a brick and cost $2500 to purchase. These days the GPS is another 'free' device we get with our pocket 'super computer', the smartphone.

---

[1] www.cameracuriosities.com/2012/02/dycam-model-1.html

# The free super computer

In fact, most of the important technologies we use today are becoming integrated into the smartphone, which isn't really a 'smart phone' at all — it's actually the most personal of personal computers. While Bill Gates aimed to have a computer on every desk in every home, Steve Jobs put a super computer in every person's pocket. The evidence is in the number of uses for the smartphone. The telephone function only gets 22 of the more than 150 interactions we have with our smartphones daily.[2] One of the most amazing things about this super computer is that it's actually free. The recommended retail price is a bit of a red herring. While there's an option to buy smartphones outright, the vast majority of us buys them as part of a deal when signing up for mobile-phone contracts, which haven't changed in price since we first started using mobile phones. The first mobile phone I signed up for, in 2001, cost me $69 a month. I recently got the new model of iPhone and it cost me $69 a month. I have all the benefits of a super computer in my pocket for no extra cost at all. We really are living in the age of free technology that's disposable because it will end up in a drawer at home once the contract expires and we upgrade.

## More than a device

Most notable about this super computer is that it does everything that all of the separate devices used to do: email, browsing, mapping, tracking, photos, scanning, searching, video, television … it does it all. In some ways it's the new digital-life control panel, a real human technology addendum. The smartphone is such an important part of our lives that most of us will turn back to get it if we realise we've left home without it. It's not a business or a social tool; it's a life tool — the missing link to a technologically driven world. The other amazing thing about this super computer — which can do what every other digital device can — is that it's very human. The tech geeks finally got their act together and gave us something we couldn't live without because they made it so human.

> The smartphone is such an important part of our lives that most of us will turn back to get it if we realise we've left home without it.

---

[2] 'The Best of Mary Meeker's 2013 Internet Trends Slides', May 2013: http://allthingsd.com/20130529/the-best-of-mary-meekers-2013-internet-trends-slides

## The 'human' device that replicates us

The smartphone has human characteristics. While it still *looks* like a piece of technology, it *acts* like a person.

It has two eyes: one on the front and one the back of its head. It can hear: it can be spoken to and speaks back to us with answers. It can think: it has a brain with more capacity than ours and doesn't forget anything. While I know what city I'm in right now, it knows where I am down to the last metre. It knows how fast it's moving; it knows when I'm sitting, running or driving. It knows how high it is (it has an altimeter telling it how high off the ground it is). It knows everything the internet (people) knows. It's connected to our collective sentience. It's touch sensitive: it interacts with human touch, just like we do. The real interface is human activity.

It's not surprising we've become so attached to the technology because, for the first time, the technology doesn't feel like technology … it feels like something human and normal. This is a big part of the reason why the smartphone is now the last thing we touch before we go to sleep at night and the first thing we touch in the morning when we wake up. (It used to be our partner!)

# The crux is human

The reason why ubiquitous and mostly free technology matters isn't just that it's so powerful. It's that it's so accessible. Early technology was so alienating that it didn't invite participation and belief in what was possible. It wasn't just the price points that kept most early computing (and industrial, for that matter) technology out of the hands of the populous; it was the interactions. The technology was difficult to understand, somewhat scary and dystopian. The old, green-screen computers with code-based logins didn't feel very human so they remained in the government and corporate world. But now that things have changed, now that the geeks have come good with their promise of a technological utopia, what people believe is possible has also changed. Our default position has changed from observation to participation. People have started to want to participate in technology and have a say in how things could be done better in business as both entrepreneurs and intrapreneurs. What businesses must realise is that when everyone has access to the same technology there's a distinct power flip. All of a sudden there's no technology gap between people and corporations and this affects the entire structure of the marketplace.

# It's getting quicker

It's not just the price decreases and relative power increases that are moving at an exponential rate. It's the adoption rates and distribution of the new communication technologies too. It's as if technology has its own agenda. And the agenda of technology is to make itself more mobile and diffused for the widest possible audience. And so each form of new technology is taking less time to infiltrate our lives and distribute itself. If we look at the history of each new communication tool and the time it took to be widely adopted, there's a clear message for business about the rate of change.

## Development and dissemination time of communications technologies

*Spoken word:* hundreds of thousands of years

*Written language:* tens of thousands of years

*Printing press:* hundreds of years to reach a mass audience

*Telephone:* 50 years to reach 25 per cent of the population

*Mobile phone:* 25 years to reach a mass audience

*Search engines:* 10 years to reach a mass audience

*Social networks:* 5 years to reach a mass audience

This sends a clear message about the ever-shrinking amount of time that business has to adjust to whatever emerges next, and that a wait-and-see strategy probably won't serve conservative industrialists as well as it may have when technology was expensive.

# Technology curve jumping

We need to remember that this is a long-term trajectory, so we can expect technology to continue to improve at an ever-increasing pace. History has shown that even when we reach the end of certain technological capabilities, different innovations have always been uncovered. Even

Moore's law has been observed as having a physical limit. There comes a time when transistors can't physically be made any smaller and exponential improvements will come to an end.

In fact, this has already happened. In the early computing era, vacuum tubes reached their physical limits. They reached a point where they could no longer be made any smaller and still have a vacuum effect. This was when we jumped the curve to the transistor-integrated circuits we currently use, those to which Moore's law applies. So when a technology reaches its limit, we jump off that technology and onto a newer technology — a curve jump, if you will. On the new curve we start a new trajectory of exponential growth and the cycle begins again. Moore's law wasn't the first accelerating computing power curve; it was the fifth curve. The next phase is likely to be quantum computing, which is currently under development.

Regardless of which technology comes next, history has shown us that something will come. And when it does, it will follow the same principles of greater power at a lower cost. It will give more tools to more people, be smaller and be cheaper than before. It will reduce the cost of access and infrastructure by the mere nature of being new technology. And that's why it changes the business landscape so much: because each innovation is increasing the rate of change, and there's no sign of it slowing.

# Technology stacking

This new layer of accessible, cheap technology is going to create a technology layer that we'll all live upon and within. It will be a technology stack similar to the new industrial landscape that began to arrive about two hundred years ago. To understand this we need to consider the idea of technology stacking.

'Technology stacking' is a term widely used by computer geeks to describe the layers of components and services that go into creating a software application.

With all forms of technology stacking — not only software or computer hardware, and not only at the digital level, but across all forms of human innovation — new layers are added to the previous elements to create more functionality, utility, depth and meaning. The best way to show this is by using an example we can all identify with. Let's take the history of roads.

## The concept of stacking

We start with a human walking track that leads to somewhere we want to go, such as a watering hole.

The track gets a little wider when we invent the wheel and have carts and chariots pulled across it.

More tracks appear as we develop civilisations and the horse and cart becomes a key mode of transport.

When the car arrives, we create road rules, speed limits and signs to avoid crashing into each other.

As car ownership widens and we start to seal the roads, we make highways, roundabouts and traffic lights.

We invent maps for directions as the number and complexity of roads increases.

We use GPS devices and live traffic reports (via the web) for more efficient movement on the roads.

And our next stack will be the self-driving car, which will do it all for us.

Each layer is needed before the subsequent layer can make any sense or be needed. While the industrial revolution created a machine-based layer of technology in business and lifestyle, we're now entering a stage where a digital layer is being added. Cheap, disposable technology will give us a new layer that augments both how we live and how we do business. The job of businesses today is to define that new layer in their industry. If it's not defined by the industry itself — if the industry lags with the new technology stack — it will be added by someone else. There's no choice.

# Omnipresent deflation

But what's happening to general prices, the non-technological part of everything we own and buy? The cost of living seems to creep up every year, our household budgets seem to get harder to balance and cost cutting by employers reduces the resources at our disposal. In this price-oriented, conspicuous consumption environment it's easy to believe the actual cost of everything is going up. It turns out that the opposite is true.

Regardless of the message mainstream media try to sell about price rises, almost everything we spend our money on is cheaper than it was last year, and the year before that and the generation before ours, if the item in question existed at all. Inflation, ironically, is a measure that inflates the truth about prices. And the truth is that all prices are going down in real terms.

## Consumer price index trickery

Wage growth has outstripped price growth or CPI in every developed nation since World War II.[3] When we overlay the growth in wages each year with the growth in prices, the pattern is clear: income growth outstrips price growth, so life is cheaper. People confuse their desired living standards with the actual cost of living.

The confusing part is that consumer price indexes don't actually measure prices because they don't measure prices in real terms relative to the increase we see in incomes every year. In addition to this, the items measured are weighted in terms of importance and changing consumption patterns. This basket is changed based on what's regarded as an expected living standard over time, as is the weighting of the items within it. Items are removed and items are added every four or five years, so it changes the goods and services that are being measured as well.

As time goes by, the CPI, which usually tells us things are more expensive, actually tells us that 'modern living' is more expensive because we purchase so much more and have access to new spending options all the time.

We're wealthier than we know and we're getting wealthier all the time simply because the dollars we earn stretch so much further every year. It turns out that life is really only more expensive because of how much we want, not because prices are getting higher. And there's about to be more downward pressure on pricing than we've already seen.

## Connections and the impact on prices

Access to new sets of information gives buyers deeper knowledge on what fair pricing looks like. Buyers can assess the market accurately and efficiently through technology. This, then, removes the bumpiness we

---

[3] www.abs.gov.au

see in prices. There was once a physical limitation to what we could know about the price of something, but this has been removed. We used to have to rely on advertising messages, shopping around and calling up buyers to compare prices. Now we're a few keystrokes away from knowing where we can get the best price on anything without error. Price comparison sites, or even barcode scanning software, puts perfect pricing knowledge in the hands of us all. This changes things a lot. It puts downward pressure on the seller's prices and margins. We all now have access to global shopping hubs, the best and cheapest in every category, ensuring we pay the price of the most efficient global operator who sells a common good. But it's not just knowing where the cheapest price is that will create a further downward pressure; it's access to lower cost forms of production for all types of work.

## Economic border hopping

We've already seen how technology prices are in rapid freefall, but the inputs for labour and manufacturing are also being facilitated via the digital revolution. Anyone can now do what once only the most privileged organisations could through democratised access to BRIC-nations labour. You no longer need some kind of special economic licence, or insight into the local geography, language or even culture, to be able to have work done in emerging markets. Once the domain of big business, now small business and independent entrepreneurs have access to a globalised and digitally connected workforce.

## The new minimum wage

As the web has emerged as a tool of commerce, socialisation and business tools, a market for labour arbitrage has emerged. Casual staff websites and staffing solutions such as eLance and oDesk ensure that everyone can gain access to labour at a fraction of developed market wages. In developing markets, anyone can have information-based work done for about ten per cent of the rate of a developed market. And I'm not talking about pure administration either. Everything is available: from accounting, to software engineering, to marketing, to legal work.

The new minimum wage for information-based work is whatever the lowest cost market will accept. *There's no such thing as a minimum wage anymore.*

Good, bad or ugly, this is the reality of where we're headed. The technology makes it possible, entrepreneurs open up the doors and the organisations do what they've always done and take the cost-cutting opportunities presented. In a connected world, the new minimum wage is the same for everyone. Now that we have the ability to border hop to get large parts of our work done, the value of the work is not bound by geography. Rather, it's bound by the market dynamics of global labour markets, not local ones.

> **In a connected world, the new minimum wage is the same for everyone.**

While it's true that geographic-centric work is less affected, it will reduce the cost structure of many businesses. When it comes to both services and production in a hyper-networked world, access is greater than ownership. And while ownership was previously the only option available, our emerging zero-barrier world will be the catalyst for changing this.

## What is fragmenting

Driven by technology, the price of everything is lowering.

## What it means for business

Selling what was sold yesterday always leads to lower prices. Making connections between the seemingly disparate is where new revenue and margins now live.

# CHAPTER 8

# A zero-barrier world: how access to knowledge is breaking down barriers

For most of the industrial era the only option for having goods and services was to own them. If we wanted to have anything, we had to buy it. This was also the way industrial society was set up. It moved society away from the traditional ideas of shared resources into consumption silo mode. The industrial era made many things affordable for the first time. The rational choice was to purchase and own, so we accumulated goods and stored them at home for when they were needed. Being able to have everything we needed, and places to store it all (fridges, cupboards, spare rooms and garages), reduced a lot of the friction that existed before industrial communities came into being and resources were shared.

## So what's changed?

Much of the friction of sharing is now coming back out of the commercial system. While vehicles gave us access to vast geography on demand, the internet is giving us access to vast information, entertainment and even physical goods on demand. Many of the things we had no choice but to buy if we wanted access to them are changing the way they come to market. Increasingly, we have an option to buy or to simply access an asset on demand. We are choosing the latter.

## Why do we even own stuff?

There are two main reasons for owning anything: utility and status. Owning something for its usefulness is pretty straightforward: you need to own it to be able to use it. Owning something for status reasons (think luxury brands and goods of ostentation) is about how it makes us feel and appear to the outside world. These are two important reasons for ownership, and neither will go away. We'll continue to accumulate artefacts, filling our homes with the items we need and want. But now we have a choice. We can now often choose to access instead of own, while at the same time still having all the benefits of ownership, and we can even have the benefits of status through access. The ability to find what we need in a virtual world has reduced a lot of the friction that comes with finding the same things in person or physically. We can seek things out with a low personal cost of time and money. We can access these items with very little friction. This reduced friction creates opportunity for temporary connections with goods and services, which, in a physical world, would be too costly and cumbersome. This means where we used to have to buy items, we can now instead pay to use them when we need them.

# The sharing economy

In a sharing economy we can enjoy the benefit of usage and status on a temporary basis. It's an obvious solution when you consider that we only use much of what we own for a fraction of the time that it's available to us, excluding such things as furniture and the fridge. Quite often, we now share or purchase collectively whatever we need, paying only for the time we use it. Instead of purchasing and owning idle assets, we can now access assets on demand.

**Instead of purchasing and owning idle assets, we can now access assets on demand.**

# Personal access

On an individual level, many of the things that existed physically have transitioned to virtual. Knowledge and entertainment have not only become virtual, but are also largely free. Wikipedia is the greatest repository of knowledge the world has ever seen. It's more accurate than any body of knowledge that came before it; it has a wider scope than any encyclopaedia; it's updated more frequently than any other source; and it's free. Most of the entertainment available online has a similar story. We used to have to buy information in physical forms (books, magazines, and so on) or go to the place of information storage to access it (libraries, museums, and so on). However, we now live in the age of the instant expert. Anyone can know about, or learn about, any topic they choose on demand.

**However, we now live in the age of the instant expert. Anyone can know about, or learn about, any topic they choose on demand.**

We don't need to buy the information, we don't need to be invited to have access to that information and we don't need to be pre-qualified by any gatekeeper to be allowed to find out what's behind those walls anymore. The barriers to knowledge, which is the key social and economic parameter, have come down and what's more, the knowledge you can gain is free. We can, if we choose to, know most facts about any topic, and much of it's not hard to find with the search tools we have at our disposal. The barriers that kept outsiders out and insiders in are being removed. Anyone who has the energy to care enough to know, can know.

# Physical access

Not only do we have free access to virtual knowledge and information, we also have access to real, non-virtual, physical goods without having to pay for them. We can now get our hands on goods that could once only be bought or rented at 'insult renting' rates. It's not just the sellers who are being inconvenienced by the shift from owning to accessing, it's all sorts of hiring businesses. Traditional business that played in the temporary access space, as well as those in the hiring and rental area (such as accommodation and cars) are also being significantly disrupted by this shift. The collaborative consumption movement means that buying is a choice rather than a necessity. We can rent cars by increments of hours now and have all the benefits of a private car on demand without the excessive cost of hiring or owning one. This is pretty significant given that the average motor vehicle spends more than 90 per cent of its available life idle in a car space. We can now gain temporary access to goods, from haute-couture handbags, to chainsaws, to private jets, to gardens, to office spaces, to bicycles. Anything that can be bought can now be accessed.

## The story of music

All goods, even those that started as physical goods, are moving towards access, sharing and temporary interaction. Music is a classic example. If we think back to how music has evolved through history, it's been on a constant path towards more seamlessly distributing itself by consistently removing the physical requirements for hearing it, making it more available and accessible.

Historically, music was first shared by way of a tribal gathering or a theatre performance. By the 1450s, when the printing press arrived, music could be shared in written form, but it still had to be performed live to be heard. Then, when the phonograph arrived in the late 1800s, music could be distributed and played in recorded form. Music became more widely available, but still only for the fortunate few. Then radio arrived in the 1920s, creating far wider access to music. The invention of the television, cassettes and CDs further broadened our access to music even before the digital era. Each layer of music distribution added to the previous layer, rather than removing it.

In the digital era of music we started downloading music to our devices, but with it still on hand. We still had to buy and download it, but it did make the music more mobile and accessible. More recently we've moved to accessing our music in the cloud. We no longer need to have it on hand, and we don't even have to own it or purchase it (or steal it). We're not even limited to listening to our own music collection. Cloud-based music services such as Spotify enable us to access all the music in the world on demand virtually on any digital device.

Increasingly, music has taken itself on a path to reduced friction, increased breadth of distribution, lower cost (if any) and simplified access. In terms of getting the benefits of music, access is far greater than ownership. In every way, owning it simply can't compete. Music is the allegory we must keep in mind for all industry. The path is one of greater access, reduced friction and wider dissemination.

### The story of 'stuff'

The story of stuff is similar to that of music and the now virtual parts of our digital economy. Things are making themselves more accessible as well. Before the industrial dawn we needed a local craftsmen nearby to make necessary items for us. We didn't travel much in those days and we had limited access to information on where to obtain whatever we needed. When factories arrived, many expensive, handmade artisanal goods became more distributed and affordable. We could buy the widget we needed from the store rather than from a craftsman. As media and retail expanded, the options we had access to became wider and cheaper until we reached the point we're at now, where the same range of products and prices is available globally as long as we're connected. And we're entering the age of desktop manufacturing with 3D printing, where we'll be able to customise things on demand and replicate 'stuff' from the physical world. More about this in chapter 10.

# Ownership is a mental state

Music and stuff hold a pattern that's the trajectory for many things as technology becomes more accessible. As computing power increases and the creation of physical things democratises, the need to own will often be substituted with the benefits of access. Owning is an emotional state that bears no true value unto itself. Nowadays we don't have to own in order to reap the emotional benefits of ownership. We've already proven this to be the case in a number of industries, so there's no reason why it won't become a reality in many more.

# Commercial access

Anyone with a smartphone has more computing power than NASA did in 1985. Anyone connected to our information network has more information at their fingertips than the president of the United States of America did just 10 years ago. These are not throwaway statements. They're serious facts that should not be taken lightly. They're more than eyebrow-raising facts; they're door openers to the major factors of production. Information is more than information; it's access to the possibilities of a commercial world. It's the first resource we need before we can do anything. Having access to near-perfect knowledge gives any person clues about how to accomplish things and organise the factors of production, even when they seem to be unaffordable. Once people know where things are and what's possible, they start to take on the types of power that were previously the protected intellectual capital of governments and powerful businesses. Once the pieces of the commercial puzzle are knowable, visible and evident, it is in the very nature of people to start playing with the pieces to see what possibilities they can offer them and their business. It's what we do as human beings. Access really is everything.

# Access to everything

While it's clear that everyone has access to much of the same information, access to certain business resources has an immediate economic impact. Access to developing nations' labour is one such factor. In the past, knowing how to go about outsourcing production was no easy task. Whether it was for human resources to perform services, or accessing a factory to manufacture something for your business, this information was both hard to find and closely guarded. The large conglomerates who started flirting with off-shoring work in the late 1970s and early 1980s closely guarded their supply chains. For good reason, this knowledge was a trade secret that gave them a cost advantage — and therefore a competitive advantage — over their competitors. In addition, it took a significant number of resources to find, organise and manage the production of anything in a low-cost market. You had to physically go to the markets in question, have personal introductions and get approval from non-capitalist government authorities. It took a great deal of time, money and political deal making. And still there was no guarantee that the quality of the output would match that of what could be produced locally. 'Made in China' used to mean 'cheap and crappy'. Now that China has become the production hub of the Western world, 'made in China' usually means better quality.

# A personal global factory

These days any business or person can find people to help them with their projects in most markets. We're not only mere clicks away from connecting directly with organisations that can perform any type of service and factories that can make any type of widget or high-end electronic device, but we can do it with far less risk. Not only can we easily find someone to make what we need, we have the added benefit of social recommendations. All of the organisations competing for our global business come with the comfort of the ratified reputation of the service provider. No-one does this better in the manufacturing sphere than Alibaba.

Alibaba is a website that started in China as a link for local Chinese manufacturers to find buyers for their products. The significance of Alibaba can't be understated. Since it was launched in 1999 more than 4.2 million manufacturers from every corner of the earth have been added to its supplier list. If it can be made in a factory, a supplier who can make it to your specifications can be found on Alibaba. In short, it means that anyone from anywhere in the world can get anything made at globally competitive prices.

No-one has to own a factory anymore. No-one has to travel to low-cost labour-market countries anymore. No-one needs local introductions to do business in international markets anymore. It's the most significant shift in manufacturing since the industrial revolution. Anyone can be an 'industrialist' if they choose to be. Now we all have access to what has historically been the most complex and costly part of the supply chain: a factory that makes things.

# The clothing company

In the early 1990s I started a clothing company. We made T-shirts and streetwear and sold them in local stores. In many ways I was competing with established leisure sportswear companies (from the surf and skate industry). Our clothes were pretty good; people liked the designs. They were in demand everywhere that we managed to get ranging in a store, which was often a challenge for a brand that didn't have any advertising support in a brandcentric industry. We had the clothes made locally in Australia. Our landed cost on a finished T-shirt was $12 per unit, which was expensive for a product we sold for $19 per unit, given we were just starting out and we wanted to bootstrap the business (that is, to ensure there was demand before we tried to reduce the cost by having our clothes made offshore).

We knew that all our competitors' (big companies) products were made in China. We also knew they landed their products for about two dollars a unit — a vast difference in margin. Whenever we tried to find out where in China the suppliers were, barriers were put up in front of us. We were told we needed to be selling many thousands of units before we'd qualify for offshore production. We never got big enough in volume terms because our product cost was so high and we didn't have enough margin to support our clothing brand. And this was a time when the social web was yet to arrive so there was no direct means of promotion. We simply couldn't compete with the established players. We didn't know how to gain access to global, cost-effective suppliers. The world we tried to do business in was full of barriers keeping us out.

The barrier wasn't about design or product quality; it was about access to an *efficient* supply chain, the secret supply chains that the big players knew about and had relationships with. The barrier was access, pure and simple. And now that barrier has been removed. Now anyone can get their T-shirts printed at the same price that Nike or Quiksilver pays.

## The two-way street

Access to developing markets, resources and labour is not the one-way street many believe it to be. It opens up possibilities for the supply side as much as it does for the demand side.

I built and launched my first dotcom business using a freelancing website. In order to build the site, I outsourced the coding on a site called oDesk. There were a lot of benefits for me personally. First, I got the services for about ten per cent of the local price. Second, it enabled a non-techie such as me to gain access to techie services. But the launch of my startup had an added benefit, a real benefit that isn't spoken about all that often: *it facilitated an important cultural exchange.*

## Meet Vasilii Racovitsa

Pictured here (figure 8.1) sharing a meal with me in my home is Vasilii Racovitsa. Now that doesn't seem like such a big deal ...

**Figure 8.1: photo of Vasilii Racovitsa**

... until you know that I first met Vasilii via oDesk where he was a freelance web developer back in 2007. Vasilii was born during the Cold War in the old USSR in a province called Moldova. (Moldova is now an independent country.) While my relationship with Vasilii started as a commercial one, it's much more than that now. In fact, it's been much more than that for many years. He's a dear friend and business confidant for whom I want family and financial success as much as I want it for myself. But I only met him in real life for the first time last year.

Besides the fact that Vasilii made my first web play come to life, he also taught me more about technology than anyone else. The truth is that the lower labour rates in eastern Europe enabled me to arbitrage my way into techie/startup land. Many people falsely believe that benefitting from lower labour rates in developing economies is a one-way street and that the people in developed economies are the only beneficiaries because we 'take advantage' of those in less developed markets. In truth we've both benefitted dramatically. Through my local connections, Vasilii now generates more than 50 per cent of his business from Melbourne — a mere 14854 kilometres from Moldova! Not to mention that his income, through accessing Western money, is now many multiples above the average wage in his home country.

Vasilii came to Australia to pitch for a large development project that's totally independent of me — a project that dwarfs anything we ever worked on together. But it was facilitated through the network I introduced him to. People would call me and say, 'Steve, can I use your guy from Moldova to get some development done?' What's more interesting is that his business employs more people in Moldova than the original startup we worked on ever did here in Melbourne. And his development team now works in every form of coding/language/mobile device you can think of.

When Vasilii was in town, it was like hanging out with a long-lost relative. He's just like the guy I used to speak to every day on Skype, a strange thing to say now that we know the virtual world is the real world. It's also a great reminder that the online and real worlds should only ever be preambles to each other and in some ways seamlessly interchangeable. While the tools this digital revolution has provided are amazing, it's the human connections that are creating a truly Sans nation state economy.

> **Sans nation state economy:** an economy where global transactions subvert national control due to their virtual nature

## The laptop corporation

The story of access isn't limited to production and digital services. This is true for all the major elements that go into the business marketing mix. We also have access to new ways of raising finance, as we'll explore in chapter 12. And we have access to an audience, as we'll see in chapter 11. A more accurate and wider view is that we're all laptop corporations if we want to be. If anyone has access to an entry-level, $500 device and an internet connection, they also have access to a media production facility, a media distribution facility, low-cost labour markets, the world's manufacturing districts, global banking and payment systems, and even bespoke capital-raising techniques from crowdfunding websites (see chapter 12). In real terms, anyone with access to the network has access to all of the important factors of production.

*Access to technology and information creates access to an everything state.*

Information not only changes what we can know and what we can do, it changes where we'll get it. We're entering the age of the infinite store, where you, I and everyone else can retail.

## What is fragmenting

Access to information removes barriers.

Knowledge is a conduit to change and commercial democracy.

## What it means for business

Everything a company can do, a person can do now too. Having a large corporate infrastructure is no longer an advantage.

# CHAPTER 9

## The infinite store: rebooting retail

Working in retail has never been harder. And I'm not talking about traditional bricks-and-mortar retail, I'm talking about retail in general. It doesn't matter if we sell online, in a store or via a combination of the two, the change in landscape, which has opened up the market, has made it more competitive. The more competition we have in any market, the harder it is to operate profitably. Again, the first rule in economics is that increased supply results in reduced prices.

It's the most basic economic fact that everyone seems to forget. In a world where choice is increasing exponentially, it presents two simple options for retailers: be the cheapest and quickest, or live deep inside the long tail.

## The physical and virtual challenges

Initial thinking as retail moved online was that online retailers were eating store operators for lunch, and this was sometimes the case. Excluding the online megabrands (Amazon comes to mind), it's much harder for everyone than it was before the web, even those who are solely online retailers. Online retailers don't have the benefit of foot traffic. Instead, they live in a search-engine quagmire with 20 chances per page to be found or they have to invest heavily in creating a fan base and community around their brand. The point is, there's no online audience that will magically drop onto their www doorstep. Meanwhile, the physical retailer faces new challenges of customer bases evaporating due to the shift to online purchasing.

## Retail was easy

If a brand chooses to do both forms of retail, it must operate in a more complex business infrastructure. Retail was once one of the most simple business models — find a geography, buy a product, sell at margin — while it's now one of the most complex. What was once a mum-and-pop business possibility is quickly becoming a sophisticated, technology-driven, multi-channel mind warp.

It's hardest for the retailers selling what everyone else sells. Selling well-known, widely-distributed products online is simply a race to the bottom, a price war that can only be won by the most efficient operator. It's quickly turning into a game of logistics more than it is about customer engagement.

The world of today is an infinite store, where everything is available at the best price possible to anyone, anywhere.

## The retail revolution

Retail is going through a revolution, but unlike many of the other industries being impacted by fragmented technology, it's not the first one retail has been through. It ought be suffering from a bit of déjà vu. Considering the move from spice market to international trade via clipper ships to touring caravans to the mall and e-commerce, this is just the next iteration in the transfer of goods and ideas to people. The fundamentals remain the same. Just as before, smart retailers need to embrace new behaviour patterns and technology to their advantage.

## What retail forgot

Retail has always been about bringing the unique from worlds afar; that is, introducing to people items they couldn't find or get in their corner of the world. From the spice market to the department store to the first iterations of the supermarket, the story of the department store is worth recalling. The traditional department store, which was only born during the nineteenth century, was about curating products from around the world and bringing them home, making available to people amazing items from before the days of travel, let alone global travel. Department stores arrived and redefined bricks-and-mortar retail as emporiums. They inspired the idea of 'shopping' as more than necessity and bridged it over to desire and aspirational living.

## The discount death spiral

Retailers forgot about enlightenment, curation and inspiration and got caught up in a TV-industrial, volume-focused price spiral. Price became the core focus of everything they did. The evidence is in all the communication materials. They even set up what's known as 'retail' communications campaigns, which are entirely focused on price and nothing more. The brand, or what I call 'reason', campaigns trailed into the background and were often removed from the corporate retail agenda entirely. They forgot that their job as retailers was to bring the world to their geography. Instead, retailers are a place where you buy cheap stuff and deals where you get two for the price of one. Many traditional retailers have put themselves into a retail price death spiral where all they've stood for were cheap prices, so what will they stand for when others sell goods more cheaply online?

## Price and range equalise

Once every person and every retailer of open-source products (those things anyone can choose to retail) are online, both price and range equalise. They become like water and find a flat surface and a market without undulation and variance. Those who don't price match on standard products simply don't sell. While it's silly to say that bricks-and-mortar retail is inferior to online retail, it's also fair to say that a physical retail store which competes on price is unsustainable.

## Same brand, different plan

The art is in understanding the different proposition of online 'delayed' versus physical or 'live' retail. Once the surface level of pricing and range is equalised, or removed from the equation, the real differentiators of how brands go to market start to kick in. In both realms, retailers have to stand for something. And that something should be the difference in every channel. Even if it's the same company, we need to go to market in different channels, in different ways; that is: same company, same brands, fragmented strategy. The value propositions in opposing worlds can only survive if they are worlds apart.

While the brand can stand for one thing and while there may be overlaps online and offline, the tactics and strategy should reflect what's possible in the opposing channels and differentiate in meaningful ways. But they must cross over in meaningful ways too.

## The questions that matter

Anyone in retail needs to ask themselves a set of important questions that weren't relevant post–World War II because in that era they were obvious questions. Stepping outside and reconsidering the dynamics of the retail world, these questions include:

- *Price strategy. Do you want to compete on price?* If the answer is yes, then it's going to be increasingly difficult to retail in physical stores. There's an extra step in the supply chain, and the economics simply don't make sense. In a market of near-perfect pricing knowledge, price-sensitive buyers gravitate to the cheapest price unless the warehouse and the store are one and the same. In many ways, this is what Walmart and Costco already do. They are more a bulk warehouse pick-up system than a traditional retailer. In general, online will win the price battle because price leadership is about low-cost infrastructure, and extra links in the retail chain do not make for low cost.

- *Product range strategy. Do you want to have a large or lean product range?* Clearly, online will win the large-range battle. It doesn't have the physical constraints of shelves and the cost of big stores. Online needs fewer places for the actual goods. In this world bricks-and-mortar retail can't win a product-range battle, it can only win a uniqueness and customised one. It's only a matter of time before widely distributed product brand owners start competing with retailers.

- *Location strategy: What's our physical location about?* For online players it's an easy decision: find a location that facilitates effective delivery. For stores it's much more than that. If the store is merely about acquiring the product, then in a connected world it has no reason to exist. A physical store needs to be a place of entertainment, education, co-creation and socialisation — a maison and experience that satisfies the five senses. Stores need to be events, not re-sellers.

- *Attention strategy: Will people use their feet or their fingers to find us?* If it's fingers (online), we have two simple choices: have an über niche audience that loves what we do because it's unique, or have a kicking SEO (Search Engine Optimisation) strategy that's first-page worthy. Both of these realities show a clear strategy: survival in retail is about being the cheapest or the nicest. Anything in between can't compete or will get lost in a world of infinite supply.

## Selling online

It's still relatively difficult to sell something online. The large majority of small-business people need help setting things up. These steps are not outrageously difficult, but they need consideration and linkages of various technology. It's not like blogging or social channels where if you can type, you can start publishing. This bridge needs to be built (and is currently being built). Once built, you'll be able to turn on a smartphone, press a button and sell to anyone in the world, accept all forms of payment and manage a storefront with lemonade-stand simplicity.

# If you make, you retail (big and small)

In the past, artisans used to sell what they made directly. The world of retail gave manufacturers, makers and artisans access to a new set of customers who could be from anywhere. The virtues of retail gave suppliers access to wider markets, more sales and bigger financial opportunities. It made sense to hand over part of the profit for access to new customers. Retail reduced the friction of selling by widening the customer base. For large tracts of the industrial era, retail was a specific industry that suppliers couldn't and didn't do. Now they can. We're quickly moving to a 'we all retail now' environment and customers want and expect to be able to go direct to brands.

Retailing is no longer about those guys over there who sell stuff; it is, and should be, about anyone who makes anything, not only because it's now possible, but because it can provide improved margin and the direct connections the market rewards. It's incumbent on those who once supplied to others for selling to know they can do the selling themselves. In an economy where anyone can make anything, having access to the people you sell to becomes a survival necessity. The power is with the distributor. We've already seen consumer goods retailers making their own 'home brand' goods to compete with their suppliers. Every supermarket in the world has a line of private labels, as do electronics retailers, and even cable television providers are funding programs to fill their channels. Now that suppliers can return the favour, it's about time they did.

## Manufacturers have to demarcate their retailers

Even today it's not uncommon for manufacturers within most industries not to have embraced the potential for direct selling. One of the most alarming reasons is because it may upset their current selling infrastructure; that is, upset their retailers or franchisees. It's a problem whereby the rights to sell have been sold. The basic reality is that any manufacturer that doesn't compete with its resellers is foolish. Exclusivity and the rights that go with it are an industrial relic. The strongest emerging retailers of the digital era don't demand it, and some — such as Amazon, iTunes and Zappos — had to fight to obtain supply from famous brands and industry stalwarts. So why would anyone provide a legacy reseller with exclusivity?

## Sorry, we don't sell online

The auto industry in Australia is one industry that chooses not to sell direct. With a long-standing network of branded car dealers, it remains loyal to its dealership network. Despite the fact that most of these franchisees sell multiple car brands, often from the same yard, the large majority of auto players in Australia does not sell cars online or direct. You can research the car and design the interior, but you can't buy it online. At the end of any online design process you're provided with a list of dealership addresses to choose from where you can go to buy the car.

The fact that the price varies by dealer is also a relic that doesn't fit in today's world. How can anyone trust a brand when they know they may not get the best deal possible, especially when the product is not one of a kind? It's as if they're pretending we don't live in a world of transparent retail prices. That type of trickery simply opens the door to more authentic brands. There's a real opportunity for auto players in developed markets to amend their retail component, and auto buyers will reward those that do.

Manufacturers in most industries need to develop a healthy form of competition with their onsellers. If their onsellers can't do a better job than they do, realistically they don't have a reason to exist. Buyers have no knowledge of, and don't care about, the way any business's retail infrastructure was originally set up. They only care about getting what they want delivered to them on their terms. And you have to love what they want more than you love your legacy infrastructure. Cross competition with buyers and suppliers should be expected in all industries because the barriers that created a linear supplier chain no longer exist.

## Don't ignore place

I've invested a large part of my adult career in fast-moving consumer goods marketing, which involves the types of products generally sold in supermarkets. One thing that really stood out to me was the limited definition of innovation. Even today, it generally takes into account only half of the marketing mix (which, as we explored in chapter 1, is the pieces of the brand puzzle — the product, the price, the place and the promotion). Most consumer-goods brands only innovate in what they make; that is, the thing itself — the widget. They make a new version of their existing product, configure a profitable price point and then sell it where they've always sold it. Manufacturers forget that innovation involves all areas of the business — not just what they make, but how they take it to the marketplace.

## Why place matters so much

Place matters because it's closest to the money. It's the final hurdle; it's where the interaction with the audience occurs. By outsourcing place to another party, you lose a significant amount of control over your brand. You lose the moment of truth. Even worse, someone else — the retail buyer, not the actual end user — gets to decide whether the new product is something they want and whether or not to range it. It's a risky way of doing business, especially when it's now not only possible, but expected, that manufacturers go direct.

With distribution systems and retail changing so much, it's an ideal time to reassess the entire marketing program, not just pieces within in. Brands and industries that have traditionally sold via third parties have to find a way of going direct, even if it means collaborating with competitors to create a new, direct channel for circumventing their traditional retailers. We live in counterintuitive times.

If you look at new technology brands such as Google and Amazon, you'll notice they innovate across all of the 4Ps, not only what they regard as their core or, more aptly, what their manufacturing arm already makes. Google is building self-driving cars, while Amazon makes and sells computers (the Kindle e-reader). Apple, through its stunning flagship stores, has become the most profitable retailer in the world per square metre.

## The location trick is over

For a long time, retailers were a kind of window to the world, representing the final access point to what was available, a lot like mainstream media did. As kids, we'd wait impatiently until the local store finally ranged that 'must have' item we saw advertised on television. If they didn't have it, we couldn't buy it — and they knew that. The more remote, the higher the price. If a retailer owned a geography, they could make abnormal economic profits. Providing access gave them enormous power because we had few (or no) other options. But the location trick is over. Being the importer is no longer enough because we can now get what they can provide from anywhere in the world at the world's cheapest price, delivered to our door.

In order to maintain relevance, small retailers will have to sell something the others don't; otherwise they'll be forever competing on price and struggling to carry a wide enough range. They need to be as far down the long tail as possible, providing a specific offer for a small and passionate audience that's far more likely to be appreciative of what they create or curate and far less price sensitive because it's being delivered by you for them and their tribe.

## Border hopping and digital reinvention

One of the terrific things the web enables is the re-birth of businesses that couldn't survive in the mass-market era, couldn't compete on price and didn't have enough appeal to remain viable. Online retail and the web are now enabling a renaissance of sorts. If you were a craftsman making handmade furniture out of Belgian hardwood, you had to hope you had enough people interested in that type of furniture within a 100-kilometre radius of where you lived and sold your wares. Today, businesses such as this that live deep inside the long tail can thrive. They have cheap access to selling to global markets; a populous with ever-increasing wealth and desire for unique artisanal products; and a unique product range, enabling them to be found in digital forums. While online retail has made many segments of the market more competitive, it's re-opening doors that were closed and providing very fertile ground for profitable niche retail. As a result, we can expect retail choice to fragment into the most micro of segments.

## Experience > item

What retailers in the physical space have to remember is that items are no longer what is being sold—they're an experience. Retailers will, in many ways, be in the business of social facilitation. They need to start creating events and experiences that are theatrical in nature. For purchasers, being there is as important as (or more important than) what they leave with in their shopping bag. The item alone is not reason enough to invest time in going into a store. The mantra must be that the experience is greater than the item. This needs to be tattooed in the DNA of physical retailers. I can't help but think that the burgeoning coffee culture has the ultimate retail lesson built into it.

**The mantra must be that the experience is greater than the item.**

## Clues in coffee culture

The city I live in is obsessed with coffee. It seems as if every second retail store in trendy inner city suburbs is now a café serving espresso from its own single origin beans specially roasted in-house. The patrons are happy to pay more than 100 times the cost of the espresso coffee they have at home, using the same beans, because they're not coming for the coffee. They're coming to be present in the physical space the coffee shop provides, which is most likely decorated the way we wish our kitchen was. They're coming to meet with friends, interact with others or chat with their favourite barista (who knows them by name). It's about watching the skilled craftsman (in this case the barista) undertake their art in front of a live audience. They're coming for the socialisation that human beings crave and to break up their day with a mini event. Coffee isn't coffee and retail is no longer retail.

The idea of retail has changed so much that when it's physical, it's not even about what we buy from the store, but the experience provided during the process. Online we can get anything from anywhere at the best price possible.

So what happens when the stuff we want can be made on demand at home? It's hard to believe, but 3D printing will make this an everyday reality.

## What is fragmenting

Retail is no longer just the end of the supply chain; it's something every business and person can do now.

## What it means for business

If you make, you must sell. The power lies with those who have a direct connection with their buyers or audience.

# CHAPTER 10

## Bigger than the internet: 3D printing

I've been mildly obsessed with 3D printing since I first learned about it. Also referred to as 'additive manufacturing' or 'digital fabrication', it's a process where a three-dimensional, solid object is created by placing down successive layers of material fused together by laser (digital light processing) and a multitude of other methods that are evolving rapidly, almost daily. Most people have now seen some footage of one of these printers in action, probably printing a useless plastic widget or a gun. You know a technology has hit the mainstream agenda when it appears on *60 Minutes*. Old media still has a place.

As far as usefulness is concerned, the technology is now starting to reach an inflection point where things get radical, blowing the minds of even the most ardent technologist. 3D printers can create complex moving mechanical parts, often in a single build process, but more radically, they're entering the realm of the biotechnology used to build human organ replacements, synthetic bones and computer-added tissue design. Add to this the ability to print various forms of computer technology, including microchips, circuit boards and capacitors, and the mind boggles. Yes, all of this is a bit like history repeating itself: making things happen with simple scanning and clicks of buttons on desks. The more important questions about 3D printing are, 'What *won't* they be able to do?' and 'How do we make money in a world where *Star Trek* style replicators actually exist?'

While researching the history of news reports about the internet, I happened upon an article from *The New York Times* by Robert Reinhold from 1982 entitled, 'Study says technology could transform society'.[1]

It was a story about computers turning into a global network where all information could be transferred, downloaded and manipulated through a few clicks of a button. We'd be able to listen to music, watch movies, do banking and send electronic mail instantly. We'd be able to connect with families around the world live on television screens, most likely free of charge. It predicted social groups forming that defied traditional demographic clustering. It even said that for most developed countries setting up a connection to the global computer network would be less than an average week's wages. It was rather fanciful thinking, it said, but it may just cause a revolution.

[1]www.nytimes.com/1982/06/14/us/study-says-technology-could-transform-society.html

As we all know, we've been delivered even more than was promised. Given that we've lived through global network formation, we need to open our minds about what 3D printing will do. It's changed everything in our physical, human-created world. It's created a fragmentation of the production process to the point where significant parts of human output are decentralised permanently.

In this sense our world becomes one, where everything is information, where knowledge is converted into actual objects and where the internet crosses the chasm from the virtual into the physical.

## A virtual physical reality

While technology has already been used extensively in the fields of dentistry, medicine, automobiles and aviation, it's now entering our homes for the first time. Famed designer, inventor and futurist R. Buckminster Fuller spoke of a future where technology would advance to a point where we could do 'more with less and less until eventually you can do everything with nothing'. Fuller spoke of this phenomenon in 1938 and coined the term 'ephermalization' to describe it.

Fuller's vision was that ephermalization would result in ever-increasing standards of living for an ever-growing population despite finite resources. His oft-cited example was Henry Ford's assembly line, which to this day has led to better products at a lower cost, in perpetuity. With 3D printing still largely on the tech-hacker fringes in terms of actual usage, the level of innovation is astounding. This non-exhaustive list provides a perspective of the potential impact of this technology and demonstrates how widely it is being embraced.

- *Cars.* Entire car bodies have been printed, both replicas and new models. The Urbee 2 is a vehicle for which more than 50 per cent was 3D printed and it can reach speeds of about one-hundred and ten kilometres per hour.

- *Tools.* Tools of every type, shape and mechanical movement have been made, all of which were printed in metals and even carbon composites stronger than most metals.

- *Camera lenses.* The current level of progression of acrylic camera lenses that perform at highly functional levels suggests that soon it will be possible to print these using glass, rivalling the quality of their commercial counterparts. This will be at a micro portion of the current cost of buying them.

- *Food.* Yes, chocolate, steak and hamburgers have been printed. NASA is experimenting with this process for long space flights. Bioengineering startup Modern Meadow has 3D printed meat that's been eaten. 3D printed food, while it sounds particularly unpalatable, has a significant potential for reducing the impact of modern agriculture.

- *Clothing.* A 3D-printable, biodegradable, flexible, synthetic fabric that feels like cloth is already here. Known as Cosyflex, this fabric is made using a spray nozzle to create layers of natural rubber-latex polymers and cotton fibres.

- *Jewellery.* Jewellery can now be printed not just from plastics, but also with precious metals.

- *Bicycles.* We already have fully functional bicycles made of pieces that click together.

- *Musical instruments.* Most kinds of musical instruments have been printed and when played they have the clarity of their handmade counterparts.

- *Drones.* These perfectly flyable aircraft, which are printed in pieces, can be as small as the palm of your hand or large and complex.

- *Rocket injectors.* A rocket injector was printed by NASA that can generate 900 kilograms of thrust.

- *Robots.* A joint team at Harvard and MIT has built a mind-blowing, self-assembling robot. It uses shape memory polymers so the bot can configure itself into the correct arrangement after it's printed.

- *Working engines.* Engines have been printed as one piece in a single build process.

- *Prosthetics.* Prosthetics can be printed for commercial or home use. Amputee Richard Van As built what he calls a Robohand to replace his lost fingers instead of paying $10 000 for a commercial prosthetic. The five fingers close when he bends his wrist, and he shared his design online to help others create their own version.

- *Body parts.* A working printed ear has come out of Cornell University that uses cells from a patient's rib. Even human liver tissue has been successfully printed by Organovo, a San Diego research firm.

- *A house.* Engineering professor Behrokh Khoshnevis of California has laid out his plans[2] to 3D print a full-size house in less than a day, including the electrical and plumbing work.

- *Another 3D printer.* The open source RepRap 3D printer has made smaller versions of itself, save a few nuts and bolts. In fact, most 3D printers could print about eighty per cent of themselves already leading us to the evolution in technology where hardware is starting to do what software is very good at: making copies of itself.

This list was outdated the moment I wrote it. It can't not be. The reason is that this technology is in the hands of people who create what they imagine at will. They don't have to wait for approval or permission. They just do it with open-source machines and software. In fact, there's no way of knowing what someone has just created in their home as a 3D printing enthusiast. What's important is what this list represents. At this early stage there's a staggering scope of possibility for what can be made. From reviewing this it's not silly to believe 3D printing could make anything. The processes used so far in 3D printing are not nearly as important as the concept that we can make things from digital instructions. We can even make things that make things. Everything — even technology, it turns out — has self-replicating seeds inside itself, just as nature does.

The fact that this part of the revolution is physical puts it directly into the 'bigger than the internet' category. All the web has done so far is change information distribution; that is, shift how we get data. Once we shift how we make things it starts to impact where and how we live as much as the industrial revolution did to the agricultural age. It affects what we can make. It affects what everyone owns because they will own their own version of everything. It affects significantly how people and companies will make money.

3D printing manufacturers claim that anything that's produced at a volume of fewer than 200 000 units will not be able to compete on price. If you stop and take a look around the room you're in right now you'll notice that the number of widgets that come from factories is astounding. These kinds of widget will very soon be made in the home. But isn't that the point? Who would want to own anything that's designed for the masses when we can have a bespoke version and make our own tweaks.

---

[2]Not yet undertaken, but technologically possible with existing methods: http://tedxtalks.ted.com/video/TEDxOjai-Behrokh-Khoshnevis-Con

# The history of technology repeats

As with all technology, the prices of 3D printers are in rapid freefall with entry-level models as low as $100. The prices are already at a point where they're affordable to pretty much anyone in a developed economy. Sure, the industrial high-end versions can run into the millions of dollars, but so do large-scale paper printing devices. The point is, with price no longer the barrier, the only missing link before these printers invade every home with an internet connection is mass pop-culture awareness. We need communities to spring up and find ways of creating in-home use. This will take people from a curious level of awareness to 'I must have one of these devices', and that desire is spreading quickly.

Add to this some simple user-centric interfaces of the process and the rest will move more quickly than we could have ever imagined. We already know how transformative digital technology can be. We've already experienced the benefits first hand through access to knowledge. We know we're living through a change that's human centric and giving the power back to the people. The accumulation of these ingredients leads to a rapid penetration of technology. We already believe. We just need to be informed of what 3D printing can do for us. All forms of retailer need to wise up and start selling them as a necessary household appliance, rather than a hobbyist niche.

While it may be hard to believe that the quality of anything and everything could be better than what comes out of a factory, there are analogies worth remembering.

In 1984 a Kodak photo-processing machine required an investment of more than $800 000 to process film into photos. Today, an inkjet printer that costs about fifty dollars can reproduce digital photos with an unnoticeable difference in resolution. This has also happened with mainframe computing to the point where the super computer that lives in our pocket is our most powerful technological device. It's clear that technology is disrupting industry and breaking down almost everything that was once mass. Just as large media has had to learn to share the stage with citizen journalism, the factory will soon be sharing the market with digital craftspeople operating out of their home. Desktop publishing is about to be joined by desktop manufacturing.

Smart entrepreneurs are already starting to build 'bridge industries' for 3D printing, which will teach and build the market in the pre–saturation phase of the coming years. Online 3D digital print shops such as Ponoko — which produces what you want using your designs or those of other people and sends the finished product right to your door—are emerging. We're also seeing 3D print shops appear on high streets, shopping centres and office supply stores, all places that could eventually provide the highest quality of 'personal manufacturing' available and match the quality of any industrial-level 3D printer worldwide.

# The home factory

The 'home office' is now parlance of yesteryear. The digital communications tools we've become so accustomed to have now invaded the entire home. They've left the office relatively freely because all types of web-enabled screens follow us around the house. Every desktop will have a 3D printer on it right next to the 2D version. Of course, we'll also end up with a 3D printer in our garage or shed to manufacture bigger items, or components such as plastic fenders for that parking miscalculation we made at the local shopping centre. The idea of 'printing a bumper bar' for your car isn't as fanciful as it may seem. Ultimately, it's a piece of plastic with a certain industrial design. If the design was download from a car company's official website, for the specific model of car, with a specific design code, and it was printed using the required input polymer formula specified by said car company during the printing, then there's no reason why this couldn't become a reality. In fact, it could be cheaper for the end user and more profitable for the manufacturer simultaneously. It's quite foreseeable for panel beaters to be replaced by car part fitters who work more like a mobile mechanic.

In fact, much of what we buy will be design. The next generation of e-commerce sites won't be shipping the products or brands we choose online to our doorstep. Instead, we'll be downloading designs from the global digital department stores, which may be Amazon or another start-up that wants to shake up the world. There's no doubt that smart brands will want to participate. It's not as if the global brands of today have a vested interest in manufacturing anymore. They outsourced that in the first shift to globalised markets and cheap labour. If manufacturing, shipping and distribution could be cut out entirely, profitability would be enhanced—but only for those who understand the shift and embrace it. Add to that the environmental benefits of reduced transport loads and wastage in the production process, and excess production of minimum runs. This requires a decision from brand manufacturers to love the customer and not their infrastructure. They need to be agnostic about the system that currently serves them, which is something most legacy industries have struggled with.

# Piracy on steroids

The real challenge for the brands that will be affected by 3D printing isn't about whether or not this new economic construct can work, but rather whether they have the gumption to embrace it. The best example we currently have on hand is the music industry. The world of MP3 downloads and music streaming should have been the domain of large recording industry houses, but instead it has ended up in the control of music newbies.

Let's imagine designer sunglasses made from plastics and perfectly 3D printable materials. There would be more designs, more often — a fashion retail match made in heaven. In fact, the rate of change will be a vital ingredient to beating the copycats because piracy could be elevated to a level that makes Pirate Bay look like child's play. An entire internet sharing actual print design files of high-end designer brands will be interesting. Monetisation methods don't immediately present themselves. They're difficult to find in a world rife with piracy, but zero-cost digital duplication is an unavoidable reality so it must be embraced with the faith of finding a way to make it pay.

It can only be imagined that this will raise legal quandaries that have previously been unthinkable. Even those brands that choose not to sell their designs won't be spared the piracy challenge. Every 3D printer will come with infrared and sonar scanners that create digital files for anything we have a copy of. We need to imagine that anything physical will be able to be scanned and uploaded via a device that clicks into our smartphone. It won't matter whether companies release the digital files of their designs or not because they'll become freely available regardless.

In order for brands not to get caught napping, they have to realise that they're not products, but identities. In fact, a 3D digital department store could be just the ticket for improving new product lead times. It could significantly reduce the inter-purchase intervals and upweight the frequency of purchase and fashion cycles. Manufacturers will soon have the potential to engage a globally distributed, free labour force, which is something most information players have in the form of content creators. They, too, can unlock the power of co-creation and the sharing of the financial upside, but they need a platform mentality to do it. They need to have the courage to hand over their brand to the audience and to cede control. Brands will have to be more curated than contrived. Brand owners will have to believe the crowd can create something that they could never imagine. Why wouldn't they? The crowd already blew our minds when it came to media; they re-imagined every form of communication and there's more to come. Brands need to allow physical mash-ups to occur to enable the best stuff to bubble up to the top. But it needs to be done knowing there isn't a clear monetisation path for co-creation. It's murky at best. The strategy needs to be one of embracing the unknown and of exploring all commercial possibilities.

It's hard to imagine that a build-stuff-on-demand world will ever exist. But it was probably hard for pre-industrial artisans to imagine what factories and production would eventually become, or how the first transistors would transform us into an information age. What's certain is that social media and citizen journalism will evolve into social design and social manufacturing. It's the way it's always been, excluding the 200-year halcyon period of the industrial era.

# Dad vs daughter

I've been thrilled to own a 3D printer for a few years now. I purchased one when they hit their Altair moment (the Altair 8800 is regarded as the first affordable personal computer and the spark of the home computer revolution). It's a pretty impressive party trick introducing someone to the basic idea of 3D printing, helping them work through their initial incredulity, showing them a little video about it, and then helping them print their first item. It's a social experiment I've undertaken on both my 70-year-old father and my four-year-old daughter.

While I was tinkering with my 3D printer in my home office, my daughter came in the room and asked me what that 'toy' was, pointing to the printer. She must have heard my wife talk about it. While it's more than a toy, I can't quite claim it to be a business necessity yet, though it will be both that and a modern life necessity shortly. I told my daughter it was my 3D printer. She didn't ask any of the curious questions I normally get, such as, 'What do you mean printing in 3D?' She just nodded her head and took it as fact. I asked her if she wanted me to print her something, maybe a toy or some jewellery. I could remember that some of the 3D-printing file-sharing sites, such as Cubify and Thingiverse, had files of really cools things for little kids. She replied simply, 'Okay Daddy,' and seemed reasonably excited about the idea of me printing her something right at that moment. Who wouldn't be? It's a 3D printer; it's the future of most everything physical.

So we scanned through the jewellery on the screen, picked out a cool and colourful bracelet, downloaded the file and sent the file to the printer for manufacturing. I pressed the print button and it started printing. During the process of finding and choosing, I was pretty pumped. I was 3D printing my little girl some personal jewellery ... on the spot ... in my home office. Once the process was underway I said, 'Look, look, it's printing it', to which she replied in a nonchalant manner, 'Okay. Thanks, Daddy,' and left the room. Sure, she was excited about the jewellery, but not the process. The process was irrelevant to her; she just wanted the bracelet.

Once the print job was complete, I called her back into my office and said, 'Look. Here it is, your bracelet. I printed it for you!', to which her reply was much like the previous one. She said, 'Thanks, Daddy,' put it on her wrist and skipped away to get on with her four-year-old life.

My father, on the other hand, had an entirely different experience. When I first informed him of 3D printing, it required a lot of explaining. I told him I'd purchased a 3D printer and he couldn't quite grasp the fact I was talking about a machine that makes things out of 'thin air' in the shape a computer tells it to. It was pure science fiction. In the first conversation we had about it he thought I was having a joke with him. To show him what it was I reached for my smartphone to upload a random 3D-printing YouTube video to do the explaining for me. He watched it, intrigued, and then again laughed it off as some kind of trick video.

It wasn't until the next time he visited my home that he truly understood what this technology meant. I showed him my little printer, which has a 15-centimetre square platform built around it, and told him I could print him anything he wanted that would fit in that space, right now. My father's a tradesman, a man of the tools who spent his life with hammers in his hands and also working on a farm. Ever the marketer, I told him we could print a tool with moving parts. He decided to print a shifter spanner, a type of wrench with a little screw that changes the size of the spanner head. During the same process I took my daughter through, he kept on saying, 'You've got to be kidding me. This is unbelievable!', adding that he never thought he'd see technology that radical in his lifetime, which is quite something given that he was only observing a hobbyist's level of tinkering on that day. He watched the entire build process. For more than one hour he obsessed with watching the magic of the digital world build him something real: something he could touch and hold. Superlatives are not available to describe how amazed he was once it was done. It totally flipped his mind.

He said, 'Can I keep it, Steve?' without realising that I could easily print another one. When I saw him a few weeks later and asked about his 3D printed spanner he told me that he keeps it in the glove box of his car to show everyone he meets and tries to explain how it was made. He went on to say that more than half the time his friends refuse to believe it was printed. If any 3D printer manufacturers ever need another brand evangelist he'd make a terrific candidate!

It's an interesting comparison to the reaction of my daughter. It's really a great reminder of the best definition we have for technology, which is, 'something that was invented after you were born'.

The stark difference in perspective between these generations is everything. The really significant element is that by the time my daughter is 14 years of age, she and every person she knows will have a 3D printer. We'll all be 3D printing in our homes every day in 10 years' time. And if you think that isn't possible, let me remind you that every social media channel you use today didn't exist just 10 or so years ago, and we all know how much that changed our economic landscape.

**We'll all be 3D printing in our homes every day in 10 years' time.**

I believe 3D printing is going to have a bigger impact on society than the internet did. Yes, it's part of the same ecosystem, but it raises even more seemingly unanswerable questions, such as:

- *How can we stop people printing dangerous items such as guns?* We can't. But all technology can be dangerous in the wrong hands. Remember that little piece of technology known as a knife? It's as old as homo sapiens and still has lethal potential, yet it lives in our kitchens. The real danger is people.

- *How can we protect a manufacturing firm from the threat of 3D printing?* We can't. It can only be embraced as a way of making the old method redundant or less profitable for a company. Manufacturers need to be beneficiaries of the advances, not victims. Technology will come anyway because it's recalcitrant.

- *How can we make money when people can make their own version of anything?* I'm not sure. But I am sure the answer will come to those who experiment in the ecosystem. I'm also sure the more human something is, the more money we will make as technology replaces itself again and again. There are already clear lessons from the music industry. The platform is greater than the product. We have to create places for people to create upon, unless, of course, the product is human, such as the 1980's pop stars who have started singing for their supper again (as they tour the globe) because their royalty streams have dried up. Human performances can't be replaced — yet.

Importantly, we need to think of 3D printing beyond widgets, tools and mechanical devices. We need to understand that a multi-material, one-process-to-print-everything is rapidly approaching.

It's quite a human process to lament the missed and seemingly obvious opportunities in hindsight. I sometimes think to myself that I should have continued coding on my 16KB RAM-only TRS-80 home computer in the 1980s and that I should have implemented some of my internet startup ideas in 1995, when I first got on the web (I finally did it 10 years later). The era for 3D printing is now. It's early days and there's enough time for any company or entrepreneur to get involved. It's the burgeoning period of possibility. 3D printing is going to impact every business. Observing its development is not enough; it requires participation.

The path for manufacturing is clearly leading to major disruption. The advantage manufacturing has is the lessons it can learn from what's already happened to the media and where it's heading.

## What is fragmenting

3D printing is taking manufacturing from the factory to the desktop.

## What it means for business

Desktop manufacturing has as much disruptive potential as the web did for information-based businesses.

# CHAPTER 11

## Screen play:
## post–mass media

Of all the industries that are being disrupted during the great fragmentation, none is being affected more than the media industry. It's fair to say it's already been fully disrupted in the sense that the power players of today are no longer the power players of the pre-web world. A new set of stalwarts has already changed things dramatically. But this doesn't mean we'll have relative stability in the coming years and decades. The process of change in the media landscape will continue. The amount of fragmentation to come will be far more significant than what we've already seen. The mere definition of media as we know it may even evaporate.

## Television is no more

Whenever I'm presenting to a group of business leaders on the topic of media, I ask one simple question to test whether they're yet to change gears into the technology age and whether they've perceived the changes that have already impacted the simplest of media tools: television.

The question I ask is this: 'How many free-to-air television channels are there currently in your country/market?'

Nine times out of ten the answer is wrong, even when I ask a room full of media, advertising or marketing executives. They go through the motion of reviewing the emergence of the new free digital channels. Some include subscription television in their reckoning. But few ever give me the answer that's our market reality today: there are currently more than 6 billion free television channels.

The truth is that there are probably even more than that. There's an infinite number of television channels available to anyone who lives in the connected world. There are a few reasons for this. The first is that you can no longer buy a television that's not web connected. Today, every new television has web-enabled wi-fi capabilities. But more important than that is the fact that in real terms televisions no longer exist. All we have now are screens, and all screens will very soon be created equal. All screens can play whatever is fed into them via digital means. The traditional main play of the television — free local television channels — is now a bit of a sideshow to what we really want to watch.

**There are currently more than 6 billion free television channels.**

## Television as an audio-visual server

We need a different view of what television is today:

*Television = on-demand audio-visual server*

It's actually a bit like a dumb terminal from the early corporate computer era. Very soon, our television will just be another one of the connected computer systems that also includes a screen.

Televisions of today can already connect with a smartphone, home computer and the web itself. Very soon they will connect to our smart homes and smart cars. We've reached a point in time where 'the end of television' and 'long live television' mean the same thing. Television has morphed into a different beast and it will survive only because it will never be what it was. It will never serve a linear purpose again. The only thing it will do that it also did in the past is create audio-visual output. Business needs to quickly revise its definition of television. It's just one of many connected display devices. It's one of the pieces of technology that delivers both connection and content on demand. And it's not something that lives in our lounge room. It's everywhere that a screen is. It's not what it used to be, and television as it was will never exist again.

# Device convergence

Device convergence has long been the holy grail of the technological world — the divine digital moment, the next big thing that always seemed to be a big prediction for the coming year. Yet, over the past 30 years we tended to see a splitting of technologies rather than a convergence with new devices performing ever-divergent digital tasks. That was until the smartphone — the pocket exception — arrived and started our current era of screen culture. While

**The smartphone, or pocket screen, is quickly becoming the control panel for a connected existence.**

we still have a number of individual technology devices, increasingly they all perform the same tasks. The smartphone, or pocket screen, is quickly becoming the control panel for a connected existence.

# Digital demarcation

The pre-internet media landscape was quite a stable set of output devices and content creations. Each platform had its output, which was clearly defined and suited to its devices and related technology. There was a small overlap, but they largely had their own job to do.

Newspapers, magazines, radio, recordings, cinema and television each had their role to play. They owned a channel, owned the content and owned the audience. There wasn't a great deal of crossover in content, although there was a large amount of cross-media ownership and large media conglomerates were formed.

That all changed once literally anyone could get their hands on the tools of content creation. Media has now entered an age of digital demarcation. The output of any and every media company is fragmenting into a multi-format experience. Most media organisations now also do what 'the other guys' (their competitors) used to do, not because they necessarily want to, but because the technology makes it possible and the audience demands it. The lines of who produces what have been blurred. As all forms of traditional mass media scramble for survival they now have to deliver multi-format content just to stay alive. They have to fragment their offerings to maintain their mass audience because their mass audience is also fragmenting. It's a very difficult task that increases costs and rarely maintains the original audience.

# Mass-media platform fragmentation

Newspapers, magazines, radio stations, television and cinema now have an incredibly wide gamut of tasks to undertake to win eyes and ears in the ridiculously competitive multi-platform world. They no longer produce their content via their chosen channel. They now have to produce it via their audience's chosen channel because audiences don't delineate between who produces what in a digital world.

Today traditional media has to create and manage output via myriad platforms. This non-exhaustive list is an example of what it has to cover: websites and content, smartphone apps, video content, news, blogs, social accounts, podcasts, email newsletters, forums, classified sites, and short documentaries. And it must ensure it's all delivered on demand and that it's responsive to any platform. This is no easy, or cheap, task.

# The legacy media challenge

The main challenge for the legacy media is that its business infrastructure and model is built around mass audiences. It has to undertake all of these new tasks to maintain its 'mass' status and audience and it needs a mass audience to feed the costly legacy infrastructure. It has to chase its audience, which is forever finding new methods and content to pay attention to.

New media players, on the other hand, don't have to do this. The benefit this has is that it doesn't have a costly infrastructure and it doesn't need a mass audience to survive. It's no wonder traditional media struggles to compete and remain viable financially. While it sounds fanciful, a budding writer with a laptop, a broadband connection, a passion and some open-source software can compete successfully against the world's biggest news(papers). All it takes today is a focused niche mentality.

# Blogs vs *The New York Times*

In the short period since self-publishing has risen to prominence, written works that are nothing more than glorified blogs have usurped the once-untouchable news stalwarts. They've been able to do this for two reasons: there's no heavy, expensive legacy infrastructure and there's no desire to broadcast.

Their power comes from what they *don't* do. In a fragmented media world, focus is far more profitable than trying to serve a mass media. The new newspapers of the web are all narrowcasters, and they're not small businesses. They chose their audience and they serve it well. The attack from new players has not been front-on; it's been occurring sideline by sideline. In fact, it's very difficult to pinpoint the difference between a newspaper and a blog because we tend to read only certain sections of newspapers. In the past, we had to buy the entire paper just to read the bits that interested us. Once newspapers moved online we could go directly to the bits we wanted to read. All of a sudden the reality of their fragmented readership became impossible to hide, and newspapers had to quickly reconfigure their advertising strategy niche. The only problem was that most of the niche positions in the market had already been filled by more nimble blogging startups.

If we look at the top blogs in traditional newspaper and magazine categories we find a cavalcade of new media darlings literally smashing old print heroes out of the park:

- *Entertainment.* The Huffington Post, Buzzfeed, The Verge
- *Celebrity culture.* Gawker, Hollywoodlife, Gossip Cop, Slate, The Superficial
- *Sport.* SBnation, The Bleacher Report
- *Technology.* Techcrunch, Mashable, GigaOm, VenterBeat
- *Business.* Business Insider, Zerohedge, Quick Sprout.

Mind you, the list of blogging categories has also fragmented to the nichest of niches, a breadth no traditional 'do it all' print player could ever cover. The list above covers only the areas traditionally covered by print. And given there are only so many channels any one person can pay attention to, we're quickly moving to the point where big and general are both fast tracking towards extinction. Not one of the 'top-10' blogs was originally created by a traditional media owner.

This doesn't mean that blogs can't have as much in-market value as traditional newspapers either. *The Washington Post* was recently sold to Amazon founder and CEO Jeff Bezos for US$250 million, while Gawker Media has a reported market value of more than US$300 million. Über-niche blogs — such as Treehugger and Celebrity Baby Blog, which were each sold for US$10 million in the 2000s — are also going for significant sums. Add to this that the 'rivers of gold' that flowed from classified ads are also being taken over online by single-minded competitors, and we've witnessed a classic 'David' victory.

## Who do you trust?

Do you trust a large media organisation that survives by running advertisements for giant global brands (who may well be polluting the earth and encouraging kids to eat food that makes them sick, or who make products with planned obsolescence) to tell you the truth about the world around you? Or do you trust a passionate 'amateur' writing a blog about a topic of interest and passion late on a Saturday night to share some valuable information with others for no money, no payoff and no vested interest other than sharing value with other people? Yes, we all have an agenda, even that lonely blogger, but the probability of agenda purity in my view sits with the independent. I know who I trust more. And trust is the currency of a connected economy where the cost of everything is tumbling.

# Screen first

The reason this chapter is entitled 'Screen play', is that in our screen-based culture the screen is now almost always the entry point for all media consumption, regardless of the category the media happens to fall into. The common connection point of media that was once screenless is now the screen.

- Before we listen to a podcast, we open the app on the little screen.
- The newspaper is now largely read online via the screen.
- Magazines have been replaced by blogs and are now read on tablets.
- A newspaper may have video content and movies.
- The radio is controlled via apps and in-car screens.
- Live events are now most often married with a screen-based webcast.

Smart screens are now both an entry and delivery mechanism for every type of media. And while we've had some clear winners in the war for the pocket, the lounge room is still up for grabs.

# Media then/media now

The main job of the media used to be about delivering content to its audience: filling the schedule for each channel, and matching the day parts of programming with the demographic profile. Whoever had the best content won the audience.

Today the most important job of major media players is to provide a platform that enables the creation of content by us that we really want to see, hear and engage with, not the average stuff that was forced down our throats over the second half of the twentieth century. As far as media companies are concerned I include Google (YouTube) Facebook, Twitter and Apple in this category. The technology industry has become a large part of the media industry now, and vice versa. In fact, we're all in the technology business now — it's just that some industries are yet to realise it — just as all agriculture and crafts were enveloped in the industrial shift 200 years ago. People either got onboard or they couldn't compete.

All of the new-media darlings are providing publishing platforms for fragmented and niche media content. They've opened up their digital warehouse, their digital factory, and said to the audience, 'Here you go. Go create something amazing. Go create something that people like you really want. Use our platform to make a lasting connection on a topic we couldn't possibly imagine or ever have your expertise in. And we'll both benefit by building an audience and making money with our tools. We'll both win together'.

## Handing it over

The media ceded control and handed over once fiercely protected assets: the tools of production and access to an audience, or more aptly, the chance to build one. And it's working out better than anyone would have imagined. The pool of creative talent runs as deep as the connected population does. They're one and the same. We all soon realised that the tastemakers didn't have some secret talent or knowledge that an audience couldn't match. It's more that before now, people had to be chosen, and we couldn't choose ourselves. Once we all had access to the tools, the truth about creativity was revealed. We all have something to offer, especially when we create it for our own micro community. So, it comes down to this:

- *media then:* protect assets and create content
- *media now:* provide platforms for the crowd.

Yahoo is a classic example of media that's unable to decide whether it's a platform provider or a content creator. It appears to be forever looking for a clear path to increased profitability.

# Platforms on platforms

In a zero cost of access media market there are now platforms on platforms on platforms ...

While the prize for owning a platform is big, it's no easy task building a primary platform. That's why both Apple and Google are in the top-5 companies in the world in terms of market capitalisation. Platform creation is difficult and incredibly profitable when it works, but that doesn't mean platforms can't be created on existing platforms. As we've seen, all technology stacks, so once a platform is viable and stable, we can build another platform on top of it. We've seen it again and again with smartphone apps that have become large and valid independent businesses (though often acquired by other big players) like Instagram, WhatsApp or any of the large blogs that used Wordpress as their platform. If a connection to an audience becomes significant and aggregated enough it eventually becomes its own ecosystem.

## How to live in niche land

Even if we can't own a platform, the play is still pretty clear: we have to provide niche content or curate the madness of the content deluge.

The reason platforms have become so successful is because the evolution of the media has told us that people don't have average interests. For example, when we go to the general store, we don't buy general items, we buy specific items. When we engage with media, we're not interested in general content, but specific content. And the breadth of what we want knows no boundaries.

Because there's so much content, we need both content creators and content curators: those who make it and those who sort it. It's something brands need to pay more attention to. While some brands are prepared to invest the long leads and compound effort to build a platform or channel of their own — such as Red Bull media — others lack the foresight, patience and willingness to invest the required resources. A valid angle of attack is to become the curator of all things good in a category, or the expert of the über niche. While it may seem like something of a sideshow, it can be both brand-building and profitable.

## People don't have average interests

When I was a teenager in the 1980s, the world I grew up in had the following media options:

- a few radio stations (only one for teenagers)
- three television channels
- two daily newspapers.

And this was no country town. It was Melbourne, Australia, a city of more than 3 million people at the time in one of the most developed and wealthy nations in the world.

As a teenage boy, I was allocated a couple of timeslots during the week where I'd get my fix of the content I really cared about: a video music program on a Saturday morning and *The Wide World of Sports* on a Saturday afternoon, both of which massively under-delivered as far as I was concerned. Here's what I got:

- *Video Hits.* This was the name of the show I'd watch on a Saturday morning to get my teenage fix of music videos. I liked alternative music and I'd be lucky if there were two songs from bands I really liked featured in full length over the three-hour timeslot of the show. That's eight minutes of footage in a three-hour show that happened once a week.

- *The Wide World of Sports.* I was totally obsessed with surfing as a teenager. *Wide World of Sports* ran for four hours every Saturday afternoon from 1 to 5 pm, with the inference being that they'd cover every sport known. And they nearly did. The problem was, I don't like 'sport'. I like surfing. So I'd invest my four hours waiting all day for the five minutes of surfing to be shown. I couldn't even tape the entire show on a VHS recorder as the tapes only went for three hours and I might have missed it! They stole my entire afternoon, and I clearly didn't get any of my weekend chores done. Surfing would always be on last, for some reason.

Fast forward to today. I have all the surfing I could ever watch, on demand, in HD, any time I want. My choice of surfing to watch now runs so deep it has fragmented to the nth level. During *The Wide World of Sports* days any surfing was good enough. Now I'm so fussy I only like watching surfing in particular surfing spots, with a particular type of surfboard with my favourite pro surfers, and often from my halcyon period of the mid 1980s. And here's the crazy thing: it's all there waiting for me online.

## Remove ~~surfing~~, insert interest X

You need to forget that the story above was about surfing. That's just my personal example. You had this experience too, before media fragmented, regardless of what you happened to be interested in: knitting, calligraphy, German folk music, wood turning, marathon running … it doesn't matter what it is, it's all available on demand with granular levels of coverage.

# Channelology

What most media and brands have not realised is that people only have so much attention to give. This occurs in two ways: first, with the depth of content and second, with the width of content. In a specific niche there's so much content that we, by definition, will miss most of it. We'd have to almost opt out of life to pay attention to all of it. People are starting to finally come to terms with the foolishness of trying to be across all the content. The trend of 'going dark'—disconnecting oneself from the internet or implementing a digital 'do not disturb'—will bubble up as a mere coping mechanism more than anything: 'I haven't seen Mary online for a while?' 'Yes, she's going dark quite often these days. She's been diagnosed with HCOS, Human Content Overload Syndrome'.

But the breadth of content is what business needs to pay attention to. There are only so many channels of content output we can follow. Channelology will become the art of managing an audience so they keep up their subscription with our channel, and give us permission to engage with them. While the number may vary by person, with the complexity of life these days there are only so many channels we can maintain—a bit like our relationships and Dunbar's number. There are only so many blogs we can follow. There are only so many news sites we can visit. There are only so many YouTube channels we can subscribe to. There are only so many industries we can be knowledgeable about. Businesses have to become a channel people care about, or get featured in one people care about. The evidence of our ability to only maintain relationships with a few channels is all around us: from the few smartphone apps that get all our attention on the phone, to our preferred social media network, to our preferred video channels. When new ones get added, invariably others drop out.

## The price of attention

We can always buy attention. Buying an audience will always be an option, but as audiences fragment, the price will rise and the effectiveness will decline. It's the pure economics of supply and demand. As time goes by there will be fewer occurrences of a mass audience aggregating. Lower supply leads to higher prices. It's funny that the first lesson in economics is the one that's forgotten most often. The alternative is to earn attention. So how do we become a channel that people care about?

## Channelling an audience

The choices for getting attention are to be newsworthy or to create valuable content. Being newsworthy is difficult because it has a giant question mark around how sustainable a strategy it is for engagement. People forget about news stories and viral sensations pretty quickly and they get on with their lives. Creating valuable content isn't about generating a mass audience. It's about being trusted by the people who care about what you build. These days people are more likely to care about the brand they support because as each day passes the products being communicated are far more niche by nature.

Due to this, the first challenge for marketers using media to communicate is to remove the millions mentality from their mind. While YouTube has provided the most amazing tools for marketers ever given, it has warped the minds of many marketing personnel as to what's required from it. And no, having a million or more views on our video is most often not required for the platform to work very hard indeed. What's needed is the specific connection, at the specific time, with the specific person at the other end of the screen.

## This ain't no Super Bowl

A real estate agency in Melbourne asked me how to get more viewers on their YouTube channel. They had a channel that listed each house for sale with a nice video showing the property on offer. Each video averaged 70 views. To them it seemed paltry and inconsequential. What were they doing wrong? Nothing. They had it all right. They only needed one buyer. The average house has nowhere near 70 seriously interested parties wanting to inspect it. They were reaching the people they wanted to reach. And they were selling the houses. They were already successfully doing modern-day marketing and they didn't know it. They got blinded by the lights of comparison and big online numbers, so much so that they forgot the objective.

## Fill the channel void

The void of channels is in the process of being filled. In our niche we need to be a channel of choice. One of the most valuable things we can have in business today is a list of subscribers, regardless of the format—email, channel sign-ups, social media followers—because this means our end users and our customers are the same people rather than a third party. A direct connection is among the most powerful things we can have in the ... surprise, surprise ... *connected age.* As e-commerce simplifies and becomes phone- and wearable-computer friendly, connection eventually leads to commerce. If we don't have a direct connection, then every time we try to make contact it will cost our brand money. And it will cost more to reach fewer people.

# The easiest way to get attention

To get more attention, invest more in a product, build something amazing and let the collective sentience take over. If we qualify in the awesomeness stakes, then our audience will do the talking for us. The old model of under-investing in the product we sell so we could afford the distribution and media costs is now being reversed. If the product is amazing, is advertising really needed? Just ask Elon Musk of Tesla Motors. Tesla Motors is a Silicon Valley–based auto startup that makes all-electric vehicles. Tesla has no advertising, no agency and no chief marketing officer and it has no plans to run television advertisements any time soon. For 2012 and 2013 all of its production vehicles were presold. (Compare this to the $25 million in media Nissan spent on their 'leaf' electric vehicle.) The buzz Tesla Motors gets (through its new omnichannel media world) because it's disrupting an entire industry with a better-looking, better-performing, safer and more futuristic vehicle is fuel enough for serious attention.

> In a connected media landscape, amazing products with no advertising beat average products with amazing advertising every time.

In a connected media landscape, amazing products with no advertising beat average products with amazing advertising every time. The truth is that Tesla could probably not have succeeded in a non-proliferated media environment. Forget how amazing the car is; they would never have been able find a market without a significant media investment. As soon as they needed to shift money from the product to eyeballs they would have lost their point of difference and remained swimming in the competitive soup of auto land.

# Curation

Given that it's both free and easy to create content, the proliferation of media simply knows no boundaries, which, ironically, creates the need for ever more channels.

Enter the curator. Once a part-time task of program directors in mass television, curating is emerging to become a powerful force indeed. Curators neither own platforms nor do they create content. They summarise what matters in a content arena. They sift through the garbage to find the gold. Given it's literally impossible to keep up, even on a single niche topic, we need curators more than ever. If there was ever an example of creating value without actually creating anything, then this is it.

Ray William Johnson—whose YouTube series 'Equals Three' (or '= 3') has one of the highest subscriptions on platform earth, with more than 10 million subscribers and almost 3 billion views so far—shows Johnson commenting on the hottest viral videos of the week. This creates value for viewers because if they subscribe to Ray, they know that no hot viral video will sneak past them.

For those with limited resources a smart play in media can be curating the good stuff to share with an audience. We don't have to be able to create cool stuff; we just have to know what it is and share it. It's like being a modern-day magazine editor of sorts.

## We're all media companies

Everyone is a media company today. While not everyone has embraced it, this is true for anyone who's connected to the internet. If we're plugged into the web, we're a valid form of media, plain and simple. If we have the ability to send a message to more than one recipient simultaneously, we're the media, even at a micro level. And it doesn't mean we have to be using the tools of citizen journalism either. People don't have to be creating traditional media output (written words, video content, audio content) to be media. If you send a text message to a group of recipients via a web app, that's media. You're delivering content to a permission-based audience. You have their eyes and ears. You have their attention, and that's the asset that matters, especially when we're living in a world of absolute channel explosion. There is only so much attention being handed out. The connection many of us already have is what large companies want most. We now live in the age of the one-person media company: 'Nonglomerate'.

## We're all nodes

The vertically integrated mega corporate is being replaced by highly distributed horizontal networks of tiny nodes. We are those nodes. In the new media landscape a corporation, by definition, must now start as a single node, nothing but one single point of interest in the vast swathe of the internet. Now that the self-selected node can choose to create and attract attention and traffic, it can grow. Traffic is a form of nutrition. That nutrition enables a single node to grow. It's a form of intellectual nutrition. From this traffic, the node becomes powerful. It adds connections and size. It becomes a virtual way point, a stopover that has something of value. It becomes more than a node, and becomes a point of interest on a macro scale. It can become part of the landscape where we all congregate and create on someone's platform: a new media company. They all start with a single connection. Before any sub channels are created, before any staff members are added, before any venture capital is raised, there was a single node, powered by a single person (or maybe a few entrepreneurs collaborating), who decided to publish something or create a digital stopover. The new media darlings all started this way. Google, Yahoo, Facebook, Twitter and every smartphone app all started when someone decided to post their content or creation online. They started with no traffic or permission from the powers that be. They said, 'Here's my address, and this is what's here'. The audience that followed gave them all their financial nutrition. They didn't need the investment first; that came after the value was created. It's a total reversal of how media companies were created during the television industrial complex. They had to invest significant sums on broadcasting rights and infrastructure. Nowadays the only investment required to give birth to a media company is an intellectual one. It's neural networks and classic biomimicry in action. More on this in chapter 14.

## On the fast track to amazing

Lots of what we see published by the crowd is rough around the edges. It's clearly homemade. While some bloggers make extra efforts with the largely free software available, there's a noticeable difference between the quality. The content from traditional media is for the most part still of better quality in terms of finish. It's the final cut. Mostly we like the human craft with unrounded edges, but in many cases resources still count — for now.

We need to remember how far self-publishing has come to understand where it's going. And where it's going, rapidly, is to a place where no media corporation in the world has access to better resources than you and I. We can already shoot in HD and super-slow motion on most smartphones. We can already publish to the world immediately, as we shoot. We already have access to the same software tools used by Hollywood studios to edit our footage. We all have access to HD cameras that can survive in outer space and 30 000 leagues under the sea — the GoPro — which can do all this and costs a mere $300. The trajectory we're on is to have more amazing tools to develop more amazing content that's even easier to use. Controlling high-quality production assets is no longer a media strategy when everyone owns them. The difference between self-publishing and publishing is moving towards unnoticeable.

# Subscription television is doomed

Business models that are no longer working manage to hang around for a long time. Just because a business model isn't dead, doesn't mean it hasn't got terminal cancer. Subscription television is one such business model. We're in the middle of a disruptive change to television. The cable television business model that emerged from the US in the late 1970s is no longer relevant. While it still exists, its days are numbered. The belief that subscription television providers can demand that people subscribe to a boundary of content in a world of boundless content is foolish. The world is moving quickly from a pay to a play subscription model, to a 'free and on demand' model. Their high in-home penetration rate is irrelevant. Lots of homes used to have encyclopaedias too. The real competition isn't other television options. It's screen time in general. And every screen, including the big one in the family room, is now web enabled. While the penetration rates of web-enabled televisions is only about thirty per cent in most developed economies, the ever-decreasing price of technology, and the relative usefulness of web-enabled screens will ensure rapid uptake just as we saw with the web during the 1990s. By the end of this decade it will be the anomaly to have a television that's not connected. And this excludes possible radical innovation in this space by the tech giants, who have their sights set clearly on the battle for the lounge room.

# On-demand subscription

The great innovation driven by the web is entertainment on demand. Time-based program schedules are quickly becoming obsolete. People no longer live their lives in boxes or maintain predictable 9-to-5 work schedules. The world doesn't work like that anymore. We want content on demand, and we only want to pay for what we use. The problem with the all-you-can-eat media buffet is that we know we're paying for things we don't eat. And in a market of perfect knowledge and myriad options, we'll inevitably find someone who only charges for what we want.

The only way subscription television can survive is if it gives free access to everything in the library — I mean every single show, movie and sports-show channel — for a fixed price. If not, it will simply be more economical to buy on demand. The element that props up many subscription television services is the access they give to live events and sports. But as soon as enough homes have connected televisions, it won't take long for sporting bodies to realise it's more profitable to run their own channels direct using

IPTV and to take all the advertising revenue they generate from 'their' loyal fans. To put it simply, the fans of a particular sport don't care how it gets fed to them or which channel it lives on. In a connected, fragmented media world, all major sporting codes will own and control their own media channels. And, just as for surfing, people will only subscribe to the specific sports they care about. It's cheaper for the end user and more profitable for the brand owner. The future of media is to have fewer intermediaries and more direct relationships using open platforms.

## We don't want your packaged deal

The idea of having to buy packages is archaic. The idea of 'packages' is a supply-centric mantra from a time when the factory called the shots, much like travel agents did. But we now live in a user-decides, mashed-up, co-created, commercial society. The idea that we can't pay for the exact channels we choose (with volume discounts, of course) is not a design for users, just for owners. People don't watch sport. They watch football or boxing or equestrian. People have specific needs, not generic ones. BBC viewers are different from Fox News viewers, so why treat them the same and bundle them up in 'News'. The package deal (on any category it appears in) is already unsustainable, but the purveyors of it are yet to realise this.

## The usability gap

It isn't connected television household penetration, or the actual capability of the technology, that's holding up the proliferation. It's the usability gap. It's still too difficult to extract the benefits that might come from a connected television. The process of getting a world of content up and running simply isn't solved yet. The clue is in what the remote controls look like. We'll know the problem is solved when the only remote control available is a smartphone, something television manufacturers are yet to find the courage to accept. The process of connecting television to available web content is still a clunky process of attaching boxes, downloading software and affixing cables. A plug and play with an intuitive interface is yet to arrive. But once we get the iPhone equivalent launched into the television space, we can expect as much radical change from whatever 'Smart TV' will be called. We can expect an entirely new ecosystem to spring up and serve the über niche. The only thing holding television back from total fragmentation is simplicity of use.

> We'll know the problem is solved when the only remote control available is a smartphone ...

# In-home demos

Once the usability gap is closed, the current adoption trajectory goes out the window. We enter an era of personal in-home demonstrations, where those who've got the new technology become the connected living-room evangelists. They give personal demonstrations of the benefits to their friends and our living rooms change very quickly. It becomes a tipping point.

Any television-related industry that's in love with its old-world system, more than where customers want to go, won't be around for very long.

# Demographics to the people

Business doesn't sell to aggregates, it sells to individuals. It always has. But the mass era helped marketers forget this. Advertising in the future (for those who still have to buy attention) is to start selling again to individuals who've already provided some form of permission to the marketer. The move is away from buying media in demographic chunks to buying the attention of individuals because we sell to individuals. The capabilities of the connected television changes things a great deal in the living room. Think about the sorts of media that will be served up once the following become a reality in every home.

- The television is connected to a web service 1000 times faster than it is today.
- The television knows who is watching it (all the individuals).
- The television is connected to every connected device in the home.
- The television is connected to every smartphone (or whatever other wearable computing devices we use).
- The television knows what we've done, what we care about, what our diary looks like and everything we've purchased online.

What then?

What happens then is that we do business one on one; that is, at a personal level. Smart marketers pre-empt and solve problems for their connected audience and do immediate and direct e-commerce. They don't sell mind-spam 30 seconds at a time hoping it may hit a 'target' and someone may buy what's on offer. It won't be the media industry and the TV-industrial complex that connect producers with potential customers; it will be the emerging data industrial complex. It may even be us, serving something relevant to our specific audience or watching a vlog on how to grow organic vegetables on the other side of the planet.

## Screens and cave walls

All this talk of screens, does make one wonder if we'll end up living in a world similar to that represented in the movie *Minority Report*, a place where every surface is a screen. While this is a distinct technological possibility, we need to remember that screens serve the same purpose as stone tablets and paper. Physical manifestation is not their purpose. The context of omnipresent screens is that they're currently the most convenient option for audio-visual interaction. If head-up displays and other forms of simple projection follow their current path of accelerating returns as mentioned in chapter 7, then screens will be about as permanent an interface as cave walls.

## Advice from a pirate

The laws of nature tell us much about piracy, or lost revenue. If we don't distribute the output, it goes bad. Stored water that isn't sent out evaporates. It's nature's form of piracy. The longer we wait to use any resource, the more we lose. We can add to this the frustration distributors have with non-global release plans, so much so that distributors are now becoming makers. Both Netflix and Amazon are starting to do the job of their suppliers. They're only doing it because they can't get what they need. The end result is a further demarcation with all things digital. In a world of infinite supply, if a company can't get it from a supplier, they'll make it themselves or source it elsewhere. The best approach from media content producers would be to embrace the reality global markets and immediacy. A drip-feed approach only works in a world full of barriers. In our present world there are none.

Anyone wishing to stop piracy of their content has to admit to the world they're doing business. Trying to do things as we did yesterday just won't work. In addition to the fact that they have to create great stuff that people want to see, they also have to make it easy to buy. They have to make it available in all platforms and forget about cutting distribution deals. People who live outside a distribution network's ecosystem will pirate what they can't buy. Everything needs to work on any device; that is, it needs to be technologically agnostic, which isn't difficult and is worth the investment. What's needed is a global perspective because we live in a single market where we all know what's available when.

# The content producers forgot

Most media companies seem to have forgotten the reasons why they did things a certain way prior to the digital era. Most of their decisions were based on what was possible at the time. The limitations on selling their goods were physical realities. The stability of the media system pre-web seems to have distorted their minds to the point where they forgot the 'why'. I'm going to reference the recorded movie business to show how their rigidity is failing them. In fact, the digital world is actually what they always wanted. Piracy is not the problem. The problem is the industry's poor memory.

## Make it easy to buy

In a digital age, the best advice anyone can give is to sell in as many places as possible. This is always the case for any mass-market product. Rewind to the pre-digital movie industry and you'll remember that the movie industry would sell their DVDs in any store that would stock them. After the cinemas, the movies went to the stores. It didn't matter which stores. As long as the DVDs were out there, the movie industry was happy. Sales representatives were judged on the number of distribution points they got their stock into, but for some reason they seem to have forgotten this fact. They now decide to hold back on potential distribution points for no apparent reason.

Why not release a movie in cinemas and the home at the same time? Yes. At the same time. The cinema is not about the movie; it's about going out. I'd happily pay an über premium to be able to watch the latest blockbuster at home on my television because it's too hard to get out with young children. The early iTunes revolt—first with music and now with movies—is the easiest example to cite. It's totally counter to what they did before the format changed. Why the movie industry doesn't embrace this and make it 'easy to buy' is a short-sighted strategy.

## It works on any device

It was much more difficult for the movie industry to have their content available in a variety of formats before digital. They had to invest in manufacturing for film, then Betamax tapes, then VHS, then DVDs and

Blu-ray … but they did it and moved quickly to have their content available in all formats. So why the change of heart now? Why don't they move as quickly as they used to? This is especially strange given that they no longer have to produce anything physical to make their content available on any device. Worse still is when it's already loaded up onto a content platform and usage is restricted depending on the device you're retrieving it from.

## Same-day global release

Content and movie producers can and should have same-day global releases. Simple. Here's the thing the movie industry has forgotten about their pre-digital, staggered global-release programs. Every new market (country) it entered had extra associated costs with it. The industry used to have to make more stock (film, VCR tapes, DVDs) to sell and it had to pay to get its content promoted on television and radio. (These days we're all immediately notified of any big movie launch once it happens.) It had to change the formats to suit particular markets. It had to ship the film on boats for more than four weeks across oceans. It wanted to be sure the movie would be a hit before it invested money into wider market expansion. It had reasons to delay global release plans, reasons largely around stock, promotions, production and mitigating financial risk. None of these reasons exist today.

## Fair price

When people get a raw deal, they find an alternative. They even cheat. They create a pirate's dilemma by fighting rather than embracing the new reality. People know the costs of content distribution are minuscule compared to the pre-digital era. This ought be recognised more than it has been in many digital channels. People will pay a fair price when given the opportunity. iTunes and other digital stores have proven that. And in the words 'fair price', I'd like to add the idea of purchase without friction: simple ways for customers to give companies their money so they can get on with enjoying the content. and not have to jump through a million hoops. In a world of zero-cost digital duplication, fair pricing should mean taking out 100 per cent of the now-removed physical production costs.

Once companies get over the fact that anything that's both digital and good will be pirated by some people, they can get on with business and just know it's a fact of life, a cost of doing business. But they shouldn't let it stop them from implementing strategies that work in a fragmenting world.

## Here's what we can expect

In the future we'll have a channel for everything, for everyone, in every format, on demand and mostly free. It's already here and it's already like that, but most people in the media arena haven't realised it yet. Once we can better devise connectivity and suitability, the legacy media industry won't exist in any recognisable pre-web format. The currently shrinking mass will be gone, save for the rare events when a populous is moved to watch some live event, be it the Super Bowl, the Olympics, an inauguration, the World Cup or some other event of geo-political importance.

# Winners and losers

As audiences fragment into a world of niche and on-demand content, anyone chasing the masses will face an increasingly difficult task, especially if they have to buy attention. The reducing supply of mass audiences will make it more expensive per thousand. More than ever, unpopular, boring products will demand mass audiences, and the price of getting mass-audience attention will be higher. The only strategy, then, for those living on the fringe of boring is to start making something more interesting and start making direct connections now.

If we could collaborate to create output that's as good as or better than that of the media gatekeepers, I wonder what else we could organise peer to peer? Pretty much anything — even finance.

### What is fragmenting

The number of media channels is exploding into über niches. Even people are now media companies.

### What it means for business

Large mass audiences will become more rare and more expensive.

**CHAPTER 12**

Too big to fail?:
the great financial disruption

While everyone knows that certain industries are ripe for change, there are others that may seem too big, too powerful and so omnipotent that they can cruise right through the shift to the technology era. It wouldn't be whimsical to think that the banking and finance industry is one of those because they're so ensconced in all that we do commercially and in life that we can't do without them—or even to think that they're too big to fail. We may even have thought that about the media, the previous purveyors of all that the world knows. The global town criers. The arbiters of timely information. And we already know how that's panning out.

## Their own private Napster

The banks have already had their Napster moment. Although the mechanics of what happened to them were different, it was a sign that their size and greed makes them believe they're infallible. They're clearly wrong. The Global Financial Crisis (GFC) brought many banks to their knees financially. It was a moment that proved they weren't the smartest guys in the room. The behaviour from the finance industry has dramatically eroded it's long-held fiduciary position of trust and stewardship. It tends to specialise in private profits and public losses. A more courageous government outfit would have let the industry fail so that a more appropriate financial species may emerge. After the GFC dust had settled, they went right back to their pre-GFC playbook.

## They lost the most important asset

Ask anyone on the street what they think of banks and how they behave with our money and their two most important requirements of trust and respect are rarely on the list. Add to that the technological possibilities emerging for peer-to-peer finance and we have a looming great finance disruption. No industry is immune to a revolution, not even banks. But in order to understand the how and why they too will be fragmented we need to remind ourselves at the most basic level what they do.

## So what do banks actually do?

The actual function and purpose of a bank is not really that complex. A bank is simply an intermediary that accepts money from one party and lends a portion of that money out to other parties who need it. A bank links together customers who have capital deficits and customers with capital surpluses. They charge the borrowing party a bit more than they give the depositing party. Banks keep the change. Or, in the most human language I can find, banking is a scorecard of who owes whom what, and making sure people pay up when things fall due.

But what if all of a sudden we could keep that score ourselves? What if, all of a sudden, we had other ways of working out how risky a trade was, or is, based on non-traditional means or via the digital trust bank? What if money were no longer an object, but a number that could live on any of our ubiquitous computing devices? What if we could do parts of our banking outside of the traditional structure? What if we could generate more cash for ourselves by dealing direct? What if we could access capital at a much lower cost than through traditional channels or have a reduced cost of capital?

We can, and we are. And there's more of it to come.

# It's virtual and data driven

Like many industries the once 'physical' side of what banks had to produce is less and almost totally irrelevant. The security of a bank is not a function of how secure its vaults are. The vaults are now all virtual, as is the impending business model. In short, banks are in the data and trust business. Now that data has been democratised, it's only rational to assume that new players will emerge and do what banks do. With the tools of banking now being cheap, more peer-to-peer finance will emerge within the business of traditional banking.

As with many industries, the supply chain is being shortened. People are choosing to deal direct. Why? Because we can.

# The leaky bucket

Like much of the change we've already seen in many industries, it won't be about a new player coming in to knock over the incumbents by doing what they do. It will happen, and is happening, in much the same way as what we've seen in retail, media and other industries: fragment by fragment. Small parts of the portfolio will be done by outsiders — newbies to the game who have probably never worked in finance or banking, but people who know they can do a better job than the greedy and the lazy who currently hold the mantle. There's a good chance the new players will be more trusted too, especially when they often come from respected brands and previous startup success, such as Jack Dorsey, who invented Twitter.

The new guys won't be banks. They'll just do a part of what banks do, or did, and do that part better. They'll use distributed computing systems, the connected society, cloud capability and user-centric models. Only this time it won't be communications, or production, or retail; it will be using money systems. Money was always going to be the last industry to be disrupted because we had to trust technology systems in other industries first. It's the part of technology we are most risk averse in.

# Circumventing banks

The data industrial complex enables systems to be hacked. The fundamental tools for banking — the ability to track, store and transfer funds — are now in the hands of the populous. Our desktop and mobile technology and distributed commercial connection system — otherwise known as the internet — provides the means for doing what banks do. The startup culture emanating as a result of the technological revolution then provides the impetus for entrepreneurs to make it happen. And it is happening.

We've already seen a number of core banking arenas be invaded by non-banking newbies. As with most legacy industries, it seems not all of the innovation in banking is coming from the banks themselves, but from startups that envisage a better way to transact using technology. The best examples we've seen so far include internet payment systems, the first one being PayPal. Crowdfunding has recently emerged as an entirely new way of funding a small business. Funding, which has long been the domain of the banks, is falling into the hands of technology startups. Square and other micropayment businesses have emerged, enabling anyone to become a merchant and accept credit-card payments, not because they necessarily solve a technology problem, but because they could see the opportunity in using available technology to make accepting money easier to small business. The banks could have, should have and would have done all of this, further ensconcing their position of power, but instead, they sat on their hands and let others

> As with most legacy industries, it seems not all of the innovation in banking is coming from the banks themselves, but from start-ups that envisage a better way to transact using technology.

build multibillion-dollar businesses by simply not paying attention to the possibilities afforded by cheap technology and omniconnectedness.

While it's true that startups only represent a tiny slither of the finance market and an inconsequential fraction of banking business, the fact that banking is starting to be done by others is what's significant. Just as music and media started, initially in small ways, to be undertaken by others, this has sowed the seed of a changing of the guard. These seemingly small finance innovations are examples of history about to repeat itself in very short turn. Finance is one area where we're very nervous about adopting new methods. It takes the greatest amount of trust of all forms of commerce. But once that trust is built, the new players will have as much chance of widening their offer as any industry, and as it turns out the banks are not doing a lot to serve their audience or repair the lost trust over years of customer neglect, not to mention the faux pas of the GFC.

# What is currency?

Before we look at what digital and crypto currencies are, there's one thing we really need to remember:

*All currency is made up.*

No currency is real. No currency since we graduated from grain receipts has any value in use, nor any intrinsic value. Even gold has limited commercial applications and is more a value parameter because it's a commodity of ostentation and limited supply. Once we remember that a currency is only used because it crossed a trust barrier, can we comprehend new forms of currency arriving that live outside the formal economic structures. Only when we remember that the sole requirement of a currency is to develop trust and have wide acceptance can we get our heads around how new digital currencies may be able to infiltrate the global digital economy.

# Digital and crypto currencies

If we look through the history of currency we notice that it's in a constant state of evolution. Since we progressed beyond the bartering system, new forms of currency have arrived, while others have faded and been replaced. Most often though, we tend to have a number of types and brands of currency in operation at any one time. We've used everything from grain receipts, to shark's teeth, shells, the precious metals, minted coins and convertible notes to government-backed paper currency (or 'fiat currency', as it's known).

> **digital currency:** a form of virtual currency or medium of exchange that's electronically created and stored. Some digital currencies, such as bitcoin, are crypto currencies (Wikipedia)

For a long period indeed, currency provided by governments in power would guarantee the amount of currency in circulation by anchoring it to the gold standard, the idea being that a currency is more trustworthy as it's the representation of a commodity with a known market and intrinsic value. That is, the government would only release an amount of currency based on its holdings of gold. But today there is not a single government using the gold standard. A curious fact about gold is that it's had much the same purchasing power when converted into currency for more than 2000 years. It's been able to buy a handmade robe or a decent suit in perpetuity. The ratio is still on the money, even today, which is something we can't claim for state-backed or fiat currency because none of the fiat currencies in the world are backed by the gold standard any more. A new globally networked commercial economy needs a currency to match. Step forward crypto currencies such as bitcoin, which are the next evolution in how we trade.

## Bitcoin

Bitcoin was the first fully implemented and distributed crypto currency. It works in much the same way as other emerging crypto currencies. Crypto currencies are simply decentralised electronic cash systems. The 'money' is created by using peer-to-peer networking, digital signatures and cryptography to generate a currency. Bitcoins are mined out of a digital network by computers plugged into a system trying to figure out a 64-digit code that unlocks 50 bitcoins at a time. The money, or bitcoins, is generally traded within the system by using specific peer-to-peer software. It's a lot like BitTorrent client software. All transactions are stored on a publicly distributed database so that the record of transaction is with everyone plugged into the system, rather than in a central storage location. It creates a form of decentralised stability and control in transactions, although the currency itself is highly volatile. A key difference with bitcoin is that the owner of each bitcoin stash is anonymous.

## The major advantages of bitcoin

- There's a cap on the amount that will ever be in circulation (21 million) so it can't be devalued by inserting more into the economy.

- There's no centralised control agency that can destabilise the currency through its economic systems.

- It's pan global and not controlled by a government (like gold).

- It's digitally native and suits the future of commerce.

- It can transfer across borders without financial interruptions and fee gouging by existing finance systems.

With economies in wild flux, banks and currencies devaluing, increasing globalisation and peer-to-peer trade, this type of currency is clearly more suited to the architecture of our emerging economy.

# It's just another technology stack

As we saw in chapter 7, all technologies stack. Currency is a form of technology, so the same principle applies to it. Why shouldn't it? Currency has already evolved a number of times based on technological advances, and digital or crypto currencies are the next rational stage in what's possible for currency. It makes sense that innovations in the exchange of goods happen. And while it seems foreign to us at the moment, the reality is that crypto currencies are more suited to the way we transact today. While it's difficult to predict the final and ultimate globally dominant currency, it's easy to see that these forms of currency are here to stay. And just like all other technology stacks it doesn't mean that the layer underneath — in this case fiat currency — will disappear overnight. The entire idea of technology stacking is that we need the previous layer to help prop up the new method; it just becomes less visible. There's a high probability we'll still need our 'home market currency' to convert back to. Just as we've seen in the past we'll have a number of forms of currency that still have value in exchange and widely adopted usage. But it's hard to see crypto currency as anything but a permanent fixture in the digital financial market.

# Why should banks care?

Yes, banks don't own currency, but the reason crypto currencies such as bitcoin are emerging is because of the banks themselves. Their opportunistic fee-taking is a counter move to the lower cost transaction (of all things) world we're moving towards. Taking advantage of the system they feed off enables new systems to emerge. Banks haven't provided simplified systems for modern-day digital trade and the net result is that this will eat into one of their revenue streams, another hardly noticeable leak in the industry bucket. It's a form of system hacking, if you like.

# Unstable yet permanent

Yes, bitcoin and crypto currencies are unstable and risky, but they're in many ways no less stable than other stores of money. While bitcoin fluctuates wildly, its overriding direction is for more users, more traders who accept it and importantly its increasing value on the long-term trajectory. The important fact is that even currency is decentralising itself and mimicking the pattern of most industries into a more distributed world by becoming again something that's not owned or controlled by anyone, but managed by the system and the people within it.

# Crowdfunding

For the uninitiated, crowdfunding is the idea of using the web to provide platforms that enable people to raise money for their projects. The platforms are generally trust-based networks where the owners of the capital decide directly who to give their money to, rather than having a financial institution make those decisions for them deep inside their corporate enclaves. It's interesting because, just like other industries, it's providing a more transparent form of business. It's direct, distributed, user-determined financing. It's more about collective cooperation and trust than it is about return on investment or capital payback ratios.

In hindsight, crowdfunding seems very logical, normal and doable in today's environment. It's the type of finance that seems to operate at a more human level. It's a type of system that promotes creativity, collaboration and the types of project that need to happen because they'll make the world a bit better and more connected. It's the kind of startup space that has us saying, 'Yes, of course. Why didn't I think of that?' If we look at it logically, it's a microcosm of what banks do, and something that we can also do using the two simple ingredients of digital tools and peer connection. It's about marrying up people who need money for projects with people who have money for projects. In a very short space of time a new finance economy has emerged where capital can be raised for every type of project possible, and all of it can now be done outside the traditional banking ecosystem.

## We are the bank

Crowdfunding is a great realisation that *we are the bank*. It's our money being handed out. It always has been and always will be, whether in cash deposits, government tax revenue funding or via our superannuation funds. It's our money they play with. It's just that the displaced, industrialised nature of our lives allowed us to forget this fact.

While there are still many jurisdictions with outdated legal restrictions to crowdfunding, we're already seeing it being employed in every arena in which money-raising is required. It's not just something that exists in the 'money for goods' realm (think Kickstarter, Indiegogo and Pozible); it's also a fixture in the money-for-business world.

Let's take a look at a couple of crowdfunding models.

## Money for goods and services

In this model, the people funding the project are essentially placing an early order for some kind of output (product or service) that's to be delivered at a later date. The format of this yet-to-be-created project becomes the topic of the pitch for funding. In this mode of crowdfunding we see a real leaning towards high technology and high creativity. It seems anything with the words drones, 3D printing and smartwatch gets drowned in money; that is, the things that generally don't exist yet and would not likely get funding via traditional channels. Things that audiences are saying they 'really want' and yet, in a pre-crowdfunding world, the projects simply wouldn't happen. The system itself creates new possibilities. While the people putting their money forward don't get a financial return, in fact the return is negative because they provide the money upfront and do not receive any interest payments. They get a social return. They get to shape the world and the things that will be in it. They get to be part of a deeper story. They get to live and create vicariously. They get to contribute financially and emotionally to something new. They get to support dreams while being part of them.

While this seems like a cute, social, web-centric way of funding, it goes beyond that. Crowdfunding is also entering the more traditional space of money movement. Serious, mainstream business ventures are being funded via new web forums for all types of capital requirements.

## Money for business ventures

In this model, crowdfunding is generally used to raise capital or borrow money, which in real terms demarcates the banks more strongly. It covers the following:

- *equity crowdfunding*: investors gain a stake in the business being funded

- *property crowdfunding*: investors receive an interest in some form of property

- *debt crowdfunding*: investors receive interest payments on their funds until they are returned from the borrowing entity.

There are many other forms of crowd business venture funding, but the existence of these tells us that even our esteemed financial institutions are not immune to the change in business landscape. Many governments are already reviewing the legalities of the capital markets to better suit a digital economy. The *Jumpstart Our Business Startups (JOBS) Act* in the US is a classic case in point. The new players are already a multibillion-dollar industry, yet every time I read the business section of a newspaper with a CEO referring to their in-market performance, they refer to their market-share performance relative to the same banks they've been competing with for decades. Just as the media industry did, they have their industrial mindset blinkers on.

# Redefining decision authority

Funding decisions in all these arenas are not based on credit scores or arbitrary banking systems. They're based on people's personal brands, the ideas themselves and the reputation the project creators carry in the marketplace. People's creative pitch and digital footprint are more important in funding decisions than their weekly income, debt position and curriculum vitae. This shift in some ways replicates our value to potential employees these days. What Google says about us is far more important than what a former employee does. Google, in many ways (because it shares our digital footprint and career-based content), can be regarded as our automatic CV generator. We're valued by what we've created in the market, not what some power-hungry boss had to say about our performance when we worked for conglomerate XYZ.

It's a clear realisation that a lot of the value that banks used to create can now be created peer to peer and that what we may value, or trust, is a totally different proposition from what they would value or trust. It tells us that finance is a means for valuing creation in society rather than a means in itself. It's the part of the fragmentation process where our money gets placed into smaller, specific niche activities that need specific types of funding.

# Unearthed economic value

As the banks got bigger and focused on bigger, more complicated deals, they opened the door to a revised finance industry for nimble, market-focused digital finance disruptors. The disruptors designed a mode of connection that would create new value for people who needed money by approaching cashed-up people who were interested in funding the unusual, the anti-conservative and the creatively risky. And the incumbents let, and are letting, it happen on their watch. As a result, small pieces of the financial framework are being disrupted piece by piece. Big, slow and established are again being eroded via new, trust-based digital networks.

# Don't expect a rush on the banks

Yes, a rush on the banks is unlikely, but banks becoming a financial sideshow, a curiosity, is just as unlikely. It's a sign that what the banks do is not so hard to do. It can be done cheaply, efficiently and without geographic constraint. It's a sign that the security that the banks once provided is no longer real or to be feared. There's no giant vault where money is kept safely anymore. It's a sign that there may be better ways of storing money and better places for allocating our money. The banks have already proven that their decisions about who to lend money to are no better than what people can decide, as a collective, to put money towards. It's not surprising we decided to start self-allocating.

# Do expect marginalisation

Our new digital world reveals unforeseeable alternatives to industry around every corner. While change is predictable, the new winners and the way they win often surprises. Small holes in the finance bucket are being created and it's hard to see the revenue leaks being repaired. The next phase of finance will be for a far less vertically integrated service. More horizontal funding structures will emerge, each taking on parts of what banks offered, in ways we haven't thought of just yet, and using means that technology hasn't quite enabled yet. Banking revenue streams will be eroded by players who are not from the finance realm. New players and network connections will continue to be weaved through our financial system. They may even crowdfund their startup to disrupt those who wouldn't fund them. It's a sign that maybe we want to allocate our excess capital to more creative, altruistic community endeavours, not only to an activity that makes more money itself.

> They may even crowdfund their startup to disrupt those who wouldn't fund them.

We want to create more value than we extract. But more than that, it's a sign that all industries need to redefine who they think their competition is, and that it's unlikely to be who it was yesterday.

It's not only industry that can expect to be disrupted by the web. It's not just people who are getting connected, but also everything else that populates our world.

---

## What is fragmenting

Pieces of the banking business are breaking away and being done peer to peer.

---

## What it means for business

Finance will become more social in nature. It will be distributed and it will match the fluidity of the digital economy.

# CHAPTER 13

## The 3-phase shift:
## a closer look at the web

In hindsight it's always easier to find the connections that made something possible. The causes are often more evident and the shift can be segmented into easily definable parts when we pay attention to what's been happening. The technology revolution has had a clear trajectory. When we view the two phases we've already been through, we'll see that the third phase is quite predictable. Not predictable in terms of who will win in the new market segment, but predictable in terms of where the technology itself will go.

# The phases

We've already lived through two distinct phases of the web from a commercial and a human perspective. The first was the connection of infrastructure and the second was the connection of people. But now, we're entering a third, and most interesting, phase: the web of things. The web of things can be defined as a world where the web becomes so omnipresent that it becomes mostly invisible. It will be a world where everything and everyone is augmented via technology and our connection to both computing power and the network itself. You may be asking why anyone would want this and how it could relate to business, but before we do that, it's worth considering how we got here as this will uncover why the web of things is a natural evolution.

## Phase 1: connecting machines

The first phase of the web was the connection of machines. This takes us all the way back to the 1960s when experiments in data transfer began. Machines and code were being built so that previously separate forms of technology (largely mainframe computers) could talk to each other and develop an interconnected network of networks. Working out ways for machines to literally talk to each other was an arduous and a difficult task of developing protocols that could cross systems and global borders successfully. All of this was being developed well before the personal computer became a common feature on desktops in the 1980s. While the internet was opened for commercial use in 1995, giving birth to the dotcom internet bubble, it wasn't until the late 1990s that we could reliably assume that the majority of computers in use were connected to the web in developed economies.

Connecting the machines was a 40-year process. All the while, the machines were becoming more accessible and distributed among the general populous. The second phase of the web was a far more rapid adoption.

# Phase 2: connecting people

It was the connection of people — the social web — that really impacted global industries faster than anyone could ever have assumed. In the early days of the commercial web, the focus was not on the people transacting, but on the commerce itself; that is, on finding ways of using the technology to skip steps and save time and money while doing business. The focus was on fulfilling an efficient market hypothesis more than it was about shifting the commercial balance of influence. The clues are in the early success stories from the first dotcom bubble. Online businesses such as eBay and Amazon, Priceline and Coupons stand as classic examples. They all focused on the new price, efficiency and direct commerce capabilities of the web. None of them launched with a community mindset, although communities became a part of their make-up.

The power of connected humanity snuck up on us. We were so used to being cogs in the industrial machine that we forget about the human need for connection.

## Are we really all connected?

Once we started to realise there was incredible value in us all being connected to each other's expertise, thoughts and creativity, we couldn't get enough. The void was filled very quickly. And while early web applications such as email and forums could be regarded as social, the truly networked social systems that connected the populous only arrived in the early 2000s. It took only 10 years for most of us to permanently connect to the web. The process we go through to find an old friend is the best proof of how connected we are today. It's telling that a social-media forum or search engine is the first place we go to for this.

## Expanding our human connection

This human connectedness to the web changed how we saw things. The power of anything social and connected on the web is a function of the people on it rather than the infrastructure itself. Now that we have our invariably permanent connection to the web, we want more. We want everything we touch and experience to be augmented, bettered and digitally enhanced. Step forward phase 3: the web of things.

## Phase 3: connecting things

'The web of things' is a world where everyday devices from the mundane to the amazing become connected to the internet. It's a cross-over virtual and physical network. Objects get connected by embedding various forms of technology, sensors or computers into them, enabling them to interdependently access the web or to access it via other available computing devices such as a smartphone. This has been made possible by the dramatic reduction in both size and cost of the sophisticated technology that enables the web. In a very short period of time much of our lives will be part of a giant feedback loop where the world around us is alive and things are self-aware, interacting, tracking and recording changes in the ambient environment and also in our every human movement.

### The tools

The tools that make the web of things possible include microchips, cameras, GPS, bluetooth, wi-fi, sensors, detectors, radio frequency identifiers and myriad other awareness nodes. The constant need for better and cheaper technology for smartphones has provided a classic scenario where the web of things can ride on the coattails of the innovation that already lives in our pockets. The smartphone's success in the market is making the web of things possible because it's the catalyst for disposable technology. Each year, the market demands that smartphones have faster, better, cheaper and more powerful functions, following the industrial model of 'Please give us what we had with the last model, but better and cheaper'. The smartphone is, in fact, the first tool we all possess that's truly connected and 'alive'.

# Evolution at warp speed

The law of accelerating technology returns doesn't just apply to tools, but also to the overriding ecosystems that the tools make possible. Each stage of progression is more accelerated than the previous one. Each phase has a shorter life expectancy than the previous phase. It took us about forty years to build and connect machines. It took us only a little more than 15 years for people to be plugged into the system. The phase of the web of things will be shorter again. When the profit motive and significant personal benefits conspire, the world changes quickly. This shouldn't be very surprising given that everything we've witnessed in the dawn of the technology age has arrived much more quickly than we would have expected. From an historical perspective, technology and its impact on our species is now evolving at warp speed. It's something we see and even feel in our skin. But it, the technology, has its own agenda, so it won't stop. The hardware we need for an effective web of things is not here yet. The technology is full of flaws, and the biggest of these is that it's currently too demanding of us.

## Inventing and stealing time

While the convenience of the smartphone is addictive and amazing, it has some clear negative effects on our being. It pretty much owns us, and we serve it. We probably haven't been as obsessed with gadgets as we are now at any point in history. There's been a dramatic shift over the past decade in the way we interact with technology. Even in the early days of the web, we used to visit our desktop computer when we needed it. Now, it comes with us and interrupts us all day long. On average, we interact with our smartphone 150 times a day.[1] Rewind to the gadget innovation of last century — the good old 1900s — and we see a different story. Gadgets from the industrial era *invented* time.

### How gadgets from the industrial era gave us more time

- *The washing machine:* no need to hand wash. Set and forget. Go and do something else.
- *The refrigerator/freezer:* no need to go to the market and buy fresh produce.
- *Gas and electric heaters:* no need to chop or collect wood. Just flick a switch.
- *Electric iron:* no need to heat the iron up on the fireplace.
- *Clothes dryer:* no need to hang the washing on the line.
- *Dishwasher:* less time needed slaving over the sink.

Now let's take our minds to the gadgets we employ today: iPods, Nintendo DS, smartphones, tablets, laptops, gaming consoles, TiVo and so on. Sure, some are extremely useful, but they tend to take more time

---

[1] www.businessinsider.com.au/how-much-time-do-we-spend-on-smartphones-2013-6

away than they invent. They give a little at first; then they take a lot. It's almost as though they take us into a wormhole of exploration that eats up more than the efficiency they create. Gadgets from the digital era steal time.

This has started to make me wonder about the time we give to our gadgets. Do we own them, or are they starting to own us? I think the challenge of technology today is about understanding how we use these tools. Are we using them to consume or to create? Will we use them to create output, or be constantly giving them all of our input? For me, this is a vital question where time is our most important asset. It's an even bigger question for entrepreneurs. The difference we make is largely a function of what we create. And in order to create something we increasingly need to pay attention to the devices around us and ensure we're in control of them, not the other way around.

# Immature technology

Considering how gadgets control our lives, to a degree, is a reminder of how immature mobile technology currently is. It's a bit like a baby that needs to be cared for, caressed and interacted with all day long so it can survive. It's not very independent yet. We have to remember that the commercial internet is still a teenager. It was 19 years old in 2014, a mere adolescent working out what it wanted in life. It's a child we love and have great hopes for, but at the moment it's a bit annoying and it sucks up a lot of our resources.

# The web of things

Our connected technology needs to split into smaller fragments to provide a more independent function, just as our industrial gadgets did. The fragmented nature of the web of things will enable technology to get on with its job of augmentation without needing our attention. It will be a welcome relief and will make technology more human than it currently is. Maybe our ears will become the killer app (for humans), instead of our hands and eyes, as in the movie *Her*. In this movie the interactions are largely verbal and without many screens. Screens are only present when needed via a head-up display or holographic image. The screens themselves as a form of hardware are no longer. For the web of things to flip to a service rather than a burden it needs to be more like the movie *Her* and less like the movie *Minority Report*. It needs to be the bellwether for screen redundancy. The next stage for the 'thingternet' is for it to become invisible. It has to be more like electricity, water and gas are in our homes, in business and in modern civilised geographies in general. Companies that enable and promote this shift will be the biggest beneficiaries of the third phase of the web. It's early days and the prize is big.

**thingternet:** 'the web of things'; a world where everything in it is connected to the internet

## It's already begun

The web of things isn't something that's coming. It's already here. The number of everyday items augmented by web connectivity is astounding. Even when we look at our own homes, we can see the momentum building: personal technology and gadgets, cars, bicycles, televisions, white goods, light globes, thermostats, athletic shoes, clothing, pillows, beds, door locks, toys and wearables — not to mention our phone (the smart hub).

## Will everything be connected?

We know from technology deflation, which was discussed in chapter 7, how cheap the augmentation of technology has become. Many of the widgets used to create this connectivity are cheaper than the packaging they're sold in. A radio-frequency identification (RFID) chip, for example, is cheaper than the glass bottle Coca-Cola comes in. Other more complex connectivity elements come at the cost of a few dollars. The price of technology is not the issue. If we add to this people's desire for everything to be connected to the web, there's no stopping it from becoming a mainstream communications phenomenon that will dwarf the impact of the social web. After all, a web of things has more direct financial implications and monetisation potential because it's the ultimate in direct marketing. Being in constant contact changes so much.

We do need some perspective here, though, as it's easy to get a bit over-excited and assume that everything anyone could or will buy will be part of the web of things. However, this is one time when some excitement is justified. Let's take the following audit of a home:

- Every water, gas, electricity and plumbing outlet (our shower, toilet and kitchen appliances) will measure and send data.

- Every product in the fridge, cupboard and bathroom medicine cabinet will be connected (mostly through packaging) and be able to provide data. The fridge, cupboard and bathroom will also know what's in them.
- Every piece of furniture, and every entry and exit point to the home will be connected. We'll have live, HD-quality cam feeds in every room on demand.
- Every toy will augment our children's playtime and provide peace of mind to helicopter parents.
- Every piece of sporting equipment will provide valued performance feedback to the weekend warrior (we already do this with our phones).
- The building materials in new houses and gardens, such as hoses and web-screen windows, will provide home hacking data.
- Municipality garbage bins will have detectors in them ensuring the web-enabled packaging of trash goes in the correct bin.

You get the picture. It's the same for retail, the city, the country, the office and the sporting club. It's all going to be connected.

## Then what?

The job of business owners then becomes not about deciding whether it will happen to their industry or product, but about how these 'aware' products can help the end user get more value because of the connection. In much the same way that smart brands quickly dreamed up ways of benefitting a connected audience on social channels, smart industries need to quickly dream up ways of benefitting people through connected things. How can they help them save energy, money and time; provide feedback; give life-hacking suggestions; and cross-reference data with other services? How can they create a mutual benefit for the brand, the end user and the community? That's the emerging job of marketers.

Everything can and will be connected, unless of course the item's brand proposition is that it's 'deliberately not connected'.

## What's first?

The connected home we spoke about above and the quantified self will provide the seeds of belief and value for everyone to embrace the web of things. The connected home and the quantified self can be defined as technology that tracks our human movements, providing data and feedback on what we do physically. Many popular smartphone apps already play in this space. The benefits we see from using gadgets such as fitness-tracking apps for quantifiable feedback are indisputable. Their popularity will provide a Trojan horse for more personal, and in some ways invasive, tracking into our lives.

# The physical mash-up

Connecting things matters because seemingly separate worlds start to collide. Disruptions caused by the technology revolution start to overlap and interact in ways we may not imagine. Connected 'stuff' has an impact on where we live and work, our shopping, retail distribution, media feeds, pricing algorithms, and on product distribution and manufacturing in a non-linear way. A world that knows what's in it, who's using what and where everything is, changes the face of commerce. It creates great layers of overlapping knowledge, and in doing so, changes what becomes important in commerce. Previously irrelevant industries and data points become a new core focus of an industry.

Let's take the connected toilet, which will have myriad sensors with the quality output of a diagnostic laboratory and could analyse all human refuse. It will tell someone they're about to get sick before they show any symptoms and it will have a DNA digital signature of each household member to warn of potentially life-threatening illnesses. A connected toilet could do this without people having to change a single life habit. It would just do it. Who wouldn't want to get an early detection of cancer? All of a sudden toilet manufacturing becomes an important business alliance for the medical industry.

As we saw with the social web, the power comes from the mash-up. Instead of mashing up the virtual to create new output, we'll start to mash up the physical through these connections to create new value and meaning. Consider these:

- The fridge becomes important to packaged goods manufacturers.

- Your wardrobe matters to clothing brands.

- The television (or screen) senses what's in the house and serves up specific and relevant media based on purchase frequencies and the products the house has in it.

Marketing becomes more a task of non-linear mash-ups than it does about vertical supply chain selling and price-based distribution models.

## If-this-then-that living

The benefits of all of this won't be the soul domain of the commercial brands and technology providers. As with anything that hopes to change the nature of how we live, the benefits in the first instance need to be human or the technology won't disseminate. Simplified apps are already emerging that give non-techies super-tech powers. The average person can code without coding and program the world around them without any programming skills.

One of the stand-out services that already does this, is IFTTT — which is an acronym for 'If This Then That' — and it pretty much does exactly what it says. The application enables users to mash up recipes, or condition statements as they are known in the geek world, which automatically makes one thing happen when something else 'triggers' an event. While the service first entered the market by providing a tool for certain social media to interact with, it's now entering the web-of-things space and already interacts with a number of hardware providers. The way services such as IFTTT will be used is by linking various web services and hardware devices so they talk to each other by instructing one connected device to undertake a certain action or output when a predetermined event occurs on that or another device. IFTTT is the start of the new world we program around us, and all we need to be able to do is read. As with social media, the tools were democratised to the simplest human operator level, so previously complex and industrial-level controls will be in the hands of everyone. This has the potential for amazing life hacks; for example, adding seasonal citrus fruit to the shopping list when the toilet data says vitamin C levels are below the optimal level.

> **life hack:** any procedure or action that solves a problem, simplifies a task or reduces frustration in everyday life[2]

## Ambient sharing

What we currently share socially is a small portion of the sharing we'll do when ubiquitous computing arrives. We won't just share what we think and portions of our social lives. We'll share our entire physical graph of movement and consumption. What smart businesses will do, is connect

[2]Collins English Dictionary — Complete & Unabridged 10th Edition 2009
© William Collins Sons & Co. Ltd. 1979, 1986 © HarperCollins Publishers 1998, 2000, 2003, 2005, 2006, 2007, 2009

what they sell and open up or hand over the software-development ecosystem to the crowd to see what they can build. To benefit from a connected world, businesses need to let go of perceived control and hand the brand over to the audience in the same way traditional media should have — but didn't — when social media arrived.

The connected home, the quantified self, two-way loyalty, gamification and real data will usurp demographic profiling and marketing guessing games forever. But getting to that phase requires companies and brands to have trust in the potential or organic commercial ecosystems. They will have to trust that the opportunity can't be totally strategised or foretold and just needs to be embraced. It will be a bit like walking in the fog: we won't be able to see the end of the trail, but as we move forward more of the path will become clear. It will take a non-predictive mindset, one that's curious to unknown possibilities.

As the people shaping the connected world (entrepreneurs and corporations alike), we now have a chance to invent the commercial implications of the inevitable web of things. The social web has now connected us and introduced a new era for startups, so we should take the lead and create physical-goods mash-ups and value equations that couldn't exist in a world without connectivity. And as for the social web, we'll only ever know what people want to track, share and do when the tools are put in their hands.

When people are able to track something, they start keeping score. We can't help but turn things into a game. While it's true that business is already a game, the gaming mechanics of industry are about to enter an entirely new era.

## What is fragmenting

Technology is multiplying. It's living not just on our desk and in our pockets, but in the things we use. We can expect everything in our world to be connected.

## What it means for business

The web of things creates new connection and incentive possibilities. New industries will emerge by linking the data between all manner of things and human behaviour.

**CHAPTER 14**

The big game:
an introduction to gamification

Gamification entered the business parlance a few years ago when some successful web-based businesses, or more accurately, web apps and web-based properties started to rise to prominence. In some ways it actually faded away as a hot digital topic before it took hold the way other arenas and terminology—such as crowdfunding—did. But this doesn't mean the predictions of what it may become were inaccurate. It was more a reflection of the diffusion of innovation rather than of it disappearing. Most disruptive innovations and technologies go through similar trajectories (see figure 14.1).

**Figure 14.1: expectation and utility curve: a personal variation on Gartner's hype cycle***

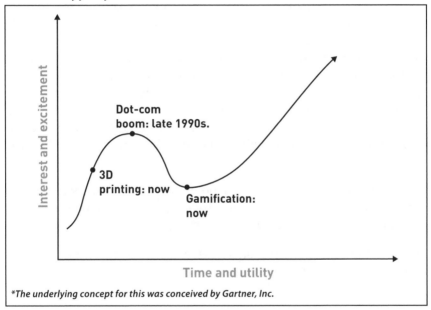

*The underlying concept for this was conceived by Gartner, Inc.*

The truth is we're still hurtling towards a gamified future of commerce. We're all still playing the games right now, but like many aspects of commerce, we go deep into the wormhole before we realise it. Gamification not only becomes possible in a connected and social world, it's inevitable. If I could draw an analogy for gamification, it would be this:

*Pong is to consoles, what Angry Birds is to gamification.*

Gamification is all about intersecting behavioural economics and game design methodology for a commercial outcome. When we think about it deeply, it's not too far removed from commerce in general. What is business other than anthropology with a scoreboard?

Gamification is much more about anthropology than it is about technology, but the two elements of anthropology and technology are starting to conspire to create new commercial platforms that, when used well, have the ability to circumvent currency while also creating purchasing power. It's going to change brand marketing as much as television did, and change the world even more. The potential is far more dramatic because this time it will impact our ability to manage ourselves and our planet better than we could without the gaming mechanics thrown in.

## Child's play

Gamification is inevitable because it's simply human nature. Keeping score is a very human quality. It's another one of those behaviours we have built into our wonderful grey matter that assists in food chain dominance. We love to count things. In many ways our ability and desire to count everything is what differentiates us as a species. Evolving from pure survival necessity we got into the habit of counting, reviewing, perfecting and keeping track of what happened and how things worked, all to obtain tiny bits of mastery. Task by task, counting days, weeks and seasons and distances helped us create intuitive survival algorithms, the rules for survival needed for the acquisition of sustenance.

Not surprisingly, it's one of the first things we learn as a child, second only to language. We invest the first 18 years of our lives in understanding numbers, counting and in the games built around them.

Then there are the modern counting behaviours that cement our gaming mentality. We count such things as:

- our salary
- our bank balance
- the value of our house, our investments, our superannuation and our share portfolio.

And we compete with others to better our score so we can win economically and socially. It's not our fault we're so competitive; it's deeply ingrained into how we 'roll'. It's slightly tragic, but these days we even count friends, followers, fans and subscribers in digital social forums.

Once we begin to count anything, it's impossible not to compete at some level. Natural game mechanics ensue as part of the process. The evolution of civilisations has become a rich tapestry of games. With smartphones and the web-of-things revolution (the third phase of the internet), things get interesting because most everything is quantifiable, and that which is quantifiable can be 'gamed'.

# Digital game grooming

We've been getting groomed into a gaming mentality in the digital world. If we look closely, there's been a deluge of gaming applications that have become part of our daily downtime rituals. The thing that's interesting about downtime is that it often finds its way into 'up time' because once the habit is formed, it knows no boundaries. We've seen many games come and go, but the aggregation of the game play in all of these is training human interaction behaviour. There are two important and different types of game style that exist in the digital realm.

## Digital meets physical games

Games in this realm involve movements made possible by the smartphone itself. They use the gyrometers, accelerometers and other sensors to detect movement. They marry someone's personal movement and physical interaction with digital mobile technology. Mobile app games of this ilk are often built around a single playing event. We may progress in levels, but each game is separate. This genre includes Flight Control, Angry Birds, Fruit Ninja, Cut the Rope, Draw Something and Candy Crush. Playing these types of game is creating personal and physical interaction with technology, training us subtly about its ability to track accurately how we move and helping us gain trust in its ability to quantify movements, even at a micro level.

## Progressive and iterative games

These are the continuous games that we play over longer periods of time. They're the games we come back to and continue to play from where we left off. They're the games that more closely represent our physical reality. They include the social nuances of life, human interactions and replications enhanced in a digital environment. This genre includes Farmville, Cityville, World of Warcraft and Minecraft, games during which we want to use digital tools and a virtual environment to create a better (yet virtual) reality for ourselves.

While these two types of game seem differentiated and separate, they're starting to overlap. The smartphone-based games are teaching us to use them to track physical movements, while the continued web-enabled game play is teaching us to shape environments based on social interaction and iteration. Both focus on forms of important mastery and both track behaviour. However, when they're put together we start to be able to gamify our actual reality. While most games haven't graduated beyond downtime, social and fun use, the human behaviour and technology are both there waiting to do this. All it requires is imaginative technologists, marketers and governments to piece them together.

## More than a niche

Most economic rationalists would argue that we've already seen the rise and fall of Zynga. They'd say the inability of Foursquare to crack the mainstream was telling. They'd claim that digital games just don't garner the loyalty required to become a serious commercial outcome. But what they're missing is the fact that most digital-based gaming hasn't had the important layer of economic incentives added. This is the missing link. Due to that, gamification in the infiltrated commercial sense is in its infancy. But it has given birth to the quantified-self movement.

**quantified self:** the use of technology to track personal activity and provide feedback to improve ourselves and our lives

## Games are for nerds, right?

Sure, we all enjoy a little mobile app–based game for a bit of fun, but isn't hardcore, continuous, long-term gaming behaviour the domain of the ultra nerd? Isn't that something for kids who live in basements and adolescents with headphones and an indoor fluorescent-light suntan?

Well, not really. Gaming is for everyone. Even adults who don't realise how seemingly ridiculous the games are that they play and follow.

## Friday night lights

During the Australian winter 80000 people turn up at the MCG (a large stadium in Melbourne) at least twice on weekends to watch Australian Rules Football matches. The people who come to watch this are from every level of education, age, sex, race and religion, all cheering and watching one of the most ridiculous games on earth. For anyone who's unfamiliar with the game, let me break it down for you.

It happens on a big circle of grass with 100 000 seats around it. The seats are there so the people can see what's happening on the grass. It even has really big lights installed so that people can watch events on this patch of grass at night. Unleashed onto the field are 36 grown men making up two teams, running around in shorts and coloured jumpers in the middle of winter. The objective of this game is to try to kick, with your feet, a football (dead animal skin filled with air) between four big, white sticks to score one point or six points, depending on where the football lands. The team that does this the most times over 120 minutes wins the game. We do this for 24 weeks of the year, and we do it every year. The only reason we watch this, is because we're not young or good enough to play ourselves. We'd sure like to; we're just not able to. Fortunately the web is a little more open to all.

Every country has its version of this behaviour. Every country sells the media rights for its league(s) for billions and has entire industries built around serving such childlike adult behaviour.

## Yes, but it's different

What people usually tell me at this point is that it's not a fair example of gaming and gaming behaviour. The average retort is that it's not the same as growing virtual vegetables and trading pigs on a social network because it's a real game with real history.

Well, not really. It's emotional. We have a non-real, emotional investment in the game. If my team, Collingwood, happens to win the Grand Final (which incidentally they have done in recent years), what do I actually gain from it personally? Absolutely nothing except for the warm feeling it gives me inside **Emotions can't differentiate between virtual and real.** my chest (and a little bit of boasting rights against my fellow football fans), which is what most digital and social games do. Emotions can't differentiate between virtual and real.

Foursquare, the retail geocheck in apps, operates on a similar human emotion. Foursquare lets me earn badges based on where I go and what I do. I compete on a ladder against friends and collect points. I'm not sure why I do that, but for some reason it's fun to track my movement. It's not very different from a travel diary. If I go to a certain place more often than anyone else who's playing I become mayor of that place and I get a nice little virtual mayor badge in my app. It can send out a tweet or post it to Facebook. The badges are cool little pictures that replicate the ones you see on the game screen. If I go to enough airports in a single month I can earn the 'Jetsetter' badge. Who cares? I do. I want to be mayor of the 'cool places' I go to. I want to be a jetsetter and gain subtle social status within my peer group. The badge isn't real. I can't wear it on my chest because it's only made of ones and zeros on a computer screen, but it's certainly real to me. A virtual badge or online recognition is not very different from being loyal to a football team's colours. All emotions are real regardless of the tools used to create the feelings. Emotions are real, just as local sporting codes are usually multibillion-dollar industries. Emotions created by virtual activity are as real as their physical counterparts.

## Emotions + incentive = shaped behaviour

In order for gaming to enter everyday commerce in a meaningful way, we need to combine the social and the financial. It needs to be about the web's ability to keep score. And score in this sense is any type of activity, movement or collaboration; not score in the scoreboard sense. Smart scoring in commercial gamification needs to become about the use of a whole bunch of tracking possibilities, such as:

- geo-locating people
- mapping intimate human movement
- finding what's near us (things, places and products)
- tracking the frequency of certain activities
- identifying the time of day, the month and the year.

In fact, it's more than that. It's about anything and everything that can be counted, measured, tracked, shared and cross-referenced.

## People won't share that stuff

And what we've seen already is that people share more than we ever thought they would. Social media is proof that sharing is a fundamental human behaviour. It's actually our default setting in civilised society. Yes, it comes with risks (many in the privacy realm) but our DNA already knows that the benefits of sharing (so far) have outweighed the risks.

We are a risk reward-based society and the evidence suggests the benefits of sharing information most often outweigh the downside. So we embrace it.

The type of sharing that deep, commercial, integrated gaming requires is far more significant. It requires us to share the most intimate and personal of activities and data. It requires us to accept push alerts. It requires us to share where we are all the time. It requires us to share what we buy, not by stealth through store cards, but openly with the companies that own the brands. It requires us to share where we will be, to have open diaries. It requires us to share medical data. It requires us to share what's happening in our home and the devices inside it. It requires us to share information about everywhere we go, everything we buy and everything we use and touch. And who we do it with. And we *will* do it. We will collect, compare and compete. Much of it we're already sharing, such as our exercising habits via smartphone apps. We'll do it because the benefits of the incentives, both financial and social, will be too good to refuse. Those who refuse will miss out.

# Bursting into reality

Digital games used to be all about fantasy. They were using futuristic technology when they arrived, and it seemed like a natural proposition for these games to be set in futuristic and fantasy settings. There were joy sticks such as those in space sci-fi films and rocket ships, and space scenes such as Galaga where we had to shoot down aliens and save the earth. We used to play these games to escape our reality for a little while, just as we do when we watch a movie. And even television was about an alternative fantasy life of sorts.

Today games are augmenting reality in all types of interesting ways. Gaming will do what general technology did. It will no longer be 'that industry over there', albeit big and profitable — not for us. Rather, gaming will become part of the day-to-day marketing program and be part of the general culture for all ages. It just won't be called a game. Just as our now revered technology nerds made their technology more accessible, gaming mechanics will be brought into our lives in simple, almost invisible ways. When they are, they'll infiltrate every industry and be part of the daily operations in much the same way that technology stopped being a separate thing in business and started being a natural layer of business infrastructure.

# Rising realism

The reality movement has entered all forms of life. It's done this because during the halcyon days of the TV-industrial complex everything was so fake — sitcoms, fake tan, processed cheese. We became out of touch with simple things such as food and how it got to our tables. Our world became one big hypermarket where everything was for sale, shelf stable, processed, bought in bulk and shiny. There were no rough edges.

The transition to this movement actually started in the mid 1990s, ironically, about the same time as the net started to hit our homes. During the hangover for the decade of excess, we started to seek out alternatives. Things started to convert into more 'authentic', non-mainstream versions. While it was partially a function of wealth — we could afford the unique — it was also a protest. Music was the first big industry to be hit with an alternative to the manufactured version we'd heard for 50 years. The grunge movement was about being real, about being stripped back. For sure some of the authentic arrivals have been totally cringeworthy — 'Big Brother', 'Jersey Shore' and 'Real Housewives' — but a lot of good has come of them too; for example, organic groceries, and decent coffee in nearly every café you walk into. Just 15 years ago coffee in a large majority of cafés was a pot of black muck and it was processed and instant: 'just add hot water'. And all of these consumer goods are not just goods, but consumption experiences.

# Doing > having

We have a deep hunger to be 'real' in most things we do these days. I mean we're sharing our total lives online and anything that isn't real doesn't make us look very cool. It's much cooler to tweet photos of the organic Ethiopian cuisine we're just about to have for lunch from some newly emerging inner-city suburb eatery than a flash restaurant because it's 'real'.

Today, the having is in the doing, not the owning. Having and owning is fake; doing and experiencing is real.

We've seen one of the top-10 trends globally on the web as collaborative consumption (discussed in chapter 8) because it connects us and makes things real. We're no longer outsourcing our joy to buying things, but gaining joy from experiencing events. For gaming to get to a permanent and commercial level it needs to do the same thing; that is, be about the events and activities we partake in. But more importantly it must interweave seamlessly into our lives and be part of what we do, just as the games of working, earning money, investing money and modern commerce are a natural part of modern civilisation. The major change of interweaving the technology into our world is well underway.

## The gaming mentality

My car is a hybrid Toyota Prius. It and most other ecofriendly cars give feedback on how our driving behaviour is saving energy. Through an energy usage screen it provides a feedback cycle of the energy being saved. This encourages the desired behaviour of driving more conservatively. I win through fuel savings and the car brand wins through brand value affirmation.

We even plays games about games. The entire fantasy league movement is now creating a personal participation reality around what was previously just an observer's fantasy: the fantasy of being Vince Lombardi.

The gaming mentality is now creeping into retail. Group buying is an early example of what's possible. While some of the preliminary models of the retail group buying model have imploded, we can view them in the same way we view early social media sites: a necessary, though failed, step in the development process. But newly 'gamed' retail plays from retailers, shoppers and external startups will continue to arrive and create new, more efficient ways to go to market.

Crowdfunding is in many ways a game that circumvents retail by offering a pre-sales channel. Yet it also starts to simultaneously game the traditional finance market. It games parts of the systems; it empowers the players on both sides of the transaction by delivering creative choice and participation.

## The sixth sense

The sixth sense has arrived, and it's our smartphone. I've already commented in chapter 7 about how human and important this life tool is to everyone who owns one. But there's more. As its name suggests, it's also very smart.

The smartphone knows a lot of stuff — really, really smart stuff that I could never have deciphered on my own:

- It knows where I am down to the centimetre.
- It knows which direction it's facing.
- It knows how high it is from the ground.

- It knows how fast it's moving.
- It can see and has eyes in the back of its head.
- It has a photographic memory: it can record everything and store infinite data (when plugged into the cloud).
- It can hear, understand and speak back.
- It can recognise my voice.
- It can communicate directly with other people.
- It can communicate directly with other technological devices.
- It can exchange money.
- It can recognise my fingerprint.
- It is touch sensitive.
- It knows everything the internet knows, or rather, what everyone else knows.

And what it doesn't know and can't do today, it will know and be able to do tomorrow. It's almost human and it has become a permanent extension of our bodies.

Whether my phone is the ultimate device that does all these jobs, or some other forms of personal mobile computing or other wearables are, our personal computing devices will continue to get smarter, smaller and more capable. They won't merely be an addendum. The simplest example I can provide to describe how much they matter to us and augment our existence, is how horrible it feels when we forget them at home or the office. It's an almost sickening feeling. We inevitably turn around to get them, even if it means doing an entire return trip. But that would never happen, because we'd feel the need to interact with them way before we arrived at our destination.

## Our decentralised nervous system

We're getting very close to having a decentralised technological nervous system. A form of biomimicry is emerging where we develop a second nervous system via external environmental sensors.

**biomimicry:** imitation of the models, systems and elements of nature for the purpose of solving complex human problems (Wikipedia)

A sensor is something that converts a real-world property such as the temperature into data that can be interpreted to give us a normal *human* measurement of it. Due to the ever-decreasing cost of sensing technology, we're creating a global nervous system that we can all tap into to create total environmental awareness at a level of accuracy people could never quite manage. It's another form of collective sentience in addition to what we now do with social media. However, this is the physical version. In essence it will become our globally displaced technological assistance system. And it's already being installed by innovative yet fragmented industries and startups. The 'smart home' will be where it first gains wide acceptance.

# Start making sense

The types of sensor we can expect to use include microprocessors, RFIDs, accelerometers, altimeters, gauges, and audio and visual scanners of every type. If you can think of it and measure it, then a sensor can do it. Sensors can measure and record temperature, light, pressure, moisture, water level, movement, proximity, density, patterns, faces, brands and everyday things in the environment. These sensors will be able to perceive the external what, how and who of our world with incredible accuracy.

Sensors, CPUs and screens will be thin, tiny and powerful. Many will be so small they're invisible. They'll come at a cost that's inconsequential — many are already at that level — so they'll be everywhere. They'll be able to detect everything we do and interact with. So all of a sudden we can use these tools for game play.

# Product = computer

Once technology is so low cost that it's disposable, it's only natural for it to appear in disposable everyday products that, when they get thrown in the bin, the technology inside them goes in the trash too. Milk, cans of cola, toothpaste, toothbrushes, pens, disposable coffee cups, bread … in other words, everything in our fridge, food pantry, bathroom and house will be 'smart'. Smart computing on everyday devices will be as common as barcodes are now because barcodes will be replaced by these devices. But they will be more common, because these sensors will appear in products and places the barcode never infiltrated. At this point we'll live in a world where the computer and the everyday product merge. It's even foreseeable to have disposable screens on the backs of cereal packets. Packaged goods will equal computers.

# Mash-up heaven

So now that we have all of these technological and anthropological elements in place, what happens next? Gamified, mash-up heaven is what happens. And it will be awesome. We move from a buy/sell–win/lose environment to a 'co-opt and collaborate for mutual benefit' one. So what could a day in the life of our gaming future look like?

Our gamified life could look like this:

- *In the bathroom.* I wake up and I brush my teeth. My new Oral-B toothbrush has a sensor in it — remember that products *are* computers now so I make sure that I brush my teeth for the required two minutes as recommended by Oral-B. But why would I do that? Because my dental plan gives me a 20 per cent discount, which is $300 a year if I do this in virtual currency. This is awesome for me because I get money and good oral hygiene. And my dental plan provider is happy because I'm a good customer due to my reduced medical risk. Oral-B are happy because I use my toothbrush more often and need a new one sooner. The sensor only works for three months (which is the recommended life of a manual toothbrush) so they get increased purchase frequency.

- *Travelling to work.* I catch the train to work. Even though I have a perfectly fine car and a free car space at my office, I do this because the incentive makes it worth the effort. The government of the day has a combined incentive for increased usage of public transport to reduce traffic congestion and to assist in the meeting of their carbon treaty targets. I check in while travelling using my registered smartphone app or RFID-enabled government issue transport card so that I'm tracked and get my tax credits.

- *Local food retail.* For my mid-morning coffee I walk past three cafés to get my java fix. The one a little further down the street offers a free coffee for every fifth check-in with my smartphone using a geo-locating app. They know I've checked in because my smartphone talks to their register (without me doing anything) when I'm less than 5 metres from it. Since I'm getting coffee anyway, why not get rewarded for my loyalty?

- *Health and fitness.* It's lunch time and I want to make sure I go for a run with my new geo-tracker-installed running shoes. I do this because I only get a new pair for free twice a year from my health insurance provider if I jog for 10 minutes at least three times a week. My health-insurance provider loves me for this because the biggest killer of middle-aged men such as me is cardiovascular disease. Every time I exercise, I'm reducing my risk to them. They've worked out an algorithm that calculates the reduced insurance payout per customer on calories burned and kilometres moved and the dollar cost of that reduction. I get free shoes (paid for by my health insurer), the sports shoe manufacturer sells more product and the insurance provider reduces its risk. Win, win, win.

- *Traffic congestion.* I finish work for the day at 6.30 pm. But instead of leaving I wait until 7 pm, giving me time to surf the net, have a coffee and a chat with someone, or go shopping. It's great because my Government Public Infrastructure App gives me an incentive in virtual currency credits that can be used to buy fuel. They have heat-mapping data that spreads traffic on our strained roads so that no-one has to sit in traffic jams anymore. They decided to do this when they realised that data-based traffic spreading and geotechnology usage would be 10 times cheaper than building new lanes on highways and extra bridges and tunnels in the city. Everyone opts in to play this game. There's massive social pressure to pay attention to our road app program because no-one wants to sit in traffic jams and not abide by the 'congestion reduction program'. We all win here too.

- *Education.* I arrive home and ask my 12-year-old son if he practised guitar. And I remember that he once convinced me to buy him the new sensor-enabled Fender Stratocaster, the one with proficiency sensor tags on the fret board, only because I knew we could link it to his Sydney College of the Arts scholarship fund. And so he perfected 'Purple Haze' by Jimmy Hendrix tonight for the first time and was awarded a significant amount of scholarship credits because the Arts school is chasing the most talented artists. So as a family we play that game to be the winner of the 'long-term scholarship game'.

- *Grocery shopping.* I decide to do my grocery shopping. I shop from my couch rather than at the store and I don't buy what's on special anymore because everything's on special. I buy based on all the games I'm registered with so that I can be a financially, ecologically smart shopper. It's all such a mind-blowing overloading requirement that instead of trying to remember what to buy, I register all of my relevant programs onto my new 'Super Market App', which automatically generates a shopping list containing all the things I need. All of a sudden I have direct relationships with brands and Procter & Gamble gives me a cross-category incentive so that I don't only buy their Oral-B toothbrush but all of their personal-care brands. Similar to Frequent Flyer points, this lets me stay in the XYZ Grocery Alliance, keeping me loyal to the brands inside it as well as the retailer selling it all.

- *Charity.* That night I'm at home and I hear a knock at the door. It's the Salvation Army doing their doorknock for the Red Shield Appeal (assumes that Salvation Army will still be doorknocking in the future). I remember their advertising campaign about the most generous suburb in Australia. 'Ah … ' I hear you say, 'but the rich suburbs will donate more … ' But they know this and make it a game any suburb can win. So they make it based on the 'number of people' who donate as a percentage of population by postcode. The Salvation Army have developed a live and ever-changing heat map you see on the screen that's super awesome because the government gives the biggest virtual dollar tax incentives to the most generous suburbs, taking the strain off the social welfare payment system, so we encourage our neighbours to donate too. Another multi-winner game play.

- *Home.* I decide to go bed and don't turn off the lights … in fact I don't turn anything off in the house. My in-home, Google Nest system senses which room I'm in (the master bedroom), detects I'm in the bed at what it knows to be bed time from its learning algorithm and organises the energy for the house. In turns off all the electric devices, and resets the thermostat to keep the home at the right temperature through the night. It sets the washing machine to start at 3 am for off-peak benefits and starts charging my electric car then too, if it needs charging. It checks my diary and notices I have an unusually early breakfast meeting and starts all the devices I'll need in the morning at 5.30 am instead of the usual 7 am.

- *Career.* Once I'm in bed and I've finished reading the latest e-book, that I downloaded, I get my self-education bonus from the government because the eye scanner on my e-reader knows I actually read the book and it's related to my tax-registered employment status. And I get 'special virtual currency', which can only be spent at Amazon and other education-related retailers … and further self-education programs incentivised by the government.

## The seed is planted

The seeds of gamified economics are deeply ingrained in our behaviour. Smaller versions of the big game have been around for many years . Gaming rule 101 states that incentives are greater than privacy. The reason we all signed up to Frequent Flyer programs and credit-card reward programs wasn't because they're a simple category for gaming mechanics; it was because they had a method of tracking things. Now that's possible for everything: every product, every home and everyone.

## Not if, but when and who

Maybe all this gaming is just what we need to make the world a little more efficient, safe and environmentally friendly... and even more fun. One thing's for sure: all of this technology is coming. The pieces of the technology needed and the human behaviour are already here. All we need to do is dream up the mechanics for our industry, brand or company and get moving. Let the games begin!

While true gaming is designed to benefit all players, sometimes businesses don't 'get it' and they give us a raw deal. When this happens, we just hack their system for them.

> ### What is fragmenting
> Gaming mechanics have left the console and are entering wider society.

> ### What it means for business
> If you can find a way to create incentives for score keeping, then currency can be circumvented or even created.

**CHAPTER 15**

System hacking: a great idea
with a bad reputation

The idea of hacking into something immediately conjures up images of crime and illegal activity. It takes us back to 1980's science-fiction films where young kids hack into government computer systems and gain unauthorised access to nuclear silos that might start World War III. Maybe your mind jumps to someone doing a rather crappy job at something they're meant to be a professional at: 'They're a real hack'. Whenever we hear the term 'hacking' being used to describe a person or an activity, our defences spring into action because we've been groomed for so long into thinking that hacking is a bad thing. What we should really be focused on is the hack itself and determining in isolation whether the hack is in fact a good one that takes us, collectively, a few steps forward.

## Hacking defined

While the word 'hacking' could be used to define a number of behaviours, I'm hoping this definition will open your mind to the good side of hacking from the outset.

### hacking

using unconventional or even inelegant methods to gain access to or get around a system to gain a more satisfactory outcome for the hackers.

Based on this definition it's fair to say that hacking can be used for good, especially if what we're hacking is an open system accessible to all and it's been designed without the end user in mind. Given that we're living in an environment that's being redesigned for and by the end user, it's time we understood that we're in the era of hacker culture.

## Hacker culture

Just as we had industrial culture, we're now entering a phase of digital hacker culture. The tools we live with, around and inside of, such as the smartphone, computers, digital networks, the internet knowledge bank — the *internet operating system,* if you will — all open us up to a world of hacking systems, a world in which we can embark upon redesigning how things are done to suit ourselves. The tools that everyone has access to are the same ones being used to hack old, outdated industrial systems. They create new possibilities where if the industry itself does not reconfigure to suit the new world, it will be done for them.

Because our world is digital, both commercially and socially, it gives us new powers to play with the system itself. Because the way we access things now doesn't involve doors and walls and buildings as much as it used to — and I mean in the real physical sense here — we can hack into the system itself. We can use the digital tools and the way we connect to the system to re-route ourselves around it and to build a new method that gives us a better outcome, regardless of whether or not it gives those in power a better outcome. We can take a look at the system and find another way virtually to get the same result physically. And we dig it.

## Hacking is inevitable

As we transition to digital platforms for most industries, every industry is either being hacked by startups entering the space, or by end users who are sick of getting a raw deal. In the days before transparent markets, industries had a far greater chance of being pricemakers. They could get away with having significant differences in prices by market or location depending on what was more profitable to them. They could decide when they wanted to launch in other markets based on what suited their budgets and marketing plans. They could even decide not to ship to a market at all if they didn't want to and there was very little the end customer could do about it. We suffered from this dramatically in Australia, as it has always been regarded as a small pond often not worth investing in.

Now, unless every market is served immediately, with the same price, with the same range and the same service, the system will be hacked. The audience armed with connection knowledge and access will hack the system to equalise the market offer. And no industry is under more hacker pressure than retail.

## Retail hacking

No industry has been hacked more often than retail. People are constantly going around the traditional retail channels to get a better deal. A number of simple system hacks have been invented by savvy entrepreneurs and eager customers who just want to get a better deal in retail. For example:

- *group buying* gave customers access to crazy prices just by pooling buyers into one time and one place
- *delivery houses* sprang up to purchase goods on behalf of buyers in overseas markets whose home markets either didn't sell the brand, or sold it at a higher price because of a lack of competition
- *coupon sites* emerged for online buyers with aggregated discount codes in one convenient online location to get better prices than could be achieved buying direct
- *comparison sites* arrived to point people in the right direction for pricing in both online and bricks-and-mortar retail, ensuring the best prices.

Bricks-and-mortar retail had the unfortunate situation of having to deal with being hacked virtually and physically at the same time. Retailers have even had to deal with potential customers coming into stores to try on clothes and test items they had no intention of buying anywhere but online, giving new meaning to window shopping. When opportunities exist to hack the system for a better deal, no matter how clumsy, opportunists will take them.

## Industry hacking

An industry is a system that has been designed by the players of that industry. If there's weakness in the system, the system will be hacked. The design, by definition, has to be for the maximisation of profits. It's always been about benefiting the players within it. All systems change over time. Their structure is modified and the architecture renewed. We're currently going through a radical redesign of the industry system. It's during these times that getting hacked has its highest probability. And we can add to that fact that others from outside the industry are most likely to be the ones doing the hacking.

An old rule in marketing has been to never launch a new product or service that will cannibalise existing revenue unless the new product has a higher margin. It's one of those marketing maxims that's no longer true. Most high-volume products are becoming more dispersed with lower margins. Not innovating because margins may be eroded simply opens up the doors for a new player who'll accept those lower margins. It opens the doors to the system hacker who will accept a smaller margin because they're doing it on a skinny and/or virtual infrastructure.

# My favourite media hack

The television industry is being hacked because of its reluctance to accept the new market realities. A key rule that it would do well to remember is that everything virtual is borderless because people will invent hacks to get around the so-called safeguards or restrictions put in place by the industry. Living in Australia means we don't get automatic access television content from the US and other overseas markets. Generally, sites such as Hulu, Netflix, and the BBC are blocked, which in all probability they do to facilitate more margin through licensing deals with each separate market. But the organisations trying to block people online because they're not in the desired geography simply doesn't work. It only takes the use of a geo-blocker to gain access. These are services that hide the physical location of where you're retrieving data from, or make believe that you're geographically located in a specific market. There are a number of these services available as web browser extensions. And as soon as one is closed down, in usual web fashion, another one pops straight up to fill the gap.

It's also a clear indication that no matter how much companies and brands try to slice up the global market into countries, we're increasingly in a truly global space. The hacks get shared. People who uncover the hacks gain social credibility by sharing the hacks with their friends, on the social networks and on blogs. Once the hack is out of the bag, it never goes back in. Once it's out there, it's out there and it's just a Google search away, which then often provides the juice needed for speedy entrepreneurs to formalise the opportunity with some new startup serving the niche in question, as with the geo-blocker business. Given that stopping system hacks occurring in an industry is nigh on impossible a better approach is to embrace the hack.

# Why we have to self-hack

In a hack-or-be-hacked world, the best plan is to face the reality and self-hack. The best example of self-hacking in the marketplace is what's occurring in our most esteemed learning institutions, our universities. Anyone can learn anything online these days. We can learn in any field of study through a variety of sources: written articles, blogs, live streamed lectures, industry journals. We can even tap into the global thought leaders of any subject. Most thought leaders in every field have a solid digital footprint these days and they're willing to share with their followers their ideas on a daily basis. A better time has never existed for learning, as anyone can tap into the best minds from around the world in any area of study. You'd think this would have the universities shaking in their boots for fear of an impending battle of relevance. Instead, they've embraced the inevitable and started hacking their own system.

# Step forward MOOCs

The Massive Open Online Course (MOOC) has recently emerged as one of the most interesting industry reinventions. A MOOC is an online course for which there are no participation restrictions and which has full open access via the web. They are courses of study, which, for all intents and purposes, are the same as the courses of study undertaken by the students enrolled in the university. They have one distinctive difference, however: they're usually free.

It's not just fringe dwellers in the education space who have embraced this reality. There's barely an Ivy League University in the US that hasn't become involved in the MOOC revolution. Harvard, Stanford, Princeton — almost every university is now involved, and there's no sign of this innovation ever going away. Enrolment rates are staggering. The first MOOC to be released by Stanford was 'An Introduction to Artificial Intelligence', launched by global thought leaders Sebastian Thrun and Peter Norvig. More than 160 000 people enrolled in this course alone. It's almost hard to believe that anyone on the internet can enrol in a course taught by the world's most respected educators from the most respected institutions and not have the thousands in fees that normally accompany such learning.

# Yes, but they're not-for-profits

It is easy to think that this example doesn't really apply because universities are non-profit organisations and that this isn't really a fair comparison to a commercial situation. That viewpoint would be unfounded. The truth is that while profits are not distributed to shareholders, universities have real costs that have to be offset by real revenues. So it's a true commercial risk and a forward-thinking move by universities. But what the founders and adopters of the MOOC seem to have understood about our new business landscape is that it's going to happen anyway. So why not fill the void ourselves and be those who can receive the new revenue streams once the system reconfigures and the profit opportunities present themselves. It's a great piece of self-hacking, if I must say so myself.

If we can hack the purchasing process and even industries, why not hack where and how we work and build a system that suits us, not just the people we work for?

## What is fragmenting

Hacker culture is not just for the tech geeks. Easy-to-use tools of connection create a hacker mentality. We're all hackers now.

## What it means for business

If a business system can be hacked, it will be hacked. It's best we hack ourselves first.

## CHAPTER 16

The job, the factory and the home: how location follows technology

Where we work has always been a key factor in determining where we live. During the earliest days of human existence we followed the herd and the seasons because we hadn't mastered agriculture. Agricultural societies made possible the growth of towns and cities, and the complex societies we call civilisations. So, too, the factory made possible the modern city of the industrial era. We have up until very recently had to live where we worked. Even when industries became globalised, we still travelled to the locations where we did business. Other than limited forms of communication, there was little choice.

Where we work has always defined where we go and, more importantly, where we live. But what happens when the output of the work, and the person doing it, can be separated and they no longer have to be in the same place? What happens when we don't have to be near the factors of production in order to organise them? What happens is we see people making personal choices about their preferred place of work and abode. The choice is no longer an economic imperative. It's no longer a choice designed by the owners of capital because we all own the capital now. It is distributed and accessible to all and that changes the physical landscape. It changes the distribution patterns of people themselves. In this sense, location follows technology. Human locations are a function of technology of the day and technological mobility.

## From the city, to the suburbs, to *wherever*

Most of the industrial-era technology was big, expensive and fixed in single locations. This meant these facilities had to be built in central locations and it also meant we had to move to these locations if we wanted to participate in the high-paid jobs they offered. This was true for both manufacturing and the emerging administrative support systems of the office. We had to go to the place of technology to undertake our work. The set-up costs were high enough that we had to aggregate around them to benefit from them, so we moved to the city en masse. We also had to live relatively close to our place of work in the city because our transport options were so limited at the time. Most of the inner-city suburbs in major industrialised nations are a clear reminder of how we lived. These houses have no driveway and they're most often homes with a very small frontage and limited living space. It's almost as if the house knew its primary purpose was to house workers, hence the name 'worker's cottage'. The fact that most of us walked or rode bicycles to work was a function of the technology available too. There wasn't much of a choice for anyone who wanted to be part of the economic benefits industrial companies provided. Get close to where it was all happening, or miss out. While there was more living space on the farm and the outlying areas of the wider city, it was too difficult to live there and get to and from work. Where we lived was defined by what we had access to.

## Along came Henry

When Henry Ford made the automobile affordable, he also invented the idea of the suburbs. All of a sudden we no longer had to live in the city to get to work. We could drive on the motorway and live in a house with much more space, a backyard, neighbours, parkland, mega malls, new schools and fresh air for growing families. Access to private transport quickly changed where we chose to live. For large parts of the late twentieth-century, inner-city suburbs — the former enclaves of the industrial worker — became run down and often slum like. Who would want to live in a tiny timber house smack bang in the middle of industry and wedged between freshly laid highways? The suburban choice, with its improved living standards, was a simple one to make. It was only when travelling in and out of the city became a horrible, traffic-induced nightmare and many of the pollution-inducing factories went offshore that the inner city had its own mini renaissance. Over the past 20 years, inner-city suburbs where I live in Melbourne have gone from being half the price of the outer suburbs to twice their price. And the reason this has happened is because technology (private transport) failed us, creating a new proximity necessity.

That said, we're about to enter a phase where living in the city becomes a choice rather than a necessity because technology enables us to choose where we live and to design our places of work and abodes around our personal requirements, not those of an industry. And the industries will go along with it simply because it will be more profitable for them to.

## The end of offices

The office itself is a weird thing that surfaced when factories did. Sure, lawyers and accountants had them, but not in the sheer quantity or corporate format in which they exist in today. The office was an addendum to where stuff got built. But as factories have been shrinking and moving offshore to lower cost labour markets, offices have been growing in size, number and inhabitants. It was to be expected as most developed markets moved from a manufacturing-based output to a knowledge-based output, a trajectory we continue on to this day.

The office was a little bit like the factory, where the parts that made it function — the office machinery if you like — was also expensive. The tools for organising business weren't cheap. It made sense to centralise things. But today cost efficiency can't be the reason to centralise office services. So why do they still exist? It can't be the cost of the tools because every piece of technology that used to make setting up an office expensive is now already in most people's homes. Xerox machines and teleconferencing facilities are not needed anymore. The much-touted telecommuting dream is finally possible, and, although it's been a slow process, it will arrive.

## What can happen, will happen

There's no disputing that every task that can be performed in an office can now also be performed away from an office. The simple things we do while sitting at a desk in front of a screen can be done anywhere that's connected. In many ways, this is even true for work that needs personal interaction; that is, the times when we need to be in the same room as the people we work with for some particular reason. This too can be done in a virtual sense, and while it's not the same as a physical interaction, for the purposes of the functionality of meetings, it can all be done virtually. So the real question on the future of the office isn't one of possibility or functionality; it's more about unveiling the true desires of the people working in offices and the people providing them. The nuances on what they want will determine whether offices will exist in the future, but indications are that there will be a dramatic shrinking of office culture and the spaces allocated to offices.

## The office staff

Offices can be workplaces that engender social encounters and where interpersonal relationships are built, and they can also be pretty uninspiring environments for getting work done. Yes, some amazing workplaces exist, but the reality is that only a tiny portion of people get to work in a fantastical environment that more closely resembles Disneyland than offices as we know them. They're the exception, and it's fair to assume they will remain so because it's only during times of abnormal economic profits that such investments are made. If we walk through history, there's a clear pattern of the most profitable industries and companies providing the sexiest work environments, and they will remain the anomaly.

Working in an everyday organisation means we have to live close enough to commute daily, most likely in peak-hour traffic. In addition, the office itself is quite expensive to run.

We have to travel to the office, which eats up valuable time. Even 45 minutes' travel each way to and from work each week day amounts to seven and a half hours a week in downtime, which is the best part of a full working day gone, evaporated, wasted in transit. This travel doesn't just take up time, it also costs staff members real money. A significant investment needs to be made in private and public transportation to get to the workplace. These are real, non–tax deductible costs that only occur because of where the office is, and our need to get to it, and for no other reason at all. It may also be that we have to invest more in housing because all the offices are aggregated in the same city locations. With everyone working in the city in relatively high-paid, white-collar jobs, the demand for housing is impacted, bidding up prices. Ironically, nowhere has been more affected than San Francisco, the home of the inventors of the technology that make remote working possible. These are all pure market inefficiencies based on the realities of yesteryear technology that can be removed by reconfiguring the office as we know it.

## History repeats

If the technology of the day has decided where we work in the past, I can't see why it won't do that in the future. The staff want it and it will represent significant cost savings for them and the business. Where we work will change again; the time just hasn't come yet. When it does, workplaces will be a fragmented combination of shrunken offices, homes, mobile locations and meeting spaces. Work will happen wherever the person doing the work decides it should, not in some arbitrary location.

## Work options

Which of these two work options would you prefer? Would you rather:

- *option 1:* turn up to an office five days a week to do your work, because, well, that's where someone decided the work should be done? You invest valuable hours and money commuting to the office every week. You make sure you turn up for the official office hours, which haven't changed in hundreds of years. Before you leave home, you get dressed in appropriate office attire, which is likely not what you'd wear if you had a choice. You buy or rent a house near where someone has chosen to locate the office, which is supposed to suit all staff, but actually suits no-one. Sound familiar? It's a bit like those TV-industrial-era mass products they used to push

or would you rather:

- *option 2:* work mostly from where you decide to work? It could be a co-working space, your home office, a company office … anywhere you can plug into the network. You live where you actually want to live, near that nice beach or lake or mountain with the fresh air and nice restaurants, or maybe in the city if that's your thing. You no longer waste any time commuting to an office to work. You don't spend any time getting road rage from fighting peak-hour traffic. Instead you come into a smaller, central office on the days you need to meet with colleagues, which is probably one day per week. When you do need to go into the office you drive in non-peak hours, making the journey more pleasant and taking a fraction of the time. You can wear what you want because as you know your clothes don't make you any more or less capable. And you can also work the hours that make sense for you and your family because you work for a company that cares more about output than office face time.

Smart people will choose option 2. Actually, you don't even have to be that smart; you just have to be human.

## Offices, control and profits

People will say option 2 won't work for a company. It would be too loose, too unstructured, non-hierarchical, without authority or control, and that too much power would be in the hands of the people. Here's a simple fact: companies like profit more than they like control.

While it would be quite an adjustment for companies, deep inside every company's DNA is a desire to reduce costs in every facet of the business. The office itself is no different from the factory, the advertising budget or staff numbers. If costs can be removed, they will be. Companies that are already large organisations have the most to gain from such a shift. The companies with the largest administrations are often from mature industries where it's much harder to find top-line revenue growth. In these situations, it's operating costs that are targeted. Reducing the office size is a solution that's available and profitable and it could even be a cost-effective way of attracting the right staff even at a reduced cost per head as it represents real savings for the employees in question. It's hard to see this not happening. Both employee history and desire itself point to reinvented, highly distributed office structures.

The time and cost benefits of staff being together every day, on demand, for when issues arise is a bit of a misnomer. For every emerging meeting or information exchange, there are usually other unnecessary meetings about the meeting, known as alignment meetings. These usually occur in place of someone actually making a decision. Or even worse, these are the meetings that turn out to be a public reading event, a time when the meeting organiser gets stakeholders in a room to go through a project or update everyone. This is often where something is presented on slides, copies of which really could be distributed to everyone to read instead of wasting everyone's time in a meeting environment. Anyone who has ever worked in an office knows that the relative benefits of immediate access to the team are clearly offset by pointless interactions and office folly.

**We'll enter an era of the cloud employee — distributed and on-call human capital — and it will be better for everyone.**

Just as the information we call on has moved from filing cabinets to in-house computer servers to the cloud, so will staff members. We'll enter an era of the cloud employee — distributed and on-call human capital — and it will be better for everyone.

# A better ~~office~~ offer

The office of the future will be much smaller, a more collaborative, creative space for interactions, not a battery farm of corporate cubicle dwellers laying digital eggs. It will be the kind of place where people actually want to hang out to connect and share ideas with others. And they will do this when *they* choose to be there. The companies that embrace the idea of a diffused workforce will need less physical space because their staff will only come in on occasion, when they genuinely need to interact in person. And because the space will be smaller, it can become a more creative space that generates value because it inspires, rather than being a human warehouse where employees have to sit under electric lights with air-conditioning. It will be a new space that's about connection and inspiration, not only about doing work. That will be done elsewhere, in a place that suits the person doing the work, not the person paying for it.

# Idea diffusion

It's true that people come to offices not just for the work, but for the social interactions and direction others can provide. But social interactions at the office are a symptom, not a reason. Wherever people gather, socialisation and idea diffusion takes place. Once we spend less time working in offices, the social needs and idea-exchange voids will be filled in new places such as shared creative spaces and co-working hubs. It's not really the interactions with other staff members that matter so much, but the interactions in general with people who don't need to necessarily be part of the same organisation. In a mash-up kind of workplace, external interactions are potentially more valuable. In a world of digital demarcation, employees who are around people with different world views, from different industries and with different domain knowledge are what companies need more of. Enforcement of existing cultural ideas from the one company blueprint can never be as valuable. Idea cross-fertilisation and diffusion is far more likely to happen when we're in new and varied environments and this is exactly what companies need in times of revolution. The burgeoning co-working space is already evidence of how this can work.

# The office is not immune

Just like everything else that's occurring around us, a democratised structure that removes power from the few and gives choice to the many is also likely to become the norm in offices. Like the other factors of production, offices and corporate working structures are not immune to the changes. The same forces are at play. A move from integrated vertical structures to distributed, choice-based, human-led infrastructure will be, and is, occurring. We went from the farm and villages to the city, then to suburbs, and next will be regional satellite centres. It's foreseeable that the next phase of where we live will consist of regional centres of great beauty that are near major cities. We'll have all the benefits of city living, without having to live in cities. This replicates the benefits of mobile technology. Our lives will be more mobile, although it won't be one-size-fits-all, and we won't leave the city for the non-city. We'll be able to make the niche-living choice that suits us, not the corporations we work for.

# The last industrial relic

I think the office is the last industrial relic. It needs to be radically changed. Even the name 'office' is wrong. It sounds official and full of rules. But if offices really added that much value, why do so many leading-edge startups not have them? Why are so many white-collar jobs being offshored to low-cost labour markets? It's because entrepreneurs and smart businesses know offices are expensive to run, they're outdated and better options exist for information workers, especially as we enter the age of projecteers, as I've already discussed in chapter 2.

While this is a simplification of the flow of jobs over time, there's no disputing that the type and structure of work we do is in a constant state of flux. Soon employers will realise they don't actually need employees. Smart companies will realise what they actually need is for tasks to be completed, projects managed and leadership provided. In a connected world they won't need to pay for people to perform these duties five days a week, on a salary, because they can access the skills on demand

**In a connected world, roles for employees will fragment into pieces and projects.**

with limited friction and wastage. This is especially true when you consider that a large amount of time that employees are paid for is unproductive downtime that's spent as being part of the organisation, rather than towards outputting for the organisation. What we need to remember is that companies pay people based on the value they deliver, not by the hours they're present. If an employee costs $x for five days' work, but it really only takes three days for them to do that work, companies should be happy to pay the equivalent of four days of the employee's time to a projecteer in view of the reduced overheads connected to outsourcing. On average, an employee costs twice their salary to carry. In a connected world, roles for employees will fragment into pieces and projects. There's no real reason why human capital can't be an on-demand resource, as are many of the other factors of production we now access instead of owning. And it's already happened with many purely digital tasks. Outsourcing labour markets such as eLance, oDesk and Freelancer are more than an opportunistic digital niche. They're proof that the employee model is changing in line with the wider economic shifts and that with the reduced friction of access labour, new models are arriving that are more fluid and independent. The biggest customers of these 'liquid labour markets' are among the world's biggest companies. The efficiency low-friction labour markets create opens up an opportunity for further independence of worlds, which is more profitable for those who need things done and those doing it.

The type of work to evolve will be that of projecteers. These people — who aren't really staff members, and don't really run companies either — are digitally facilitated freelancers with skills that are in demand from the new economic landscape, such as UX Consulting, app developers, big data scientists, community managers, cloud services specialists, online course teachers and 3D printing designers, as well as jobs that don't exist yet. They're niche roles for an increasingly fragmented world.

The greatest fallacy in modern politics is the idea of saving jobs. There aren't many people who hunt bison for a living in this day and age and saving jobs is a simple misallocation of taxpayers' dollars. A far more effective approach is to recognise and facilitate the shift in creating new jobs. Structural unemployment is a perpetual and ever-moving beast, and it occurs at a more rapid pace when the fundamental structure of society changes. The breadth of tasks people will do for a living in the coming years will astound, and it's a massive opportunity to re-humanise the work we do and the way we do it.

Not only will projecteers gain a deeper satisfaction for the work they do than an employee would, they will also gain a greater revenue clip for the time they have given. Meanwhile companies will save on the cost of having the work done. In addition to this, neither party will be mentally chained to the other, resulting in a more creative work and life ecosystem.

Even the most complex of projects can be undertaken virtually — projects that employ all the tools of the new digital world, even when the participants are living worlds apart.

## What is fragmenting

Technology has always defined where we live, and now people will redistribute where they live more widely because technology enables and demands it. Living in cities will become a choice, not a necessity.

## What it means for business

We need to redefine how and where the work gets done, how products get to people and where operations are based. A non-clustered, distributed mentality is needed.

**CHAPTER 17**

A stranger from Romania:
building a real Lego car

Sometimes it isn't until after you've gone through an experience that you realise what you've just lived through, what it means and what it becomes an example of. I had an experience where I met a stranger from Romania. This is my personal example of the great fragmentation.

It started with the kind of request you get every day, a request for money from a stranger in a developing economy. He assured me he would put it to good use and that I would benefit from helping him. I gave him the money. He kept his word. It wasn't really what anyone expected — including me. But yes, there's more to it than that.

# A new low for the internet

The first request from Raul Oaida to connect wasn't one you get every day. His request-to-connect message on Skype said, 'Hi, I'm building a spaceship'. He had me right then. It's not every day you get a request to connect online with such an old-school kicking copy line that has such cut through. So I clicked on 'accept'. Who wouldn't? I thought maybe he'd been reading my thought-leading blog posts, or seen some of my startups or published articles. But the sad truth was that he was far more savvy than that. He wanted to connect with famed technologist, venture capitalist and trained astronaut Esther Dyson.

Through some diligent online investigating, Raul discovered I had a tenuous connection to Esther. We were connected via LinkedIn and Twitter as we'd met at the WPP Stream Conference (the world's biggest media-holding company's digital event). She was a board member of WPP and I was in a senior position at one of their advertising agencies. Raul wanted to use me to get to her. Mind you, he did in the end get to meet Esther in person. But I have to say it was a new low for the internet: astronaut-stalking via social media! He wanted Esther to invest in a rocket project he had concocted called Project October Sky. His plan was to build a suborbital rocket for about ten thousand dollars using some new techniques, just because he thought he could.

He finally connected with Esther (he found her email via other means) and she answered his email, but decided not to invest. He didn't give up. In fact, he told me he had sent the same Skype request to more than 100 other investors and technology pundits before I accepted.

# Digital tenacity

I quickly learned that Raul doesn't give up easily. After others declined to invest, Raul started asking me to back his project. I told him I was small fry in the world of venture capital and technology, but he just wouldn't go away. Every day, the moment I logged in online I'd hear that little sound Skype makes when you receive a message — 'whooooop' — mere seconds after I was connected. It was as though he was waiting for me or had some kind of alert already set up. Mind you, this would be around midnight in Romania. So we started chatting on Skype every other day. I quickly learned that he'd already done some projects that proved his technical capabilities, if not tenacity. He'd already built a small jet engine in his backyard, a steam engine from a bicycle pump, and he'd learned to fly a plane. He could get stuff done. He was starting to turn me into a believer, not because of what he said, but because of what he'd already done. He showed me the proof via the live video chat over Skype and his YouTube videos. A few short years ago, none of these tools existed so he would have had no way of proving himself. He also sent me his PDF plan of Project October Sky.

# Marketing rocket science

I concluded I couldn't really justify investing $10 000 into the project, but advised Raul I'd be happy to do something smaller together such as a minimum viable product if it could benefit both of us. He came up with the idea of sending a helium balloon into the near space field. He told me we could get more than 30 000 metres into the sky and film the curvature of the earth for under $1000. He went on to tell me that he wanted to do it for scientific and experimentation reasons, and that I could take on the marketing. In simple terms, if I'd fund it, he'd give me the filming rights and the decision on what to send up into space and film. I was surprised we could undertake the project so cheaply considering almost half of the cost went into purchasing a GoPro camera.

So I added a bit of marketing rocket science to the project plan. It's the oldest trick in the playbook and is known as borrowed interest: attaching the activity to something with pre-existing fan bases. I decided we should send a Lego space shuttle replica into the near space field to pay homage to the end of the space-shuttle era, albeit in toy form (see figure 17.1). This would ensure that we'd get every space-shuttle fan and Lego fan to view our project.

**Figure 17.1: anyone can get into space**

*Source: © Raul Oaida*

It's not even ironic that a teenage kid from Romania and a marketing guy from Melbourne could put an object into space, more than 30000 metres high, film it and retrieve it on earth for a little over two weeks' average Australian wages. Our final cost was a little under $2000. About ten years ago this would have cost more than $100000 to undertake. A high-definition camera that could withstand the knocks and temperature variations would have been totally out of reach. The GPS device we used cost a mere $39. We even bought the helium balloon on eBay from the US and had it shipped to Romania — an impossible task in a pre-web world. It's little wonder the real innovations in the revised space race are coming from private operators as their relative costs are also in rapid freefall.

The project gave us global attention. The video spread virally on YouTube and it also earned mainstream media coverage. Millions of views online has become a bit of a calling card in much the same way as Ivy League school MBAs did in the past. I'm of the opinion that one view of a technical or business project is worth 10 views of a funny cat, mainly because it leads to something. It's a trajectory rather than a distraction.

## The Super Awesome Micro Project

In order to leverage the momentum, we thought we'd do something to take it to the next level. We came up with the idea of building a full-size car out of Lego. It would drive and have an engine made out of Lego that ran on air. While this sounds kind of crazy, we knew we could do it before we even started. It was a classic marketing hack because all of the parts that made up this project already existed. It was just that no-one had put the parts together in this way before. People had built full-size stationary or ornamental cars entirely from Lego. People had built little engines out of standard Lego pieces from the technic range, and pneumatic engines had been built before. We'd even seen a very small one made from Lego online. The art was in re-organising these pieces to create new meaning. Yes, it would take money, time, skill and planning, but it was there for the taking.

We costed up the project and came up with a budget of $20 000 to do it and an estimated lead time of three months, both of which turned out to be a fair bit off the mark. But I truly believe that if people didn't have the innate ability to underestimate the cost and time of projects we'd still be living in caves. We should be thankful human nature is so naïve when it comes to project estimations or we'd never undertake them. I wasn't sure I wanted to invest that amount of money into building a giant toy car for an adult, so I decided to use my personal network to crowdfund it. Given the investment was a techie-hacker style project with no clear return on investment or product, it was even too radical for crowdfunding websites. So I went to Twitter (see figure 17.2). With a single tweet I raised $20 000 from 40 local patrons, all non-millionaire, everyday people participating in the technology revolution.

**Figure 17.2: the pitch tweet**

**Steve Sammartino** 🐦
@sammartino
Anyone interested in investing $500–$1000 in a project which is awesome & a world first tweet me. Need about 20 participants... #startup
12:07am - 1 Mar 12

I also released a faux prospectus to send through to them that was designed for advanced people just like them. It didn't even tell people what the project was. Half of the people who invested did so without any more information than what they got from the pitch tweet.

The fact that I funded this project so easily is an indication of what reputation from previous projects and personal brand can do, even at a micro level. Speaking of micro, I called it the Super Awesome Micro Project, a counter-intuitively long brand name that everyone liked and remembered. In a world where everything is becoming smaller and sound-bite oriented, it felt like the juxtaposition of a ridiculously long project name would serve the purpose of providing a mnemonic device — a little bit like 'supercalifragilisticexpialidocious'. The name made people curious enough to call me to find out more. It was here that the pitch came into its own. When they asked me why they should invest in our air-powered Lego car for no return on investment, this is what I gave them:

*During the height of the GFC the three heads of the largest car companies based in Detroit boarded private jets to fly down to Washington to beg congress for money. They did this because they didn't know what the future looked like. And here we are crowdfunding an ecofriendly car made from toy pieces, built by a teenager in Romania. Boom! That's what the future looks like. So join me and let's be a lesson to an industry.*

Sure there's a fair amount of hype in this one. But every person who heard it put up some money to get involved.

Raul then invested the best part of the next 18 months bootstrapping the promised outcome of a drivable Lego car. There were no technical blueprints, no technical assistance from qualified engineers and no help from anyone. He did it himself near on 18 hours a day. Everything he knows about technology he taught himself from what he could read on the internet or watch via online videos and that great self-educating device known as YouTube. He learned on the job, a clear reminder that fragmented informal education is becoming a powerhouse for generating high-calibre people. It takes education to the next level of democratisation, beyond what public schooling did. Not only does anyone with web access have the potential to learn anything from the world's greatest minds, we can now choose our own syllabus.

> He learned on the job, a clear reminder that fragmented informal education is becoming a powerhouse for generating high-calibre people.

Once Raul had completed building the life-size car we shipped him and it to Australia to meet its makers, the patrons who supported him and made it possible. Getting a visa for Raul to enter Australia was no easy task. Romania is regarded as a high-risk country for illegal immigrants. Our first couple of applications were rejected by immigration because of his unique status of not being a student and not technically being in paid employment. It wasn't until we applied for special consideration that we were able to get a work visa. This serves as yet another example that the formality of the industrial governmental structures does not serve well a world of pan-global startup projects and border hopping.

By this time the budget was clearly blown. I'd invested more than 100 times my original expected personal allocation of funds, granted that the outcome was grander than our initial vision. It ended up being a 3-metre-long Hot Rod capable of 20 kilometres per hour with a 100 per cent standard Lego piece pneumatic engine. And yes, we had to rebuild a significant portion of it in Australia. Let's just say the car has some naturally occurring crumple zones.

We eventually got the car working and did a test drive to create some footage of the beast in action. We launched the Super Awesome Micro Project to the world with a short web video on YouTube. Just search for 'Life size Lego car that runs on air' to watch it. In order to maintain some symmetry to the project commencement, I launched the car to the world with a single tweet in reply to the original crowdfunding tweet. It was the only promoting I did to get the video underway. The other 40 patrons then retweeted my tweet and we uploaded the YouTube video to a homepage with some background information. That's it. For a brief moment it became a global phenomenon, achieving millions of views in a very short period and featuring in all forms of news around the globe.

The marketing high ground isn't just about what you've built; it's also about the way you built it. It's the angles of interest it creates. That's what drives attention in a world that's deluged with data. The Super Awesome Micro Project had many angles to it. They included:

- *A connected world.* Pan-global projects are only possible in a post-internet world.

- *Globalisation.* A digital world enables people to circumvent nation states with broadband cables. It eliminates physical boundaries.

- *Technology.* Projects that are heavy in the use of technology get more air time now. Just review the business and the technology sections of *Forbes*, *The Wall Street Journal* and *The New York Times*. The overlap of stories in these two previously separate sections of interest tells the story.

- *Social media.* It used the new media tools of connection. The story came from the people first and then graduated into the mainstream media second. The mainstream media now feeds heavily from the micro media.

- *Building with a toy.* The fact that the project was constructed with a 'kidult' toy inspires deeper age-agnostic engagement.

- *The age gap.* A teenager and an adult teaming up on a hacker project is an example of the evaporating accuracy of demographic profiling.

- *Teenage genius.* If we throw the word genius and the word kid into one sentence, it always equals free media.

- *Crowdfunding.* A rapidly growing space that gets more than its share of attention. The industry itself looks for examples to prove how it's responsible for changing the landscape.

- *The car industry.* When an industry is struggling, any form of innovation (regardless of its usefulness) is used for comparison stories. The Super Awesome Micro Project was covered in car media channels the world over.

- *Environmentally friendly.* Examples of different forms of energy production and usage, especially pertaining to transport, even if the technology is very old (in our case pneumatic engines), provide a platform for reporting and debate.

- *The maker movement.* As the web graduates from virtual to physical, the maker movement and manufacturing 2.0 seek out people using lean methodology to make things and undertake projects with physical output.

- *New web tools.* Whenever I talk about this project to the media, I remind them that all of the tools we used to connect upon and to manage the project with did not exist 10 years ago. It surprises many people.

- *Developed world meets developing world.* It was highly unlikely that I would have met Raul. When I was his age our countries lived at opposite ends of the Cold War. The fact that it's the uptake of collaborations among individuals to close the income gap with developing nations tells us much about the power shift from the few to the many. I knew it would get all the attention in the world so long as we could get the car built and operational in the way we intended.

If you've got a project launch right (in terms of a media hack or something with a launch mentality) it should only take a few hours to determine whether or not it's going to work. Videos that are getting shared a lot and starting to go viral on YouTube often have a view count that stops at 300 or a bit above that number. To quote Google, the owner of YouTube:

*Sometimes you might see that the video view count isn't showing all the views you expect. Video views are algorithmically validated to be fair to both content creators and advertisers and to maintain a positive user experience. This process assures that the video views are quality views ...*

A viewcount that's frozen at 300 is one of the great success indicators of a project being launched through YouTube. It means it's being viewed so often, and shared so frequently, that YouTube has to check that nothing dodgy is happening. This is something every launch should hope for. It means the project has probably gained the attention it desired.

## The hourglass strategy

When considering all the launch elements that went into the Super Awesome Micro Project, it made me realise that the shape of launches needs to look different. The funnel has long been the visual marketing reference of how to launch a product. First, the funnel was referenced for wide-birth marketing and communications campaigns of multimedia output, all pointing at a single thing. It was then spoken about in terms of being flipped and letting brand evangelists do the talking for you. But both of these launching methods feel too limited to me. Good launches now look like an hourglass in shape: I call it the hourglass launch strategy (see figure 17.3).

**Figure 17.3: the hourglass launch strategy**

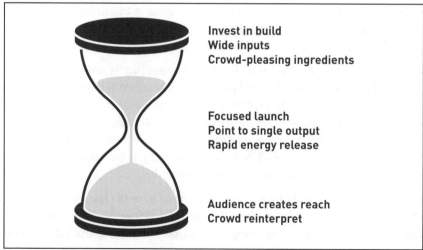

Invest in build
Wide inputs
Crowd-pleasing ingredients

Focused launch
Point to single output
Rapid energy release

Audience creates reach
Crowd reinterpret

In simple terms, we need a lot of inputs that are notable: things worth talking about, points of interest. We invest our capital in producing these at the expense of launch and promotion costs. This is the top half of the hourglass. This is the stuff that really matters in a world of excess supply and a connected populous.

Then we launch the product itself. We take it to the market as it is, in its pure, natural state. The energy is focused on a single point of interest or distribution.

And from here the market decides how worthy the product is of its attention, time, spreading, interpreting, mashing-up or even that other financial implication of actually purchasing the product.

If what we've taken to the market is deserving, its exposure widens. The market takes it to the places where it deserves to be from a communication and awareness perspective, but very often from a distribution and collaboration perspective as well. The attention it earns opens up commercial opportunities as the connected world seeks out methods to leverage the output. People arrive on our digital doorstep wishing to distribute it, sell it, license it, adapt it and build it. The number of amazing outputs post-launch are the metaphorical equivalent of the number of amazing inputs we put into it pre-launch, which is something a heavy promotion campaign will never deliver. This is even evidenced by what happens to amazing advertisements without an amazing product to match. The advertisement is what gets built upon. The advertisement gets the parodies and mash-ups, not the product itself.

If the hourglass strategy doesn't work, the world probably doesn't need or want what you've given it. Before we decide on any launch, it's worth remembering we live in a world where what we create is most often above the layer of necessity. And as with the 300 YouTube views, when we get it right, we often know within an hour as well. This is a classic lesson for marketers trying to promote something. If they focused more energy on creating something amazing, and less on trying to tell an amazing story about an average product, they'd find they get more attention. They'd save an enormous number of marketing promotion dollars.

A real flip has occurred in the post-industrial marketing landscape. Most times large organisations put their investment in the wrong place. They invest large portions into trying to tell an inspiring story about an average product or service. Instead, they should be investing more in making what they're selling and letting the digital conversation take it to the world. What's strange is that if we have an amazing advertisement that people love, the advertisement becomes the thing of interest, not the product it's meant to serve. Maybe people find the advertisement entertaining and inspiring, and want to share it with everyone they're connected to. They want to ask people if they've seen it and talked about it. In this instance, the advertisement becomes the actual product because it achieves the attention that the product should have received. But that's not the point because it's the product that the advertiser is trying to sell. I like to refer to this as the Super Bowl mentality. When people say, 'that's a great advertisement' I have a couple of questions for them:

- What brand was it for?

- Are you going to buy it?

Unless we have a name and a yes, the advertisement is less than great. It may well be entertaining and worth remarking on, but advertising is not cinema, regardless of how many creative directors may try to extract budgets to make it so. Its primary purpose is to inform and change behaviour or, heaven help us, actually sell something. If it doesn't do that, then it hasn't done its job.

# The human motive

Neither Raul nor I give a hoot about cars or Lego. They're both tools for proving a point. A lot of people ask me what the commercial outcome of the project was meant to be. The answer is that there wasn't meant to be one. The desired outcome of the project was the project itself; that is, the fact that we wanted to do it and we did it. While we knew it could have commercial benefits, they were symptoms, not reasons. Now that we want for nothing in developed countries, now that we have everything we need physically, it's the emotional output that matters most to people. It's passion projects that keep us up late working with a smile on our faces. They actually always mattered the most. It's just that we're starting to remember that and our economic circumstances now enable it. It's this idea that creates gifts to humanity in the technology age. It's why resources such as Wikipedia, Linux or even the blogosphere exist. It's about people who have undertaken projects to create value for others, often to the point where they set up platforms that others can make fortunes from. The gift Sir Tim Berners-Lee gave the world with the world wide web itself has been the platform for some of the quickest and biggest fortunes ever created on planet earth. It's the real human needs of connection, collaboration and community that drive us; the need to feel valued, appreciated and wanted. And while many people mistake financial achievement as a means of filling that void, the smart money is on embarking on projects that aim for human fulfilment.

# An open-ended strategy

There's also a deeper strategic reason for embarking on projects with unknowable commercial benefits. It's only when we explore without agenda and embrace randomness that serendipity can occur. When a person or business has the presence of mind to not believe it knows everything, only then can discovery occur. It's high time business became more humble. In times when the future is moving so fast, often on unexpected trajectories, business would do well to resist the temptation to forecast everything and to allocate capital to pure exploration. I find it strange that we only tend to see this in the technology and natural resources sector, when the potential upside of discovery is just as dramatic in any field. It's human to explore. It's why we live on every corner of the earth. It's during these explorations that new lands with untold wealth and never-before-seen natural resources were found. It's obvious that exploration creates a more bountiful ecosystem than the profit imperative ever could. Yet, we tend to ignore it in most established businesses because it takes courage that most executives do not have, and that corporate cultures do not allow. If we focus on profit, then what we see is selling more of what we already have, and reducing the cost of what we already make and leveraging resources we already control. While these are all totally valid concepts, they rarely lead to new fields of endeavour and the profit of tomorrow.

In a world where anyone, including any kid, can use technology to do anything we have to ask who our corporate competitors really are. Is market share what we should be measuring?

## What is fragmenting

Distributed tools are circumventing geography by connecting the globe with like minds.

## What it means for business

Our audience, employees, supply chain, revenue sources and other inputs are no longer in predictable geographic clusters. The market is now self-selecting.

# CHAPTER 18

# Market-share folly and industrial fragmentation: industrial metrics

The development of modern marketing and all forms of corporate management has led to a set of metrics that enable managers to assess how well they, their brands and their company are doing. Most are borrowed from nature, from the basic measurement tools we used in the agrarian society to ensure we had enough to eat or trade in the subsequent season. They make sense now and they'll make sense a thousand years from now. Simple models of assessment such as yield and growth rates spring to mind. But one that is an industrial-era measure is that of market share. How much of a market does a brand or company hold in percentage terms? Is it increasing or decreasing and what does that tell us about the relative performance?

# Market-share folly

The problem with using market share as a measure is that it can provide companies with a false sense of what's actually occurring in the market. For market share to be measured, a set of assumptions used to build the measurement framework is needed. Companies first require the following elements:

- They have to clearly define the market.

- The market must be defined in terms of a product or service.

- The market is then often split into smaller product or service segments of the wider market.

- There must be clear distribution channels, from where their sales come, from which market share can be measured.

- There must be a defined set of competitors who also serve that market. They need to know who they are, and they need to sell in and around the same measureable channels.

- There needs to be a measuring tool. Historically large research companies such as AC Nielsen have a system in place to do the measuring.

All of the requirements needed to find market share tell us the story of how this can be a misleading and problematic measure in times of revolution. When all the factors of production and all the distribution methods are being disrupted, it's important to be careful when deciding what to measure. Often the things we measure — the channels, the product type, the systems — are those that evaporate when the pace of change is rapid.

## The key assumption = we know the market

Market-share folly can mislead a company into believing it's doing better than it is. It focuses attention in the market as the way it is, or was, rather than how it will be — a defined market that's knowable, predictable and has a pre-defined set of players who usually play by the industrial rules developed over the past 200 years and who probably all use the same go-to-market methods. This means all the players most likely share the same production methods, the same selling channels, the same advertising and promotion methods, the same supply chain, the same employee backgrounds and the same customer base. The assumption is that the market is known and defined. It's a linear factory mindset and it's no longer applicable. In times of revolution, as markets evolve rapidly, companies need to widen their perspective and focus on customer-need states.

## Software is eating the world

Inventor of the first graphical web browser 'Mosaic' and now venture capitalist Marc Andresseen famously said that 'software is eating the world'. His inference is that any industry that can be disrupted by the use of software, will be and that all industries are being attacked by a new breed of entrepreneur — the four-dollar tech startups, as I like to call them. Anyone with a laptop computer and the $4 needed to buy a café latte and get free wi-fi can be an immediate entrepreneur.

**Any industry that was built to any size in a preconnected world either has been, or will be, disrupted to the point where it no longer represents its former self.**

They don't even need to be software engineers; they can outsource that to any of the millions waiting on global low-cost labour market websites. These entrepreneurs want to hack existing industries. They seek to find the inefficiencies existing industries operate under, and reconfigure them with a technology edge. Their goal is to remove the inefficiencies and build a new market for themselves. They aim to make old markets more liquid and transparent, providing deeper access to the end user. And the way they do this is by ignoring most everything about how it was done, what was built and how customer connections have been made. In fact, they have to; there is no other way to disrupt. They have to approach the market from where they can't be seen and attacked by the incumbents. They want to do what new industrialists wanted to do eight generations before them. Any industry that was built to any size in a pre-connected world either has been, or will be, disrupted to the point where it no longer represents its former self.

## Did they see them coming?

Smart corporations need to be watching the flanks to see where their industry is heading, not the other corporations they've been competing with since before the technology revolution. The list of examples of brands and industries that got whipped out by side-winding newbies is long, and it's only going to get longer.

Do you think the market-leader incumbents saw these competitors coming?

- *Wikipedia.* It's clear that *Encyclopedia Britannica* and *World Book* would not have seen this coming. No-one did. Not even the founder, Jimmy Wales, whose first email message to friends upon launching Wikipedia asking them to make a wiki entry said, 'Humour me and please write an entry about something you have some expertise in'. Not only did they do it, it turns out the crowd knows more than the experts. Wikipedia is not only more up to date, but more accurate than encyclopedias. The problem with this example of disruption is that there's no longer a business model at all for encyclopedias.

- *Google.* The Yellow Pages, the brand now famous for delivering giant yellow doorstops and recycling-bin fillers, would not have been measuring its performance against search engines. Nope. Neither would the newspaper classifieds. The truth is they serve the same need: a directory of life solutions. And by the time the Yellow Pages reconfigured its output it was far too late.

- *Airbnb.* The hotel industry would never have taken into account the calculations of peer-to-peer accommodation as part of its market. It doesn't even own any real estate! It's unimaginable to believe that executives at the Hilton chain or the Starwood group of hotels would have considered Airbnb a threat, and certainly not a threat in the section of the market they define as high-end, luxury or business appropriate. Yet Airbnb has both unexpected luxury and growing numbers of business travellers as its audience. So much so that it's now valued at more than US$10 billion (and it was only born in 2008).

- *Uber.* The first disruption to the car-rental and taxi-cab industries was the share car. This caught them napping and major players had to make acquisitions to buy out the threat. So the question now is, are Hertz, Avis and others measuring Uber in their relative market performance, a competitor that doesn't have to buy cars and doesn't have the costs of the hire-car industry, or even the car-share market? It only has a few of the costs of the legacy players, but with many of the customer benefits. It's even disrupting the most recent disruptor (the car-share market) in a very short time frame.

- *Tesla*. Surely a new car company can't compete with the more than 100 years of expertise of Ford, General Motors (GM) and others? Surely a startup from Silicon Valley that's never built real hardware — American steel — and only ever messed around with 1s and 0s can't build a car that could be a serious option as a family sedan? In this case the competitor is measurable in market share, but while Ford and GM are taking an experimental approach to electric vehicles, the new kid in town is taking it a bit more seriously. In 10 short years it has already achieved half the market capitalisation of Ford and GM ($30 billion vs $60 billion). And it's done this with only two car models being released to the market.

- *iTunes et al.* This example is even more telling as the music industry (the big three: Universal, Sony and Warner) actually had a chance and still missed it. Music downloads were not part of their market-share calculations until well into the 2000s, by which time the game had already been won by others. The near miss with Napster was a pure gift of prophecy that they chose to ignore. The market wanted new delivery methods. iTunes should have been the result of a collaboration with the music industry stalwarts, as should Spotify, Rdio and a host of others. Instead, music newbies took centre stage. The industry was too busy fighting lawsuits to see the opportunity to remove massive parts of their cost infrastructure by going digital. They were too busy competing to ship thirty-dollar pieces of plastic instead of finding ways to deliver new music to music fans.

# Redefining industries through infrastructure

When we look at it closely, we see that what was once mandatory in certain industries is now becoming optional. This is further proof that access is more important than ownership. In the accommodation game, we no longer have to own buildings. In the transport game, we no longer have to own vehicles. In the music game, we no longer have to sign artists or have stores. In the knowledge game, our curators are the crowd. In each of these examples pieces of the infrastructure have been removed in ways we would never have thought possible.

As markets are redefined, companies have to go further back to the actual need and much closer to the user's needs to ensure they don't get disrupted in unforeseeable ways. What spaces are there where you can rest your head? What options are emerging in the short-trips travel market? Where do people hear music these days? Where do they go to seek information?

Companies have to widen the circle of industry reference before they can understand whether or not they're measuring relative success without being blindsided.

## Collaboration with competitors

When the landscape of an industry is changing, it's often better to collaborate than it is to compete because industries and the way people connect and transact with the new ground needs lots of development. Sometimes it's better when competitors invest effort in transitioning the customer base to the new method rather than stealing from each other.

This is no more prevalent than in the social-media space. The two largest competitors, Facebook and Twitter, actually collaborate via their open APIs. This enables a Facebook status update to appear in Twitter and a tweet to be automatically posted on Facebook. This may seem trivial now because we're so used to seeing the cross-interaction, but it's a radical departure from the industrial way of thinking. It's akin to the ABC having a box in the corner of its screen with NBC playing in it. The open market allows for cross-fertilisation and growth of a new market. By collaborating with each other the space they compete in — their ecosystem — gets bigger.

## We'll just buy the winners

A popular corporate strategy has long been to buy the innovators. It worked well for traditional media, traditional retail, packaged goods and the auto industry. It's also something the tech industry of Silicon Valley, and elsewhere, is not immune to doing — making a plan to buy the new winners and threats. This a strategy that's absolutely valid when there's a shared infrastructure and go-to-market strategy, but it can fall short when the prize of winning is big and the price of missing it destroys an old business model. For example:

- What if the new star is not for sale?
- What if we can't afford to buy them?
- What if they get bigger than we ever were?
- What if they put us out of business before we get a chance to react?

Contending to buy potential threats is not a smart play when the new winners are more profitable and yield a higher return on investment. Especially when the acquisition target's business model is highly unlikely to plug into the old one and synergy is highly unlikely.

# The pace of change

Companies have to disrupt themselves. With the knowledge that the landscape is creating a more fragmented environment, the best strategy is to embrace the inevitable. Companies have to be the creators of the new revised infrastructure in their industry. They have to try to put themselves out of business; that is, to have a skunkworks mentality. It can't be about new products or incremental innovations. It needs to be about building new methods with which to go to market, not just new things to put into the market. The change we're living through is environmental, rather than about the species that live in the environment. So it requires much more than improvements on the existing; it requires new systems.

What smart companies are doing is creating external environments for radical innovation. The Google X lab, for example, carries out research and development that's breaking totally new ground. The aim of the Google X lab is to create 10-fold improvements in the technology they release. As with all classic skunkworks, they're in a different building so that the existing business culture doesn't infect their purpose.

> **skunkworks:** a small, independent, loosely structured group who research and develop a project primarily for the purpose of radical innovation (Wikipedia)

# Internal venture capital

If the new players in the market are consistently being beaten by startups, why not join them? There's no reason why any large company can't redirect R&D

capital into a skunkworks, or their own venture-capital arm. Outsourcing is not a new concept. It's used for creative advertising development, manufacturing, administration, legal and accounting. Almost every function of a business can be and has been outsourced, so why not innovation through the employment of venture funding? An industry realm focused venture-capital fund sponsored by an industry about to be disrupted may be the best investment it can make in surviving the upheaval.

For large corporations to maintain their position they need to jump the curve instead of making small, financially-safe innovations. That's no longer enough. The R&D focus needs to be a 10-times better mentality, such as the venture capital industry, whose business model is to invest in organisations that aim to change the shape of an industry. But this takes serious courage, the type that most career corporate managers don't have.

# Cold War era thinking

It's funny how what's happening in the geopolitical environment and the business environment are often aligned. It seems that the shift we've seen in modern warfare is much the same as what's happening in business. During the Cold War era we knew who the enemies were. The US and USSR both played a game of trying to out-resource each other, creating an aura of power as both led the way in the arms race, a quantifiable game where both parties employed the same techniques, though they did have opposing political philosophies.

Then, in the new century, not long after the web arrived the enemy changed. Terrorist cells not using any of the traditional resources and infrastructure have become the biggest threat to Western civilisation. Even modern warfare has fragmented away from the nation states to what could possibly be described as a startup mentality by using skinny resources to infiltrate a market. In much the same way as large businesses have been disrupted, the impact of the new player was largely unexpected and came without too much warning. It's always most difficult to find an enemy you can't see, or even worse, one that you don't take seriously when it first appears because it is too small and has nowhere near the resources of the big boys.

During the Cold War era, big brands played the same game, trying to out–'Super Bowl' each other with their giant advertising campaigns and product launches (for example, obtaining the rights to the Rolling Stones song 'Start Me Up', which was used in the commercial for Windows 95). But big brands and companies need to pay attention to what's happening on a global scale, not just in business but in all forms of battle, whether they be corporate or nation state. The smaller more nimble invisible competitors are the ones we really have to be careful of.

# Ignore resources and self-disrupt

The move in focus should be defined as this: move from an industry focus (large industry agglomerations) into small user-centric models. Pieces of the market are breaking away from the historically vertical structure of industries. As we move to a more horizontal marketplace, ownership resources pale into insignificance compared to direct access to users. Whatever industry a business is in, it can be sure that someone is working hard now to fracture it with their new connection method. What we can be sure of is that the new technology and environment will make the disruption inevitable. Business can be in control of the choice to self-disrupt its own system before someone else does it for them.

All change has unexpected downsides. With industries being flipped upside down and lives being tracked, it can feel like our private lives are being invaded by others. But privacy erosion, in real terms, is nothing new.

## What is fragmenting

A technology based economy enables demarcation of industry. It's hard to see how people's product and service needs will be fulfilled in new ways.

## What it means for business

It's foolish to try to define your competitors in a market. The real innovation in any industry is likely to arrive from firms outside the expected competitive realm.

**CHAPTER 19**

# The externality reality:
# is this the end of privacy?

A favourite term of economic rationalists is 'externality'. In economics, an externality is a cost or unexpected consequence of a new form of activity. The problem with most externalities is that they usually arrive after the fact, once the new behaviour has already set in and been widely distributed. In addition to this, externalities aren't usually priced into the market or regulated in the short term. They tend to become the focus of heated political debate sometime after the innovation that led to them. Environmental pollution was the core externality of the industrial era. Many claim that the erosion of privacy and the emerging data industrial complex are the pollution of the technology revolution.

# Digital footprints

The mobile revolution has enabled some supposedly new forms of human behaviour. The ability to leave a footprint of everywhere we go is one of these. We now have the ability, intended or not, to geo-locate ourselves. We can share whatever we think, do and buy, and wherever we go. While these footprints are left with most of our digital-based activities, the footprints themselves are not like those we leave on the beach. First, digital footprints are hard to see because there are so many of them. But we need to remember they rarely get washed away, and someone else owns the beach. It leaves us with a set of circumstances that seem, on first impression, like a first for humanity: the end of privacy.

A lot of non-digital natives believe the concept of checking in, or sharing personal activity live on the web, is kind of weird. They believe the mobile web is going too far. The truth is that this form of human behaviour is not new. It's just a new form of existing human behaviour that hasn't changed much in millennia. There's a belief that these new forms of immediate digital connection are putting the private lives of all people into question. But there's a simple fact about privacy that straddles all communication, and it's this:

*The ideas of communication and privacy are naturally juxtaposed with each other.*

If we look at this more closely, we come to understand that every iteration in our ability to communicate takes away an equal amount of privacy. The reason we continue to choose connection over privacy is simple:

*Improved communication improves the living standards of our species.*

# Geo-locating isn't weird

We've had and used maps for centuries to guide us. Even the simple idea of a cave painting or a book is a form of geo-locating. It's telling a story of what we saw, or what we found, or where we were. There is no doubt that these forms of documenting our experiences seemed weird when they first arrived. The only difference with a geo-locating mobile device is that it has improved accuracy and immediacy. In fact, all iterations of documentation of events have done the same thing — they've become more accurate, distributed and immediate. The trajectory of where communications is going hasn't changed — better, faster, cheaper and more available. Geo-locating is merely another technological curve jump, a moment of 'wow, this is way more accurate and available'.

# A history of privacy concerns

Having privacy concerns about new forms of communication is not a new thing. When street numbers were first introduced in the Austro-Hungarian empire in the early nineteenth century there were riots in the streets. Segments of the population were up in arms and fought against the government for making public where they lived. In the end, when people decided they wanted their mail delivered more than they cared about where they lived being a known quantity, things quietened down.

We can add to this a long list of privacy erosions whereby the end benefits outweighed the losses, creating a largely opt-in society. See table 19.1.

**Table 19.1: privacy erosions and benefits**

| Privacy erosions | Erosion benefits |
| --- | --- |
| passport | ability to travel across borders |
| phone-book listing | ability to be connected |
| drivers licence | ability to use public roads |
| car registration | access to private transportation |
| tax-file number | access to free public services |
| Medicare number | access to free health services |
| credit cards | access to deferred and safer payment |
| loyalty cards | access to benefits of loyalty |
| social web | access to community |

This list could be much longer, but it provides a clear path that shows that we'll gladly hand over personal information when the benefits to us are greater than the cost of the losses, something business needs to remind itself of in a data-rich world. If the benefit of participation isn't worth it, people will remove themselves. What digital brands such as social media must remember is that, often, what they provide doesn't have the monopoly powers of government tracking innovations and many other privacy eroders, so how those in the data business behave will become a significant brand health measurement in the future. In a digital society with many connection options, there are often low barriers for exiting. Social media is one such example, especially given it's in the substitution phase of its existence, rather than the void-filling stage.

# Types of privacy

In reality, our formerly non–digital enabled papers (or documents), such as passports and driver licences, are being digified. Opting out of data trails is turning into an opting-out-of-civilisation kind of choice.

There are really two forms of privacy: what you do in your personal life and what you do as part of community participation.

## How communication improves the human plight

Knowing more leads to all of us either having more or having access to more. Sharing, collaborating and specialisation are ways of reducing scarcity and increasing efficiency. We intuitively share data and lessons because we know subconsciously they're what put us atop of the food chain. The challenge in the short term is coping psychologically with new methods that seem out of place.

## We have a choice

Ultimately, these so-called 'weird' behaviours of sharing, collaborating and pinpointing our location and activities are chosen ones. We can choose not to take part in any of them. We can choose not to participate in the culture. But the choice to self-exclude most often leads to reduced self-opportunity and benefits.

Human tracking is a normal and historically relevant activity for improved civilisation and living standards. While recent technology has given it a jolt regarding what's possible, my advice is simple: we're all better off when we embrace the evolution and share in the benefits.

## Privacy vs secrecy

Our increasingly public lives through digital living raises important questions about secrecy. What everyone tends to forget is the difference between secrecy and privacy. They're not the same. Privacy and secrecy are totally different things. Most things that are private are not secrets. But they are intimate, sensitive and of a nature that in most cases doesn't concern others. We all know what happens when we go to the bathroom and we all know how our parents made us. Neither of these is a secret, but they need to remain private. Much of what we do online — which is now a natural part of our evolved human conversation — is private. And that's how they should remain.

> Most things that are private are not secrets.

What we, as the owners and constituents living inside the technology, need to do is create a society that has regulations which are above any government organisations. We need to create a digital culture that clearly delineates between privacy and secrets. We need to create boundaries around our digital infrastructure where privacy is not invaded on demand by authorities, just in case they find a secret (a relevant secret at that). The only way it will happen is if the majority stands up and lets the authorities know it wants a new set of boundaries. It isn't without a small amount of irony that the tools that need to be reviewed are the ones we need to use to create the boundaries we want. Isn't that what civilised societies do: set boundaries that create a better, safer, fairer society? If we fail to create this delineation between secrecy and privacy, our basic, important, intellectual and progressive freedoms are at risk. What's made public should surely be the choice of the publisher. A one-to-one digital communication should remain as such. Information sent to a service provider should also remain as such.

Industries being impacted by technology to the point where our entire lives become public tells us that business is becoming inextricably linked to technology.

## What is fragmenting

Private information is being unlocked from the filing cabinet and shared freely online. Our private lives are becoming increasingly public.

## What it means for business

People will share private information as long as the incentive is greater than the personal cost.

# CHAPTER 20

# Business = technology: the 4Ps revised

After the journey we've just been on it's time to review the 4Ps, which were introduced in the very first chapter. These are the factors of production, the marketing mix — the only real elements that exist in the business environment. As we review each of these you'll be taken back to each of the individual parts of the mix and reminded of how significantly the world of business has changed. Every single one of the Ps is unrecognisable compared to the pre-technology digital age. Let's indulge ourselves in a review of them one by one.

# Product

The products (and services) we buy, use and engage with have changed forever. We no longer have to accept mass products made for average people living average lives. We can instead find exactly what we want on demand from anywhere in the world. And if it doesn't exist we can find someone to make it, or we can make it ourselves. We can mash things up. Mass products that do exist will continue to decline into commodity pricing, unless the mass product is 'customisable' once we have it in our hands. Just compare your smartphone interface to anyone else's. No two in the world are the same. We can get any product we want from any geography via the infinite online retail stores and we can co-create using the tools that have been handed over to us by the smarter brand houses out there — the ones that have realised the brand is actually 'ours'. From sports shoes to media, products are increasingly coming from platforms where the final product is not what we buy, but a set of ingredients we can use to make our own recipe.

And as far as radical technological ingredients go, we can expect that 3D printing will have as much impact on the products we use as the digital web does on the media we interact with. Bits are being turned into atoms and desktop manufacturing will change the way things come into being and will change our lives. The services of the future are quickly becoming a cross-referenced, mashed-up, gamified bunch of system hacks that suit the end user. The best option for any business is to say, 'Here you go. These are our pieces of the puzzle. Put them together again your own way'.

Everything we know about products has changed and the future isn't even designed yet. Stability is an illusion. The art of product design is to be able to have the courage to live with collaborative and counter-intuitive uncertainty.

# Price

The price of everything is getting lower, cheaper, more affordable and more distributed so that everyone can afford what's important. High technology prices are quickly heading to free, disposable, inconsequential … call it what you will, but price is no longer a barrier for the most vital parts of our economy. We all have NASA-level powers today. The current path of technology is to become cheaper, smaller and more available.

Contrary to what the tabloids say, life has never been cheaper. In developed markets wages continue to grow at rates above inflation year on year. Everything is getting cheaper and prices have never been more reasonable in real terms. And this will continue. New access to BRIC-nations labour will add more service providers to the labour market via digital connections enabling everyone — not just large corporations — to border hop and lower the costs of doing business and making things. Sites such as Alibaba

**Price is a function of demand and supply, and the supply of everything is getting bigger and even infinite.**

will continue to open up low-cost manufacturing to those previously excluded, creating an increased oversupply of everything and forcing prices down. In simple terms, we just have to come back to the very first lesson we ever had in economics, the one I keep on ranting about and everyone seems to forget: price is a function of demand and supply, and the supply of everything is getting bigger and even infinite. We have infinite supply, and two-thirds of the world's population is yet to arrive on the web and add to that supply mix. But that isn't far away as the costs of getting connected are dropping.

We can add to this the perfect pricing information we have and a new ability to bid prices down via comparison and system hacking. New methods of finance and funding as discussed in chapter 12 are deeper recognition of a dramatically shifting price structure. Everything is pointing towards a future with lower prices. If your business thinks it's hard now to maintain profitable pricing, you'd better buckle your seatbelt, because the trend is set to continue thanks to the forces at play. Profitable pricing in the future will be more about having the most efficient distribution system or about mashing up the seemingly disparate technologies to create new things that previously didn't exist. Selling what someone else sells will just leave you swimming in commodity soup.

# Place

Location is no longer relevant unless what people are buying is an experience, a live event or an irrevocably human experience.

Retail as we know it is over. Gaining access to generally available products at the best prices will be the domain of the online buyer. The cost of bricks and concrete is just too big and expensive to carry. Links in the distribution chain are being removed as our bits of information find a more efficient path in the same way that water does. The retail revenue leaks we've seen in the traditional space will become more of a tsunami.

Distribution has never been more fragmented or important. Having direct access to a customer base needs to be part of the innovation strategy of any company that wants to survive. Outsourcing the moment of truth (the place where the money changes hands) to a retailer or distributor is now a very dangerous game. The greatest amount of control now, more than in the history of business, belongs to the distributor. We only have to look at the power of Amazon, Apple and the new media giants to see that. They all go direct to their audience, not via someone else. Add to this the fact that every person is quickly becoming a retailer and can sell whatever they make (even their labour) with simplified humanised technological tools.

Distribution is now non-linear and undefined so it's hard to tell whose job it actually is. Makers are now sellers, and sellers are now makers. The vertical supply and distribution structure is now an integrated and networked system where a vertical flow pattern no longer applies. Companies need to pay as much attention to how they sell things as they do to what they make and sell. Selling where you've always sold is now a path to invisibility. The industrial retail mentality of the supply chain is now unrecognisable. Distribution, or 'place', has been totally revised.

# Promotion

The days of buying an audience on demand are evaporating before our very eyes. The 30-second road-block launch now belongs in a marketing museum. Even buying an audience via search and social tools is not a direct or possibly valid substitute. The media landscape has forever changed from an interruption business model providing free entertainment and interruptions with messages from sponsors to a permission business model, where the audience and business choose to have a relationship and interact with each other with known and expected interactions.

Audiences must be earned and advertising is not enough. The offer is the thing that matters, and when a brand has something significant enough on offer, something we care about, we'll do the rest from there on. Smart brands need to concentrate less on making cinematic and comedic advertising addendums and focus more on what they actually provide; that is, the reason they exist. In a world where we can pay attention to what we want according to our own schedule, the model of mass advertising and buying a place in people's hearts just doesn't work anymore. Media is omnichoice on demand and über niche. Using it to sell a message is not nearly as effective as it once was. Audiences will increasingly fragment into their niche worlds. This means aggregated mass audiences will become a rare commodity. If we need to find a mass audience, we can only expect the price of that connection to increase. There are only so many Super Bowls in a year.

The media is no longer a path to promotion. The path to promotion is about having something in the market that's worth talking about and then participating in that conversation when the market wants interaction. In the words of the Cluetrain Manifesto, 'Markets are conversations'. And conversations always occur within a human voice, not a corporate PR brochure.

The way we promote is not the way our industrial mass market did yesterday.

## Selling potatoes

During the industrial revolution, the prize in business went to those who embraced industrial-era economics. Working the field by hand didn't compete with the combine harvester. Bespoke automobiles hand-built by craftsmen couldn't compete with the production line. The US went from having more than 2000 car 'builders' in the early 1900s, to 44 in 1929, and then to 11 in 1976.[1] And when the television hit the lounge room the travelling circus could no longer compete with The Tonight Show.

We're all in the technology business now, whether we like it or not. There's no choice, regardless of whether the business sells microchips or potato chips. Yes, even potato selling is influenced by technology in the same way that making and selling everything is. The savvy potato farmer has integrated digital systems for irrigation using live feeds from web-enabled weather reports. They price their product using global indicators

[1]The History of the Automobile:
http://l3d.cs.colorado.edu/systems/agentsheets/New-Vista/automobile

from commodity trading websites, and change the range of what to plant based on what's hot in the leading gourmet restaurants. So, next season he moves to baby kifler, which is far more profitable. He has a geo-map of all the places he sells to, creating the most efficient run for his delivery, and accepts new forms of direct payment via his smartphone. The point is that technology isn't about what we sell anymore. It isn't 'that segment over there'; it's the entire economic structure that we live within. No business can choose whether something is relevant to them because everything is relevant to everyone.

# The end of 'big'?

Being big for the first time in a long time is now often a disadvantage, certainly if the business in question was born before the 1990s. The advantages of being big are being removed. For industrial-era companies, their former economics of scale are quickly becoming the economics of fail. Big makes a business too fragile and dependent on volume and size. Businesses built around the idea of supply-chain scale are at risk because as part of a vertical-based infrastructure they depend on each other for both throughput and stability.

On the other hand, businesses that are large, but networked, systems — built around the concept of horizontal distribution and integration — can be big or small. Because what they build is a collection of nodes. A failure in the system — a rogue node, if you will — does not break the chain itself. It doesn't stop the system. The chain doesn't break because there is no chain. Instead it re-routes itself to another node, keeping the system working.

The emerging form of big, a big that can work in our new environment, is the platform. This is made up of small parts loosely joined to each other. The new big provides platforms to the many and is inclusionary by nature. By inviting participation, the new big allows itself to become distributed pieces of the economic infrastructure. But it will not have control over many of these. It will build things that are built upon, not owned outright. It's not the sellers, but those who provide economic and entrepreneurial democracy, who will have the scale — which will be something like an open-source scale — advantage going forward.

The new big is a bunch of smaller pieces of the collective.

There's a very strong possibility that the future of large business has to become the sum of its parts financially, but not operationally. The two will have to be kept separate to maintain their nimbleness, or risk becoming victims of the accelerating pace of change. Keep the segments separate and aggregate the profits; don't aim for false efficiencies in operations. Avoid the development of a monoculture, a viewpoint where a company thinks it has all the answers, which is something no company can do in times of rapid change. Instead, maintain an independent skunkworks mentality of self-hacking and disruption. The structure can't be that of the industrial model; it just doesn't work anymore.

## The 'now' question

It gets heavy carrying an irrelevant past into the future. The key question big companies need to ask themselves is this:

*If we were setting up shop today, which parts of our business would we not include? Which parts would be in-house, what would be outsourced, what would our culture be and what would we not invest in?*

This is the same question startups ask before they disrupt an industry, and the same question that's being asked about every established industry, if not by the incumbents, certainly by those wanting to eat their lunch. If you don't do what they do, they'll end up doing what you don't do and put you out of business.

## Survival is about evolution

For any species to survive it has to evolve. It has to adapt to its environment as it changes or it can be left behind, or even worse not survive the transition as the landscape changes. There comes a time in every species' existence where it has to climb down from the trees — or its corporate ivory tower — get down to ground level and make its way into unchartered ground. The time to do this is when there's no longer enough nutrition (revenue) in the place that has been feeding us up until now. People have been particularly good at this for millennia. We followed the herd and we even fashioned small craft to cross oceans to find warmer, more hospitable, fertile ground as our climate changed. In real terms, the climate has always been the ultimate arbiter of where we need to move to, and as much as we think we can manage the climate, or work around it, it's always in control.

And business is really just one type of climate. It's also a climate that's out of our control. And the climate is going through a tectonic shift for the ages where the conditions will never be the same again, at least not in our lifetime. So the decision for the more mature species in the business environment is quite simply to make way for new ground. Leave the old baskets, structures and huts behind (our infrastructure). They'll be far too heavy to carry on the long trip into the future where the world is more fertile. The new ground will provide for those who have the faith to make the trip. And it's not as if the trip is into unknown territory. The startups that now shape a business technology world have already taken the trip. They've made it to the new ground, and it's good ground. It's fertile and they've even provided the old-timers with some charts and some rough ideas on how to get there. Sure, the ground is still changing, but many have crossed the chasm and it is doable. All they need is some courage to get there.

## A lab or a factory?

Businesses need to decide whether they want to be a lab or a factory. There are some clues into which one may work best in the new business environment when we review what each one is.

- *The factory* believes it already makes something that people want. It can't handle dramatic changes to the product or the formula because it was built to make specific, predetermined things. The factory's core focus is on scale, cost reduction and efficiency. It wants what it wanted yesterday, but cheaper and faster. The factory is the biggest investment the company makes. The people who work in and around it serve the factory, not the other way around. There's very little room for movement, change or creativity. It's more about the boxes of stuff to sell that come out the other end. The factory took a lot of money to invest in, so we need to churn out lots of stuff from it for a long time to get a payback. We're in it for the long haul, and it will work out better for the factory if things don't change too much.

- *The lab* knows the answer's in there somewhere; it just doesn't know what it is yet. Many experiments will be undertaken in order to find something that solves a certain problem, and while there are some ideas around solutions, there's no answer just yet. The ingredients are flexible and easily changed, as are the methods being undertaken. The thing that really matters isn't so much the ingredients, but the people mixing them up, the imagination they have and their interpretations of the possibilities. Each experiment they do leads to another idea and provides some real-world feedback as to how things interact. The focus is on human capital as opposed to financial capital, so we can have lots of labs working on different things at the same time and finding answers. If the lab fails it's okay. It's part of the learning process. And failures are very low cost. Every failure becomes an idea that can be crossed off the list and gets us closer to the answers we seek.

In times of change it's pretty clear that a lab mentality is what's needed. The lab is an approach that doesn't pretend to know the answers or believe that the world is stable. It's an approach where the playbook is in fact to not pretend to know what's next, but to understand that speed is the asset, creativity is greater than finance and collaboration is more powerful than control. The marketing model of the technology age is a model that must remain in a constant state of flux. What organisations need is a culture and structure that can cope with flux, one that revises how it goes to market based on what it learned today.

## The great fragmentation

While at various points in this book it may seem like I'm dancing on the grave of the industrial revolution, and singing a happy song about the end of powerful industries or even corporations, I'm not. What I'm doing is trying to help everyone realise that what made companies big yesterday is likely to be their unravelling tomorrow. The tools of life and business are now in the hands of everyone. Mass is quickly fragmenting into a world of niche, smaller and more distributed things. And big businesses that need a new survival manifesto need to embrace the fragmented nature if they want to stay 'big'.

We are entering the age of post-scarcity abundance. The great fragmentation isn't just great because it's huge or amazing — although, in fact, it really is. It's much more than that. It's a move to a more equalised and humane society where the power to know and the power to participate are being handed back to everyone. Both economically and socially, just about everything is being democratised for good. I think it's better than good ... I think it's great.

# Recommended books and documentaries

Most people who read this book will have a pretty good handle on business principles and the great business books worth reading, so I thought I'd mix it up a little. Given we are living in a time of true revolution, we need to look outside our own realm, become exploratory and open our minds through the understanding of different fields. To help you do this, I've pulled together a reading and viewing list of work that helped me to see the world better. I've done this because the truth about business is that the patterns within it come from worlds outside it.

## Books

*The Art of Game Design: A Book of lenses*
Jesse Schell

*Billions & Billions: Thoughts on Life and Death at the Brink of the Millennium*
Carl Sagan

*Brand Hijack: Marketing Without Marketing*
Alex Wipperfurth

*The Cluetrain Manifesto*
Rick Levine, Christopher Locke, Doc Searls, David Weinberger

*The Demon-Haunted World: Science as a Candle in the Dark*
Carl Sagan and Ann Druyan

*How to Create a Mind: The Secret of Human Thought Revealed*
Ray Kurzweil

*The Intelligent Investor: The Definitive Book on Value Investing. A Book of Practical Counsel*
Benjamin Graham

*One Up On Wall Street: How To Use What You Already Know To Make Money In The Market*
Peter Lynch

*The Prince*
Niccolo Machiavelli

*A Random Walk Down Wall Street: The Time-Tested Strategy for Successful Investing*
Burton G. Malkiel

*Rework*
Jason Fried, David Heinemeier Hansson

*The Road Ahead*
Bill Gates, Nathan Myhrvold, Peter Rinearson

*Stuff White People Like: A Definitive Guide to the Unique Taste of Millions*
Christian Lander

# Documentaries

*Connections* (series 1-3, 1978-1997)
Series presented by James Burke.

*The Corporation* (2013)
Film on the concept of the corporation.

*Cosmos* (1980)
Series presented by Carl Sagan.

*The Day the Universe Changed* (1985)
Series presented by James Burke.

*Dogtown and Z-Boys* (2001)
Film about 1970s Zephyr skating team.

*Downloaded* (2013)
Film about Napster.

*Eames: The Architect & The Painter* (2011)
Film about industrial designers Charles and Ray Eames.

*Enron: The Smartest Guys in the Room* (2005)
Film about the American energy corporation Enron.

*Everything is a Remix* (parts 1-4)
Web series by Kirby Ferguson.

*Exit Through the Gift Shop* (2010)
Film from graffiti artist Banksy.

*Inside Job* (2010)
Film about the global financial crisis.

*No Maps for These Territories* (2000)
Film presented by William Gibson.

*Something Ventured* (2011)
Film about venture capitalists.

# INDEX

3D printing 11–12, 113, 117–127

access and accessibility 11, 26, 27, 31, 61, 66, 69, 84, 86, 88–89, 109, 111, 112, 121, 137, 144, 145, 156, 169, 171, 187, 199–200, 201, 202, 203, 207, 208, 212, 214, 223, 234, 236–237, 240, 244, 245, 252, 253 *see also* barriers; communication; digital; social media
—factors of production 27, 98–99, 102
—knowledge 93–102
adoption rates 85
advertising 4, 5, 12, 16, 17, 26, 32, 52, 57, 61, 68, 70, 89, 98, 111, 131, 135, 142, 146, 147, 194, 211, 219, 226, 227–228, 229, 234, 239, 254; *see also* marketing; mass media; promotion; television
Airbnb 235
Alibaba 27, 98
Amazon 77, 111, 136, 148
antifragility 15
Apple 111, 136, 137
artisanal production 3, 96, 109, 112, 124; 239, 257, 258, creativity

audience 134; *see also* crowd
—connecting with 52–55, 70–71, 101, 111–112
—vs target 49–50
Away from Keyboard (AFK) 38–39

banking 155–165, 192; *see also* crowdfunding; currencies
barriers 72, 81, 93–102, 110, 121, 148, 158, 245, 252
Beck (musician) 53
big as a disadvantage 255–256
bioengineering 118, 119
biomimicry 190
biotechnology 117, 119
bitcoins 159–160, 161
blogs 134–135, 144
borrowed interest 220
brand 51, 52, 55, 67, 70, 75, 98, 105, 106, 107, 110, 111, 138, 228, 239–240
business strategies, 6–7, 18, 41

change *see* disruption and disruptive change
Cluetrain Manifesto 254
co-creation 123, 124
coffee culture 112–113, 188
Cold War 239–240

collaboration 4, 18, 37, 39, 61–62, 71, 95, 111, 144, 151, 161–162, 186, 188, 192, 212, 225, 227, 228, 236, 237, 245, 251, 258

collaborative consumption 95, 188–189

collective sentience 23–24

commerce, future 181–196; *see also* retail and retailers

communication 5, 6, 12, 22–23, 76, 81, 85, 106, 122, 124, 157, 174, 190, 207, 226, 227, 243, 245, 246, 254; *see also* advertising; promotion; social media; social relationships
— channels 140–141, 143–144
— tools 5, 15, 23, 24–25, 117, 131, 141, 143, 177, 204, 220, 225, 251, 253

community vs target 49–50

competition and competitors 17–18, 105, 109, 110, 235–236, 237, 237–238, 239, 240

component retail 53

computers 17, 23, 43, 56, 81, 82, 83, 84, 86, 117, 121, 124, 127, 132, 159, 169, 171, 172, 186, 191, 193, 199, 212, 234; *see also* connecting and connection; internet; networks; smartphones; social media; software; technology era; 3D printing; web

connecting and connection 15, 22, 23, 25–26, 27, 36, 37–38, 39, 40, 43, 54, 57, 62, 68, 69, 70–71, 72, 74, 75, 76, 77, 88–89, 93, 98, 109, 113, 117, 121, 132, 136, 137, 138, 141, 143, 144, 151, 157, 162, 164, 165, 169–178, 200, 204, 212, 214, 224, 225, 229, 234–235, 240, 243, 245, 252,

254; *see also* social media; social relationships
— home/world 90, 108, 131, 175–176, 178, 214, 224, 227
— machines 169
— people 169, 170, 188–189
— things 170, 171–178

consumerism 3, 4, 33, 57–58, 65, 93–94

consumption silos 93

content, delivery of 136–141, 142–143, 149

coopetition 62

corporations 26–27, 101–102; *see also* industrial era; retail and retailers; technology era

costs 4, 11, 16–17, 22, 26, 32, 42, 51, 54, 66, 67, 81–83, 85, 86, 87–90, 93, 95, 96, 97, 98–99, 101–102, 113, 118, 119, 121, 123, 133, 134, 136, 141, 142, 144, 150, 156, 161, 171, 174, 191, 192, 193, 203, 207, 208, 209, 210, 211–212, 214, 215, 220–221, 222–223, 224, 229, 234, 236, 243, 245, 252, 253, 257, 258, 259; *see also* finance; price

co-working space 62, 213

creativity 4, 12, 26, 27, 37, 55–56, 57, 61–62, 82, 137, 161, 162, 163, 164, 165, 170, 189, 202, 212, 213, 215, 228

crowd, contribution by the 54, 123, 137, 144, 178, 226, 235, 237,

crowdfunding 17, 70, 102, 157, 161–163, 165, 181, 189, 222, 223–224, 225,

cryptocurrencies 160–161, 192

culture
— hacking 199–200
— startup 16–17, 157

currencies 158–161, 192; *see also* banking

deflation 81–90, 174
demographics 65–77, 147–148
device convergence 132
digital 121, 122, 133, 224, *see also* computers; internet; music; smartphone; retail and retailers, online; social media; social relationships; technology; web; work
— cohorts 37–38
— era 26, 70, 81, 95–96, 109, 149, 150, 173, 200
— footprint 77, 163, 164, 202, 243
— revolution 11
— skills 42–45
— strategy 41–42
— tools 26, 37, 39–41, 42–45, 55, 59, 61, 71, 76, 81–82, 86, 89, 94, 101, 118, 122, 133, 137, 144, 162, 171, 173, 178, 183, 191, 199–200, 215, 229, 225, 233
— world 38, 61, 125, 133, 149, 165, 183, 215, 224,
disruption and disruptive change 4, 6, 15, 23, 41, 95, 121, 127, 131, 142, 145, 157–165, 176, 181, 233, 234–236, 237, 238, 239, 240, 256
DNA as an operating system 34–35
drones 119
Dunbar's number 35–36, 140

e-commerce *see* retail and retailers, online
economic development, changing 11–18

education 11, 13, 15–16, 223
employment, lifetime 13–14; *see also* labour; work
ephermalization 118–120

Facebook 21, 24, 26, 36, 49, 62, 136, 237; *see also* social media
finance, peer to peer 156, 165; *see also* banking; crowdfunding; currencies
Ford, Henry 208
4Ps 5–7, 110, 111–112, 251–259
Foursquare 184, 185–186
fragmentation 9, 18, 27, 45, 77, 90, 106, 127, 133, 151, 165, 173–174, 178, 196, 204, 215, 229, 240, 247, 258–259
— of cities 72–74
— industrial 233–240
— Lego car example 219–229

gadgets 171; *see also* computers; smartphone; tools
games and gaming behaviour 178, 184–189
gamification 181–195
geo-location 186, 193, 243, 244, 245
glass cockpit 54
Global Financial Crisis (GFC) 155, 158, 192, 223
globalisation 72, 82, 160, 224
Google 26, 111, 136, 137, 164, 226, 235

hacking 199–204
hourglass strategy 226–228

IFTTT (If this then that) 177
industrialists (capital class) 3, 207–208
industry, redefining 235–237

industrial era 3, 4, 7, 12, 14, 15, 17, 18, 22, 26, 44, 56–58, 61, 77, 81, 93, 109, 124, 172, 207, 211, 213–214, 224, 233, 243, 254–255; *see also* consumerism; marketing; retail and retailers
— hacking 201, 234
— life in 31–33, 45, 45, 51, 93, 171
influencers 74
information-based work 89–90, 127
infrastructure 105, 109
— changing 3, 4–5, 6–7, 11, 41, 42, 51, 66, 69, 86, 108, 144, 169, 187, 201, 213, 236–237, 238, 239, 246, 255, 257,
— declining importance of 7, 11, 45, 102, 110, 122, 170, 236
— legacy 7, 110, 134
innovation 3, 6, 16, 26, 51, 69, 85, 86, 110, 111, 118–120, 145, 157, 158, 160, 171, 172, 181, 191, 202, 203, 221, 225, 237–238, 239, 240, 243, 245, 253
intention 71
interest-based groups 71, 72–76; *see also* niches
interest graphs 71, 72 74–76, 77
internet 6, 14, 25, 26, 36, 38, 39, 43, 51, 75–76, 84, 93, 101, 117, 118, 121, 123, 126, 127, 133, 140, 143, 157, 169, 171, 173, 174, 183, 188, 190, 199, 202, 203, 219, 223, 224; *see also* access and accessibility; connecting and connection; social media; social relationships; web
Internet.org 26
In Real Life (IRL) 38–39
isolation 37
iTunes 236; *see also* music

Jumpstart Our Business Startups (JOBS) Act (USA) 163

keyboards 38–39
knowledge economy 42

lab vs factory 257–258
labour 53, 55, 89–90, 97, 99, 123, 214, 253; *see also* work
— low-cost 82, 98, 100, 101–102, 122, 208, 214, 234, 252
language 49–51
layering 86–87
legacy
— industries 6–7, 17, 109, 110, 122, 157
— infrastructure 7, 110, 134
— media 6, 25, 134, 151
Lego car project 219, 221–229
life
— in boxes 31–33, 35, 45
— in gaming future 192–195
— hack 177
living standards 3, 31, 33, 72, 88, 118, 208, 243, 246; *see also* life
location *see* place, work

making 113, 117–127; *see also* artisanal production; retail and retailers; 3D printing
malleable marketplace 52–55
manufacturing 207–208, 225; *see also* artisanal production; industrial era; making; product; 3D printing; tools
— desktop 121–127
marketing *see also* advertising; consumerism; 4Ps; mass media; promotion; retail and retailers
— demographics, use in 65–77
— industrial era 57–70, 77, 112, 147, 233–240

—language 59–60
—mass 57–70, 77, 112, 147
—metrics 233–234
—new 70–77, 233,
—post-industrial 227–228
—predictive 65–70
—research 76
—target 67
—traditional 59–60, 65, 69–70,
   201
mass media 57, 66, 67–68, 69–70,
   75, 124, 131–151; *see also*
   advertising; marketing; media;
   promotion; television
—after 131–151
materialism 3, 33, 93–94
media 131, 133, 143–144; *see also*
   communication; legacy; mass
   media; newspapers; niches;
   television
—consumption 67–68, 69–70
—hacking 202
—platform vs content 136–138
—subscription 145–146
Metcalfe's law 25
MOOC (Massive Open Online
   Course) 203
Moore's law 81, 86
music 53, 69, 95–96, 123, 127, 155,
   236, 237

Napster 69, 155, 236
Netflix 148
netizens 39,
networks 25–26, 74–76, 117–118,
   143–144, 255; *see also*
   connecting and connection;
   media; social media; social
   relationships
newspapers 6, 134–136, 138, 163,
   235; *see also* media

niches 55, 57, 58, 66 –67, 72–76,
   108, 112, 121, 134, 135, 136–140,
   141, 142, 146, 151, 164, 184, 202,
   213, 214, 215, 254, 258
nodes 143–144
nondustrial company 17

Oaida, Raul 219–229
oDesk 99, 100
office, end of the 208–215
omniconnection era 70
open source 11, 107, 120, 121, 134,
   115, 228

parasocial interaction 34
payment systems 157–158
Pebble 70
phones, number of mobile 11; *see
   also* smartphones
photography 121
Pinterest 74–75
piracy 123–124
place 5, 110–113, 253
—of work 207–215
platforms 134–138
pop culture 66
power-generating technologies
   11–12
price 5, 110, 120, 121, 150, 252; *see
   also* costs
privacy 243–247; *see also* social
   media; social relationships
product 5, 51, 148–149, 174–175,
   251, 191
—unfinished 52–55
production 5, 6, 26, 97, 151; *see
   also* industrial era; product;
   3D printing
—mass  118–120, 207–208
projecteer 14–15, 214–215
Project October Sky 219–221

promotion 5, 6, 253–254; *see also* advertising; marketing; mass media; media

quantified self 184

Racovitsa, Vasilii 100–101
remote controls 42–43, 146
RepRap 3D printer 120
retail cold spot 58
retail and retailers
— changing 105–113, 149–151, 251–259
— digital 109–110, 200–201
— direct 109–112
— hacking 200–201
— mass 66–66
— online 59, 102, 105, 107, 108–109, 110, 111, 112, 122, 141, 170, 181
— price 106–108
— small 111–112
— strategies 107–108
— traditional 58–59, 105, 106–107, 109, 111, 201, 254–255
rewards 185–186, 187, 194–195
robots 119

Sans nation state economy 101
scientific management 12–13
search engines 37, 85, 105, 108, 170, 235
self-hacking 202–203
self-publishing 134
self-storage 33
sensors 190–191, 193–195
sharing 62, 93–97, 177–178, 186–187, 245, 247; *see also* social media; social relationships
smartphones 38, 39, 52, 54, 70, 82, 83–84, 97, 108–109, 123, 125, 127, 132, 133, 137–138, 144, 146, 147, 176, 171, 172, 182, 183, 184, 187, 189–190, 193, 199, 251, 255
smartwatch 70, 162
social graphs 71, 72, 77
social media (digitally enhanced conversation) 21–27, 62, 99, 176, 177, 185–186, 224; *see also* Facebook; social relationships; Twitter; YouTube
social relationships 35–36, 71, 113, 169, 209; *see also* social graphs; social media
— digital 36–38, 39–41
software 38, 52–53, 54, 82, 86, 89, 120, 134, 144, 146, 159, 177–178, 234–235
speed 85–86
subcultures 72
Super Awesome Micro Project *see* Lego car project
Super Bowl mentality 141, 151, 228, 239, 254

target 49–50
tastemakers 57–58
technology 7, 43, 84, 117–118, 121, 259; *see also* computers; digital; open source; social media; smartphones; social relationships; software; 3D printing; work
— deflation 81–90, 174
— era 4, 6–7, 17, 70, 81, 155, 235–237, 240
— free 81–83
— revolution 11–18, 157, 171–172, 176
— speed 85–86
— stack 86–87, 160
teenagers, marketing to 68–69

television 4, 6, 27, 32, 34, 51, 57, 58, 60, 61, 66, 67, 75, 82, 83, 95, 109, 111, 117, 131–132, 133, 138, 142, 144, 145–146, 147, 149, 150, 174, 176, 182, 187, 202, 254
Tesla Motors 142, 236
thingernet 174
thinking and technology 56–57
times 172–173
tools 12, 21–22, 23, 27, 38–39, 43, 61, 127, 156, 186, 192, 228, 229, 253, 258; *see also* artisanal production; communication; computers; digital; making; smartphones; social media; 3D printing
— changing 85–86, 118
— old 22, 61, 65–66, 125, 209
trust 135–136, 155, 192
Twitter 23–24, 62, 76, 77, 136, 222, 237

Uber 235–236
unlearning 4, 12
usability gap 146–147
user experience 5, 39, 59, 61, 226

volumetric mindset 33

wages
— growth 88
— low 99, 100
— minimum 89–90
web *see also* connecting and connection; digital; internet; retail and retailers, online; social media; social relationships
— three phases of 169–178
— tools 171, 225, 229
Wikipedia 235
work 13, 14–15, 96, 111, 214–215
— digital era 21–22, 41–42, 208–215
— industrial era 207–208, 213–214
— location of 207–215
— options 210–211
words *see* language

Yahoo 137
YouTube 27, 136, 141, 221, 223, 224, 226

# Learn more with practical advice from our experts

**UnProfessional**
*Jack Delosa*

**The Game Changer**
*Dr Jason Fox*

**Winning the War for Talent**
*Mandy Johnson*

**It Starts With Passion**
*Keith Abraham*

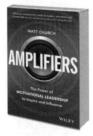

**Amplifiers**
*Matt Church*

**Understanding Y**
*Charlie Caruso*

**Above the Line**
*Michael Henderson*

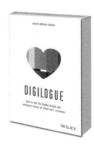

**Digilogue**
*Anders Sörman-Nilsson*

**Start with Hello**
*Linda Coles*

Available in print and e-book formats

WILEY